WORKBOOK

Student Notes and Problems

PHYSICS 20
Alberta

CASTLE ROCK
RESEARCH CORP

Publisher
Gautam Rao

Contributors
Wayne Ladner
James Strachan
Rob Schultz

Rao, Gautam, 1961 –
STUDENT NOTES AND PROBLEMS – Physics 20 Workbook (Alberta)

1. Science – Juvenile Literature. I. Title

Published by
Castle Rock Research Corp.
2340 Manulife Place
10180 – 101 Street
Edmonton, AB T5J 3S4

2 3 4 FP 11 10 09

Dedicated to the memory of Dr. V. S. Rao

STUDENT NOTES AND PROBLEMS WORKBOOKS

Student Notes and Problems (SNAP) Workbooks are a series of support resources in mathematics for students in grades 3 to 12 and in science for students in grades 9 to 12. SNAP Workbooks are 100% aligned with curriculum. The resources are designed to support classroom instructions and provide students with additional examples, practice exercises, and tests. SNAP Workbooks are ideal for use all year long at school and at home.

The following is a summary of the key features of all SNAP Workbooks.

UNIT OPENER PAGE

- summarizes the curriculum outcomes addressed in the unit in age-appropriate language
- identifies the lessons by title
- lists the prerequisite knowledge and skills the student should know prior to beginning the unit

LESSONS

- provide essential teaching pieces and explanations of the concepts
- include example problems and questions with complete, detailed solutions that demonstrate the problem-solving process

NOTES BARS

- contain key definitions, formulas, reminders, and important steps or procedures
- provide space for students to add their own notes and helpful reminders

PRACTICE EXERCISES

- include questions that relate to each of the curriculum outcomes for the unit
- provide practice in applying the lesson concepts

REVIEW SUMMARY

- provides a succinct review of the key concepts in the unit

PRACTICE TEST

- assesses student learning of the unit concepts

ANSWERS AND SOLUTIONS

- demonstrate the step-by-step process or problem-solving method used to arrive at the correct answer

Answers and solutions are provided in each workbook for the odd-numbered questions. A SNAP *Solutions Manual* that contains answers and complete solutions for all questions is also available.

NOTE TO STUDENTS

Answers to problems are provided in the appropriate number of significant digits. To achieve similar answers, follow this procedure when performing calculations:

- Use as many significant digits as possible when entering values into your calculator.

  e.g., use $9.81 \, \text{m/s}^2$ vs. $9.8 \, \text{m/s}^2$ for the acceleration due to gravity

- Retain all digits in your calculator for intermediate steps before reaching your final answer

$$\begin{aligned} \text{e.g.,} \quad F &= ma \\ &= 10.2 \, \text{kg} \times 9.81 \, \text{m/s}^2 \\ &= 100.062 \, \text{N} \end{aligned}$$

- Round off to the correct number of significant digits in your final answer

$$\begin{aligned} \text{e.g.,} \quad W &= Fd \\ &= 100.062 \, \text{N} \times 1.4 \, \text{m} \\ &= 140.0868 \, \text{J} \\ &= 1.4 \times 10^2 \, \text{J} \end{aligned}$$

Please note: Intermediate steps presented in solutions in this book will not show all of the digits that were retained in the calculator. This is done for clarity—to make the solutions easier to follow when reading through them.

e.g., In the $F = ma$ example above, the answer is used to calculate work.
Finding force is therefore an intermediate calculation needed to find work.
The solution will read as follows:

$$\begin{aligned} \text{e.g.,} \quad F &= ma \\ &= 10.2 \, \text{kg} \times 9.81 \, \text{m/s}^2 \\ &= 100 \, \text{N} \\ W &= Fd \\ &= 100 \, \text{N} \times 1.4 \, \text{m} \\ &= 140 \, \text{J} \\ &= 1.4 \times 10^2 \, \text{J} \end{aligned}$$

At most, in intermediate steps, one additional digit may be presented beyond what is significant.
This may appear in some of the solutions presented.

In the end, no matter which approach is used to solve a problem, final answers will be different in the last digit—the digit that requires estimation and rounding. This is acceptable, since that is the whole idea behind significant digits. The final digit contains uncertainty.
If two answers are presented that are different in the final digit, both answers should be considered correct solutions for the problem.

CONTENTS

Circular Motion, Work, and Energy

Oscillatory Motion and Mechanical Waves

Answers and Solutions

INTRODUCTION TO PHYSICS

When you are finished this unit, you will be able to...

- demonstrate an understanding and appreciation of the role of physics in society and will be encouraged to develop the skills and methods employed by physicists.
- describe the major branches of physics that comprise the discipline
- compare and contrast physics with other disciplines
- identify the unique characteristics of physics
- give examples of the continuing development and refining of physics concepts
- demonstrate knowledge of physics-related careers in local, regional, and global workplaces
- describe some of the tools and activities of physicists, in particular a reliance on mathematics and experimental design
- gather and organize data, produce and interpret graphs, and determine relationships between variables

Lesson 1: THE NATURE OF PHYSICS

NOTES

The word *physics* comes from a Greek word meaning "of nature."

The science of physics is the study of matter and energy and of their interactions. Of all the natural sciences, physics encompasses the greatest range of topics, from the properties of subatomic particles to the movement of stars and planets.

Matter, energy, sound, light, and many other topics all make up what we know as physics. Some of these subtopics are:

- Mechanics—which deals with energy and force and their effects on objects.
    - Kinematics—related to dynamics, kinematics is the study of *how* objects move. Kinematics tells us how to calculate an object's motion: speed, acceleration, and so forth.
    - Dynamics—the study of the effects of various forces on objects. Basically, it is the study of *why* objects move, and includes areas such as gravity, momentum, and Sir Isaac Newton's laws of motion.
- Thermodynamics—the study of heat, its effects, and its conversion to and from other forms of energy.
- Wave Motion—the study of transmission of energy from place to place using a variety of wave types.
- Optics—the study of light: how it moves, how it is transmitted, how it is transformed, and how it is perceived.
- Modern physics—advanced topics based on relatively recent discoveries, ideas, and technologies.
    - Relativity—the idea that space and time are not absolute, but based on one's frame of reference.
    - Nuclear physics—a modern branch of physics that deals with the structure of the atomic nucleus.
    - Quantum mechanics—there are certain things that Newtonian mechanics (see above) fails to explain: the movement of subatomic particles, condensed matter physics, and other advanced topics. Quantum mechanics offers a better way of addressing such issues, but it is notoriously complicated.
- Electromagnetism—the part of physics that deals with electricity and magnetism, their interactions, and their effects.

The work of physicists is critical to the development of new technologies. Today, physicists are found in all manner of fields: academia, medicine, telecommunications, computers, environmental management, space science, industrial design, and so on. Here are just a few of the things that physicists are working towards:

- Fusion Power: When two atomic nuclei are forced to combine into one heavier nucleus, an extraordinary amount of energy is generated. Physicists are working towards a way to use this process to generate power, which would be safer, cheaper, and more environmentally sound than nuclear fission (atom-splitting) reactors.

- Nanotechnology: This is the application of technology on an extremely small scale—small enough for interaction with individual atoms. Nanotechnology could potentially revolutionize health-care, power generation, computer technology, and a host of other fields.

- Space Exploration: Humans have already walked on the moon, lived in orbiting space stations, and sent machines to Mars to collect data. The next challenge is to create a machine that can return to Earth from Mars, bringing physical samples of rock, soil, and atmosphere that we can study. We might even see manned missions to Mars in our lifetimes.

Physics encompasses the entire physical universe, and is thus the basis of all other natural sciences (biology, chemistry, etc.).
Ernest Rutherford, one of the world's first nuclear physicists, once said, "In science there is only physics; all the rest is stamp collecting."
However, while physics may lie at the heart of the other sciences, it is not the best way to describe chemical or biological processes. Becoming an expert at making bricks does not make one an expert at building houses out of them; likewise, a physicist may know all the forces and particles that comprise an atom, but not know its effect on the human body, or its place in a complex molecule.

The truth is that the sciences are becoming more and more dependant on each other, and each plays a key role in our understanding of the world around us. It is increasingly common for scientists to take on interdisciplinary roles.

Biochemists, for example, study the effects of chemistry upon the human body, and can use this knowledge to develop medicines.
Biophysicists develop machines used to study the human body (MRIs, X-Rays, etc.), and research human and animal motion, genetics, and a host of other topics.
Physics is an attempt to describe the fundamental processes of the universe in quantifiable terms. This means that physics relies heavily on mathematics: algebra, geometry, and trigonometry. The idea is that we can use math to predict real-world outcomes.

Because so many variables can affect the outcome of an experiment (temperature, friction, gravity, etc.), experiments in physics must be done very carefully to make sure that all possible factors are considered. Experiments are designed to minimize, or account for, outside influences. Data collection can involve any number of devices, from ordinary metre sticks to billion-dollar particle accelerators.

Before we begin our study of physics, let's talk about:
- significant digits
- scientific notation
- graphing

Lesson 2 SIGNIFICANT DIGITS AND SCIENTIFIC NOTATION

NOTES

Physics involves collecting data. This involves measuring, and every measuring instrument has a limit to how precisely we can make a measurement. Because of this, the digits in measurements and calculations that we know with certainty are also limited.

The digits that we know for certain, plus an estimated digit, are *significant digits*.

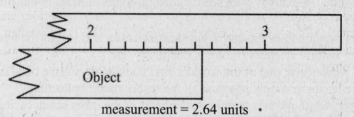

measurement = 2.64 units

We can clearly see that the object is between 2 and 3 units. By counting, we can also determine that it is just over 2.6 units. However, our ruler does not count hundredths. We can see that the object is not quite halfway between 2.6 and 2.7; therefore, we estimate the length at 2.64.

Value of reading = 2.64 units (3 significant digits)
2 and 6 are certain
4 is estimated

ADDITION AND SUBTRACTION OF MEASUREMENTS

A sum or difference cannot be more precise than the least precise measurement.

e.g. 2.71 m + 30.2 m = 32.9 m

Although both of these measurements have three significant digits, 2.71 m is measured to a hundredth of a metre, while 30.2 m is measured to a tenth of a metre. Tenths are less precise than hundredths. Therefore, the answer, 32.9, is given to the nearest tenth of a metre.

MULTIPLICATION AND DIVISION OF MEASUREMENTS

A product or quotient has the same number of significant digits as the measurement with the fewest significant digits.

e.g. $2.7 \text{ m} \times 21.9 \text{ m} = 59 \text{ m}^2$

Any number (digit) from 1 to 9 is a significant digit.
Zeros may or may not be significant.

ZEROS

- Zeros at the beginning of a quantity (measurement) are not significant.
  - e.g. 0.027 m has 2 significant digits; these zeros are not significant
- Zeros that are sandwiched between significant digits are significant.
  - e.g. 2.07 m has 3 significant digits
- Zeros at the end of a quantity may or may not be significant.
  - e.g. 20.0 m has 3 significant digits; 200 m has 1 significant digit

In the case of 200 m, we cannot be sure whether or not the zeroes are significant. The instrument could have read "200.012", and we then rounded to the nearest metre. In this case, the zeroes are significant. On the other hand, the instrument could have read "210.012", and we rounded to the nearest hundred metres. In this case, the zeroes are not significant.
- To show that 200 m has 3 significant digits, write it as 2.00×10^2 m
- To show that 200 m has 1 significant digit, we write it as 2×10^2 m

The notation 2.00×10^2 m and 2×10^2 m are written in scientific notation.

The quantity 20.0 m has 3 significant digits. When a zero follows a decimal point, it is significant. It does not have to be there to show where the decimal point is, so the only reason for it being there is that it came from the measuring apparatus.

To avoid this complication, numbers are often expressed in *scientific notation*. Scientific notation is also used to express very large and very small numbers.

SCIENTIFIC NOTATION

Scientific notation is a useful way to express some values. Scientific notation allows us to show the proper number of significant digits without ambiguous zeros at the end. It also allows us to express large and small numbers in a convenient way.

Here is how it works. First, establish whether the number is greater than 1 or less than 1. In the last example, 200 m is greater than one.

Next, we need to find out how many places we would need to shift the decimal to get a number between 1 and 10. In this case, we would need to shift the decimal over 2 places. This gives us 2.00. To show that we have moved the decimal, we multiply our number by 10 to the power of the number of places we have moved the decimal. To continue our example, our number would now be 2.00×10^2 m.

Now we can show how many significant digits our number has.

If it only has one significant digit, we can write it as 2×10^2 m.
If it has two significant digits, we can write it as 2.0×10^2 m.
If it has three, we can leave it as 2.00×10^2 m.

NOTES

LARGE NUMBERS

Physicists often work with very large numbers, and scientific notation is usually the best way to express them.

For example, astronomers frequently have to work with extremely long numbers—light speeds, planetary distances, etc. Let's say an astronomer is studying an object that is 234 561 000 km from Earth. It is lot easier to write (and to avoid errors) by expressing this in scientific notation:

$$234\ 561\ 000 \text{ km} = 2.35 \times 10^8 \text{ km (to 3 significant digits)}$$

SMALL NUMBERS

Scientific notation also works for numbers under 1. For example, a physicist has calculated the weight of a tiny object as 0.000 012 5 g. We shift the decimal place to the right instead of to the left, until we are left with a number between 1 and 10—in this case, 1.25. We then multiply the number by 10 to the *negative* power of the number of decimal places moved—in this case, 5. Our number, expressed in scientific notation, is:

$$0.000\ 012\ 5 \text{ g} = 1.25 \times 10^{-5} \text{ g (to 3 significant digits)}$$

PRACTICE EXERCISE

1. How many significant digits does each of the following measurements have?

   a) 7.03 m

   b) 0.075 m

   c) 6.00 m

   d) 200 m

   e) 4.20×10^2 m

2. Write the following measurements in scientific notation.

   a) 0.003 40 m to 3 significant digits

   b) 700 m to 2 significant digits

   c) 559 m to 2 significant digits

   d) 552 m to 2 significant digits

   e) 4.05 m to 2 significant digits

3. Add the following measurements. Express your answer in scientific notation.

   a) 70.0 m + 2.32 m

   b) 552 m + 7.1 m

   c) 460 m + 29.8 m

4. Multiply the following measurements. Use the correct number of significant digits.

   a) 75 m × 0.82 m

   b) 9.63 m × 1.9 m

   c) 6.20×10^2 m × 20.0 m

Lesson 3   GRAPHING

A common process in physics, as well as other sciences, is to determine the relationship between variables. To do this, we manipulate one variable to see how it affects another variable while keeping all other variables constant. The variable we are testing is called the responding variable. We are seeing how one variable responds to a manipulation of another variable if all other variables are kept constant.

A good way to analyze this relationship is to plot a graph (the responding variable vs. the manipulated variable). In the following example, the responding variable will be labelled B and the manipulated variable is A. The units are invented.

Units of A = eb
Units of B = tz/s

Data:

A (eb)	B (tz/s)
2.0	3.0
4.0	6.0
6.0	9.0
8.0	12.0
10.0	15.0
12.0	18.0

RULES FOR GRAPHING DATA

• Label the axes.
  – The manipulated variable should be placed on the *x*-axis and the responding variable on the *y*-axis.
  – Labels should include the units of the variables and any common exponents.
• Scale each axis.
  – Use a scale that will use as much of the graph as possible when the data is plotted on it.
  – Use a scale that is easy to read.
  – Make sure that the scale is evenly spaced; that is, each division on the graph paper has the same value.
• Plot the data points and draw a smooth line of best fit.
• Give the graph a title. It always works to title a graph as the responding variable vs. the manipulated variable.
• If a linear relationship (straight line) is suggested, use a straight edge to draw the line of best fit. If the points do not exactly line up, have some points above the line and some points below as shown in the following diagram. This is an averaging technique (averaging out errors).

NOTES

Title: **B vs. A**

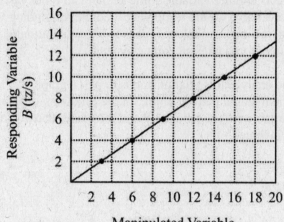

Responding Variable vs
Manipulated Variable
(*B* vs. *A*)

SHAPES OF GRAPHS

In the analysis of experimental data, it is helpful to be able to recognize the relationships that the shape of the line of best fit suggests.
It is hard to tell if a graph shows an inverse or inverse square relationship by just looking at the shape. Usually further analysis is necessary.
This analysis involves curve straightening.

$B \propto A$ $B = kA$

direct relationship

$B \propto A^2$ $B = kA^2$

exponential relationship

constant relationship

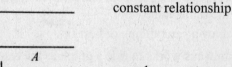

$B \propto \dfrac{1}{A}$ or $B \propto \dfrac{1}{A^2}$

$B = \dfrac{1}{A}$ or $B = \dfrac{k}{A^2}$

inverse or inverse square relationship

CURVE STRAIGHTENING
B vs. *A*

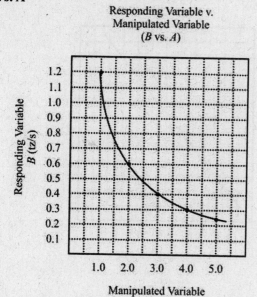

Responding Variable v.
Manipulated Variable
(*B* vs. *A*)

Responding Variable
B (tz/s)

Manipulated Variable
A (eb)

Data:

A (eb)	*B* (tz/s)
1	1.2
2	0.60
3	0.40
4	0.30
5	0.24

We do not know by looking at the above graph if it has a mathematical relationship of:

$$B \propto \frac{1}{A} \qquad \text{or} \qquad B \propto \frac{1}{A^2}$$

In order to determine this, if we complete the following data table and draw the graphs:

$$B \propto \frac{1}{A} \qquad \text{and} \qquad B \propto \frac{1}{A^2}$$

A (eb)	*B* (tz/s)	$\frac{1}{A}$ (eb)	$\frac{1}{A^2}$ (e²b²)
1	1.2	1	1
2	0.60	0.50	0.25
3	0.40	0.33	0.11
4	0.30	0.25	0.063
5	0.24	0.20	0.040

NOTES

Straight line:

B vs. $\dfrac{1}{A}$

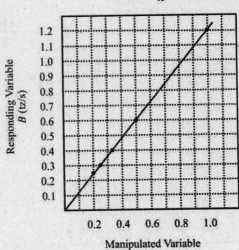

$\dfrac{1}{A}$ (eb)

Not a straight line:

B vs. $\dfrac{1}{A^2}$

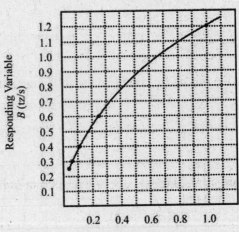

$\dfrac{1}{A^2}$ (e²b²)

It is clear that A vs. $\dfrac{1}{B}$ produces a straight line.

This tells us that $B \propto \dfrac{1}{A}$ and not $B \propto \dfrac{1}{A^2}$.

FINDING THE SLOPE

An important process in analyzing experimental data is to find the slope of a linear graph.

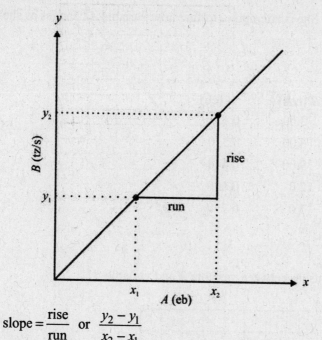

$$\text{slope} = \frac{\text{rise}}{\text{run}} \quad \text{or} \quad \frac{y_2 - y_1}{x_2 - x_1}$$

To find the slope, choose two points on the line of best fit.

- Choose these points as far apart as is convenient, and choose points you can read easily.

- If your graph passes through the origin (0, 0), you may use it as one of the two points.

- Make sure you are using points on the graph. Do not use data points unless they are on the line.

PRACTICE EXERCISE

1. A student collects the following data. She is attempting to find how variable *A* changes as she manipulates variable *B*.

B (tz/s)	*A* (eb)
3.00	0.151
6.00	0.310
9.00	0.448
12.0	0.600
15.0	0.750

a) Draw a graph showing the relationship between variable *A* and variable *B*.

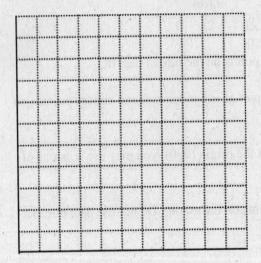

b) Find the slope of the graph.

c) What is the mathematical relationship between *A* and *B*?

2. A student collects the following data. He is attempting to find how A changes as he manipulates B.

B ($\times 10^{-2}$ tz/s)	A (eb)	$\frac{1}{B}$ (s/tz)
2.1	4.0	
1.4	6.0	
1.1	8.0	
0.7	12.0	
0.35	24.0	

a) Draw a graph showing the relationship between variable A and variable B.

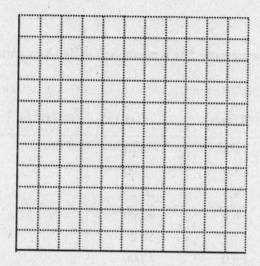

b) Complete the $\frac{1}{B}$ column in the previous table, and draw the graph showing the relationship between variable A and $\frac{1}{B}$.

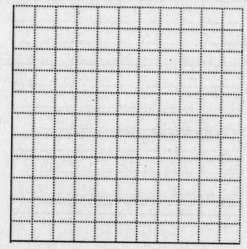

c) Find the slope of the graph you just drew.

d) What is the mathematical relationship between A and B?

3. A student collects the following data. She is attempting to find how variable A changes as she manipulates variable B.

$B\,(\text{tz/s})$	$A\,(\text{eb})$	$B^2\,\left(\text{tz}^2/\text{s}^2\right)$
1.5	2.25	
3.0	9.00	
4.5	20.25	
6.0	36.00	
7.5	56.25	
9.0	81.00	

a) Draw a graph showing the relationship between variable A and variable B.

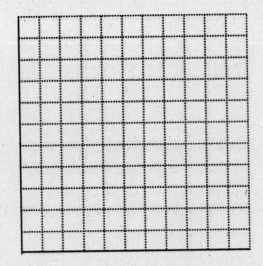

b) Complete the B^2 column in the above table, and draw the graph showing the relationship between variable A and B^2.

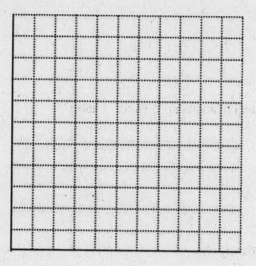

c) Find the slope of the graph that you just drew.

d) What is the mathematical relationship between A and B?

NOTES

KINEMATICS

When you are finished this unit, you will be able to...

- qualitatively and quantitatively define displacement, velocity, and acceleration
- operationally define, compare, and contrast scalar and vector quantities
- qualitatively and quantitatively explain uniform and uniformly accelerated motion when provided with written descriptions and numerical and graphical data
- quantitatively interpret the motion of one object relative to another, using displacement and velocity vectors
- quantitatively explain two-dimensional motion in a horizontal or vertical plane, using vector components
- explain that scientific knowledge is subject to change as new evidence becomes apparent and as laws and theories are tested and subsequently revised, reinforced, or rejected
- explain that the goal of science is knowledge about the natural world
- explain that the process for technological development includes testing and evaluating designs and prototypes on the basis of established criteria

19

Lesson 1 INTRODUCTION TO KINEMATICS

There are objects in motion all around us. The sun appears to move from east to west across the sky. A plane takes off from the airport. We see students walking down the hall. Trees sway back and forth as they are driven by the wind. The hands of the clock are in motion. How are we to describe motion?

Kinematics: the study of how objects move

Kinematics is the study of how objects move.

TERMINOLOGY

The Greek letter *delta*, Δ, is a symbol meaning "change in"

Displacement: $(\vec{d})$ is the change in position of an object.

Velocity: $(\vec{v})$ is the rate of change in an object's position.

$$\vec{v} = \frac{\Delta \vec{d}}{\Delta t}$$

Rate of change describes the change, in terms of the time the change takes

Acceleration: $(\vec{a})$ is the rate of change in an object's velocity.

$$\vec{a} = \frac{\Delta \vec{v}}{\Delta t}$$

A vector quantity has direction as well as magnitude

The quantities displacement, velocity, and acceleration are vector quantities. A *vector* quantity is a quantity that has direction as well as magnitude (size). This means that displacement, velocity, and acceleration are described using magnitude and direction. For example, if an object is moved 20 m, we do not know its new position. However, if it is moved 20 m east, we know its new position—we know its displacement.

Displacement, velocity, and acceleration are vector quantities

There are two additional terms that are often used to describe motion. These terms are:

Vector quantities use symbols with an arrow, such as $\vec{v}$ and $\vec{a}$

Distance (d) refers to how far an object has moved.

Speed (v) is the magnitude of velocity.

Average speed is the distance moved divided by the time of motion.

$$\text{average speed} = \frac{\text{distance}}{\text{time}}$$

$$\text{average speed} = \frac{\text{distance}}{\text{time}}$$

or

$$v = \frac{d}{t}$$

average velocity

$$= \frac{\text{displacement}}{\text{time}}$$

The quantities distance and speed are scalar quantities. A scalar quantity is a quantity that has magnitude (size) only. For example, if an object is moved 20 m, we know the distance moved but we do not know the displacement.

A scalar quantity has only magnitude

Distance and speed are scalar quantities

PRACTICE EXERCISE

1. A man walks 275 m east and then turns around and walks 425 m west.

   a) What is the distance travelled by the man?

   b) What is the displacement of the man?

2. A little girl takes her dog for a walk around the perimeter of a city park with the dimensions shown.

   a) What is the distance travelled by the girl and dog during the walk?

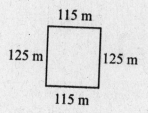

   b) What is the displacement of the girl and dog at the end of the walk?

3. An object travels 11 m north and then turns around and travels 25 m south. If the total time of travel is 52 s, what is the average:

a) speed of the object?

b) velocity of the object?

Lesson 2 INSTANTANEOUS VELOCITY AND SPEED

Knowing the average velocity and average speed of an object does not give us any information about how fast an object is moving at any given time. It gives an average, as the term indicates.

Instantaneous velocity and instantaneous speed are the velocity and speed at some given time (at some instant).

Uniform motion is motion in which the speed or velocity remains constant (unchanging) over time. Uniform accelerated motion is motion in which the acceleration remains constant (unchanging) during any time of observation.

In order to describe these two types of motion graphically, begin by creating a table using a column to represent the values of your manipulated variable, and another to represent the corresponding values of the responding variable. Use the column of manipulated variable values to create values along the *x*-axis of a graph. The column of the responding variable values provides the *y*-values that create the two-dimensional locations of your plot points.

In the case of time and motion studies, your manipulated variable values will be determined by the scope of time in which the positions and velocities of an object are being observed. When comparing position and velocity in relation to time, your data chart can have two different columns representing your responding variable values, each corresponding to the instantaneous values of an object's position or velocity at the time indicated by the data.

NOTES

We will use the terms *velocity* and *speed* when we mean *instantaneous velocity* and *instantaneous speed*

Uniform motion is motion in which the velocity remains constant

Uniformly accelerated motion is motion in which the acceleration remains constant

UNIFORM MOTION

Activity 1

1. Design an experiment to study uniform linear motion.
2. Collect data that will allow you to determine the relationships between position, velocity, and time.
3. Analyze your data by drawing a position-time graph and a velocity-time graph

Data:

Time (*x*)	Position (*y*)	Velocity (*y*)

NOTES

Position-Time Graph

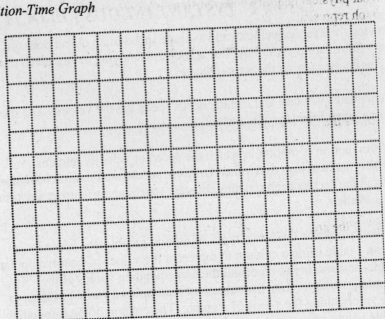

Velocity-Time Graph

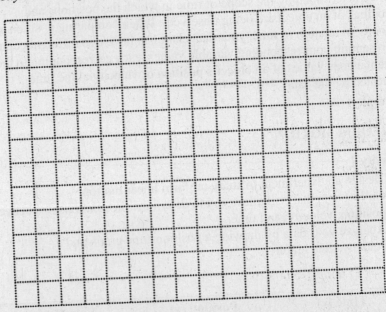

Use the graphs you have drawn to answer the following questions.

1. What is the slope of your position-time graph?

2. What physical quantity does the slope of your position-time graph represent?

3. What is the uniform velocity of the object used in Activity 1?

4. That is the area under your velocity-time graph?

5. What physical quantity does the area under your velocity-time graph represent?

The units used on a graph should directly indicate what the values of the plotted coordinates measure

Use the formula $\vec{v} = \dfrac{\vec{d}}{t}$ to work through the following examples.

Example 1

An object travels at a uniform velocity of 25.0 m/s west. What is the displacement of the object after 10.0 minutes?

Solution

$$\vec{v} = \dfrac{\vec{d}}{t}$$

$$\vec{d} = \vec{v}t$$

$$= (25.0 \text{ m/s})(6.00 \times 10^2 \text{ s})$$

$$= 1.50 \times 10^4 \text{ m west}$$

NOTES

Example 2

After 3.0 h, an object's displacement is 2.60×10^2 km north. What is the average velocity of the object?

Solution

$$\vec{v} = \frac{\vec{d}}{t}$$

$$= \frac{2.60 \times 10^2 \text{ km north}}{3.0 \text{ h}}$$

$$= 87 \text{ km/h north}$$

Example 3

An object travels a distance of 5.0 m in 2.7 s. What is the average speed of the object?

Solution

$$\vec{v} = \frac{\vec{d}}{t}$$

$$= \frac{5.0 \text{ m}}{2.7 \text{ s}}$$

$$= 1.9 \text{ m/s}$$

PRACTICE EXERCISE

Formula: $\quad \vec{v} = \dfrac{\vec{d}}{t}$

1. In 11.2 s, an object is displaced 1.00×10^2 m west. What is the average velocity of the object?

2. An object is travelling at a constant velocity of 10.0 m/s west.

    a) How far will this object travel in 4.5 s?

    b) What is the displacement of this object at 4.5 s?

3. An object is travelling at a constant velocity of 9.8 m/s west. How long will it take this object to travel 2.5 m?

4. A man runs at an average velocity of 1.30 m/s south for 98.0 s and then walks at an average velocity of 0.45 m/s in the same direction for 90.0 s. What is the average velocity of the man during the total time of travel?

5. An object is dropped from a height of 64.0 m. If the object takes 3.61 s to fall, what is the average velocity of the object?

6. Given the following position-time graph of an object moving east, find the velocity of the object at:

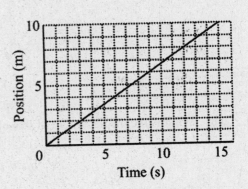

a) 8.0 s.

b) 12.0 s.

c) 1.0 s.

28

7. Given the following position-time graph of an object moving north, find the:

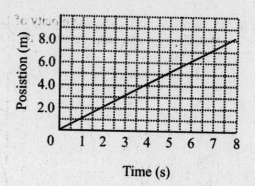

a) speed of the object at 6.0 s.

b) velocity of the object at 6.0 s.

8. Given the following velocity-time graph of an object moving south, find the:

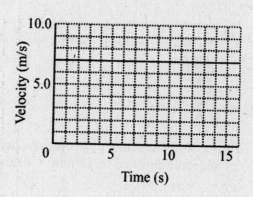

a) displacement of the object in 10 s.

b) distance travelled by the object in 10 s.

9. Given the following velocity-time graph of an object moving west, find the:

   a) displacement of the object in 5.0 s.

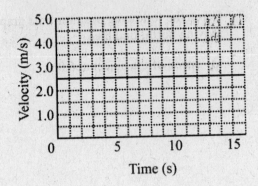

   b) distance travelled by the object in 5.0 s.

10. An object travels at a constant velocity of 5.0 m/s north for 31 min, after which it travels 7.0 m/s in the same direction for 15 min. Calculate the average velocity of the object.

11. An object travels at a constant velocity of 8.0 m/s north for 25 min, after which it travels 5.0 m/s in the opposite direction for 15 min. Calculate the:

   a) average velocity of the object.

   b) average speed of the object.

12. Object A travels at a constant velocity of 2.0 m/s east, and object B travels in the same direction at a constant velocity of 3.0 m/s. If object B starts 1.0 min after object A, how much time will it take object B to catch object A?

13. The following data were obtained by moving an object at a constant velocity to the right.

Time (s)	Displacement (m)	Displacement during time interval (m)	Average Velocity during time interval (m/s)
0	0		
0.10	0.012		
0.20	0.024		
0.30	0.035		
0.40	0.047		
0.50	0.060		
0.60	0.072		
0.70	0.085		
0.80	0.097		
0.90	0.108		
1.00	0.120		

a) Complete the data table.

b) Draw a position-time graph for this data.

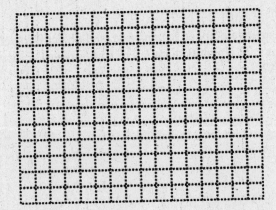

c) Draw a velocity-time graph for this data.

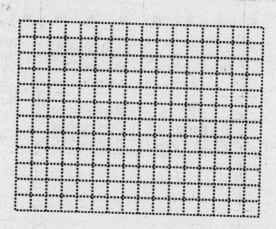

d) Use the slope of your position-time graph to find the velocity of the object.

e) Use the area under your velocity-time graph to find the displacement of the object in 0.95 s.

14. The dots below represents the position of an object every 0.10 s as it moves east along a horizontal straight line.

$t = 0$

●   ●   ●   ●   ●   ●   ●   ●

a) Complete the following data table for the motion of this object.

Time (s)	Displacement from $t = 0$ (m)	Displacement during time interval (m)	Average velocity during time interval (m/s)
0			
0.10			
0.20			
0.30			
0.40			
0.50			
0.60			

b) Draw a position-time graph for your data.

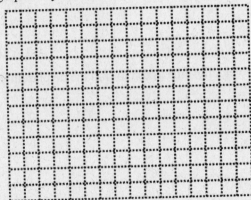

c) Draw a velocity-time graph for your data.

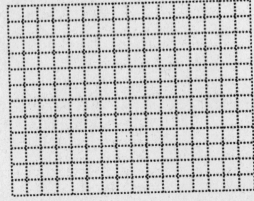

d) Find:

    i)   the velocity of the object using your position-time graph.

    ii) the displacement of the object using your velocity-time graph.

Lesson 3 UNIFORMLY ACCELERATED MOTION

NOTES

In uniformly accelerated
motion, the acceleration
is constant

Acceleration is the rate of
change in the velocity

Uniformly accelerated motion is motion in which the acceleration of an
object remains constant (unchanging).

Remember that acceleration is defined as the rate at which
velocity changes.

$$\vec{a} = \frac{\Delta \vec{v}}{\Delta t}$$

or

$$\vec{a} = \frac{\vec{v}_f - \vec{v}_i}{t}$$

where $\vec{v}_f$ = final velocity

$\vec{v}_i$ = initial velocity

t = time interval

Activity 2

1. Design an experiment to study uniformly accelerated linear motion
   (keep the motion in the same direction).
2. Collect data that will allow you to determine the relationship between
   acceleration, position, velocity, and time.
3. Analyze your data drawing a position-time graph and
   a velocity-time graph

Suggestion:
Use a data table similar to
those used in the problems
on uniform motion

Data

36

Position-Time Graph

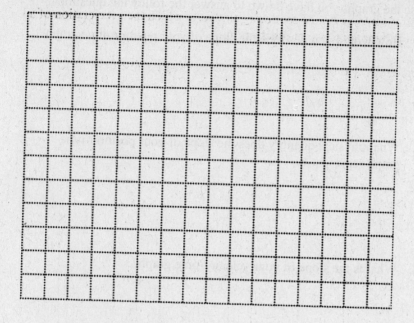

Velocity-Time Graph

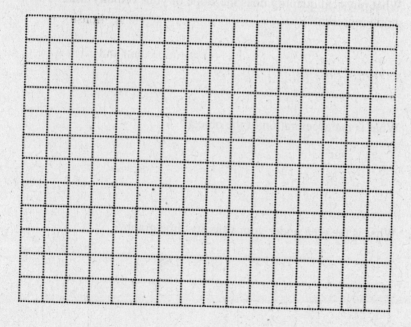

The average velocity of the interval for uniformly accelerated motion occurs at the mid-time point of the interval. Take this into consideration in plotting your graph.

NOTES

Analyze the units
being used in the
graph very carefully.

Questions
Use the graphs you have drawn to answer the following questions.

1. How would you describe the slope of your position-time graph?

2. What physical quantity does the slope of your position-time graph represent?

3. What is the slope of your velocity-time graph?

4. What physical quantity does the slope of your velocity-time graph represent?

5. What is the acceleration of the object?

6. What is the area under your velocity-time graph?

7. What physical quantity does the area under your velocity-time graph represent?

INSTANTANEOUS VELOCITY (OR SPEED)

The slope of a position-time graph represents the velocity of the object. For the position-time graph you drew, the slope could not be calculated because it was constantly changing. However, we can find the velocity at any given time (instantaneous velocity) by drawing a tangent line to the curve at the given instant, and then finding the slope of the line.

Example 1

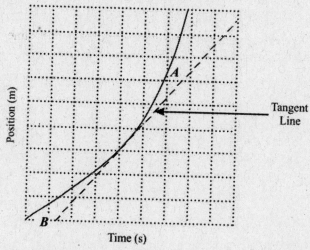

A tangent line only touches a curve at a single point. Mark a point on the curve for the time in which you are interested. Draw a straight line that only touches the curve at this point. In the given illustration, you can see that angles *A* and *B* are equal when this line is drawn.

GRAPHICAL ANALYSIS SUMMARY

1. Slope of position-time graph is the velocity.

2. Slope of velocity-time graph is the acceleration

3. Area under a velocity-time graph is the displacement.

PRACTICE EXERCISE

1. Use the position-time graph that you drew for Activity 2 on page 37. Find the velocity of the object for which you collected the data at:

   a) 0.4 s.

   b) 0.7 s.

2. Given the position-time graph of an object moving east, find the velocity of the object at:

   a) 0.40 s.

   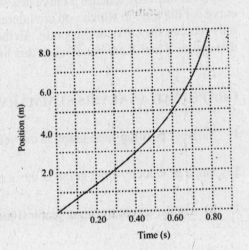

   b) 0.60 s.

3. Given the following velocity-time graph for an object moving north, find the:

   a) acceleration of the object.

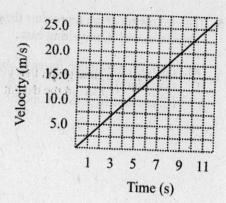

   b) displacement of the object in 7.0 s.

4. Given the following velocity-time graph for an object moving east, find the:

   a) acceleration of the object.

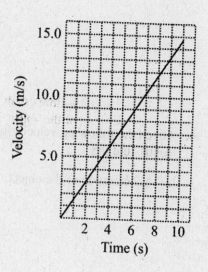

   b) displacement by the object in 10.0 s.

5. The following graph represents the motion of two objects, A and B, travelling east.

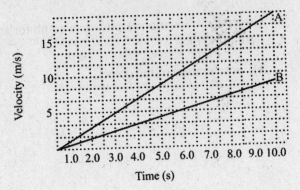

a) At 5.0 s, how much faster is object A travelling than object B?
(Express answer as a proportion.)

b) How much farther did object A travel in 5.0 s than object B? (Express answer as actual distance.)

6. Given the following velocity-time graph for an object moving south, find the:

a) acceleration of the object.

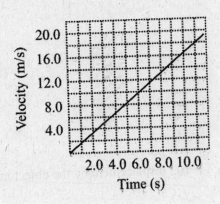

b) displacement by the object in 10.0 s.

7. Given the following velocity-time graph for an object moving west, find the:

   a) acceleration of the object.

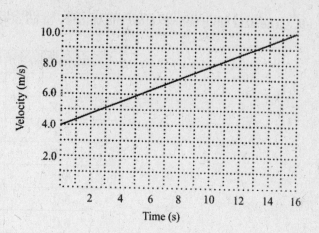

   b) displacement by the object in 16.0 s.

8. Given the following velocity-time graph for an object moving east, find the:

   a) acceleration of the object.

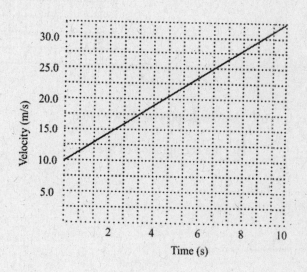

   b) displacement by the object in 10.0 s.

9. The data table below shows the velocity of an object moving north at intervals of 1 s.

Time (s)	Velocity (m/s)
0	12.0
1.0	15.3
2.0	18.6
3.0	21.9
4.0	25.2
5.0	28.5
6.0	31.8

a) Draw a velocity-time graph for this data.

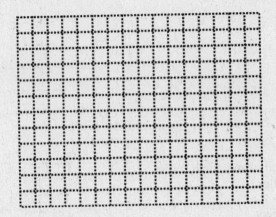

b) Use the graph you drew to find:

   i) the acceleration of the object.

   ii) the displacement of the object during the 6.0 s period defined by the data table.

10. The dots below represent the position of an object every 0.10 s as it moves west along a horizontal straight line.

$t = 0$

●● ● ● ● ● ●

a) Complete the following data table for the motion of this object.

Time (s)	Displacement from $t = 0$ (m)	Displacement during time interval (m)	Average velocity during time interval (m/s)
0			
0.10			
0.20			
0.30			
0.40			
0.50			
0.60			

b) Draw a position-time graph.

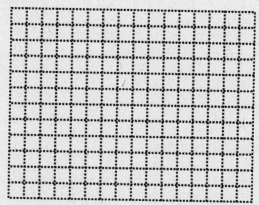

c) Draw a velocity-time graph for your data.

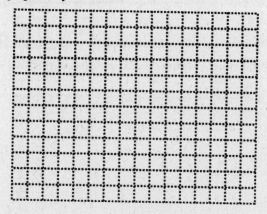

d) Find the acceleration of the object by using your velocity-time graph.

11. The following data were obtained by moving an object to the right at a constant acceleration.

Time (s)	Displacement from $t = 0$ (m)	Displacement during time interval (m)	Average velocity during time interval (m/s)
0	0.00		
0.10	0.02		
0.20	0.09		
0.30	0.20		
0.40	0.36		
0.50	0.56		
0.60	0.80		
0.70	1.09		

a) Complete the data table.

b) Draw a position-time graph for these data.

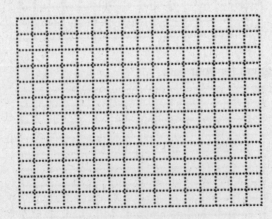

c) Draw a velocity-time graph for these data.

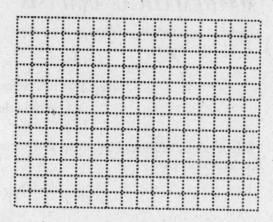

d) Draw an acceleration-time graph for these data.

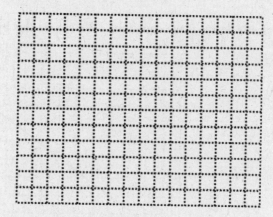

e) Find the velocity of the object at 0.30 s and 0.60 s by using your velocity-time graph.

Lesson 4 UNIFORMLY ACCELERATED MOTION— MATHEMATICAL ANALYSIS

Acceleration is the rate of change in an object's velocity

$$a = \vec{a} = \frac{\vec{v}_f - \vec{v}_i}{t}$$

where $\vec{v}_f$ = final velocity

$\vec{v}_i$ = initial velocity

There are three additional equations that are used to describe uniform accelerated motion:

$$\vec{d} = \left(\frac{\vec{v}_f + \vec{v}_i}{2}\right)t$$

$$\vec{d} = \vec{v}_i t + \frac{1}{2}\vec{a}t^2$$

$$\vec{v}_f^{\,2} = \vec{v}_i^{\,2} + 2\vec{a}\vec{d}$$

Let's derive these equations. We can do this by graphical analysis.

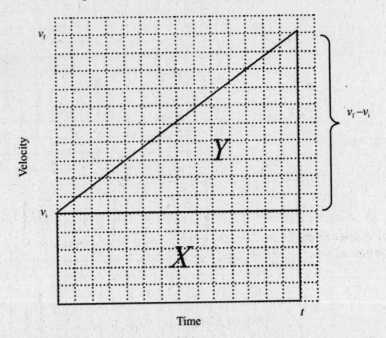

The displacement is the area under the velocity-time graph.
Therefore, the displacement is the area of the rectangle X plus the area of the triangle Y.

$$\text{area of rectangle } Y = \frac{1}{2}t\left(\vec{v}_f - \vec{v}_i\right)$$

$$\text{area of triangle } X = \vec{v}_i t$$

$$= \frac{\vec{v}_f t}{2} - \frac{\vec{v}_i t}{2}$$

Total area of X and $Y = \vec{v}_i t + \left(\dfrac{\vec{v}_f t}{2} - \dfrac{\vec{v}_i t}{2} \right)$

$$= \frac{\vec{v}_i t}{2} + \frac{\vec{v}_f t}{2}$$

$$= \left(\frac{\vec{v}_f t + \vec{v}_i t}{2} \right)$$

$$\vec{d} = \left(\frac{\vec{v}_f + \vec{v}_i}{2} \right) t$$

$\vec{d} = \vec{v}_i t + \dfrac{1}{2}\vec{a}t^2$ can be derived in much the same way.

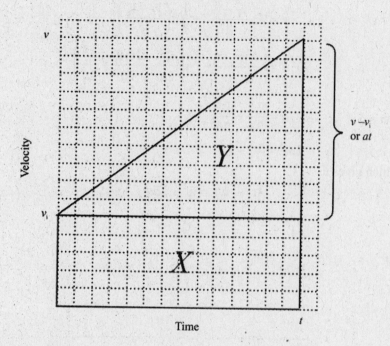

The displacement is the area under the velocity-time graph. The area is represented by a rectangle X and a triangle Y.

$$\text{area of rectangle } Y = \vec{v}_i t$$

$$\text{area of triangle } X = \frac{1}{2}\left(\vec{a}t \right)t$$

$$= \frac{1}{2}\vec{a}t^2$$

$$\vec{d} = \vec{v}_i t + \frac{1}{2}\vec{a}t^2$$

$$\vec{d} = \left(\frac{\vec{v}_f + \vec{v}_i}{2} \right)t$$

$$\vec{a} = \frac{\vec{v}_f - \vec{v}_i}{t}$$

$$\vec{v}_f - \vec{v}_i = \vec{a}t$$

$$\vec{d} = \vec{v}_i t + \frac{1}{2}\vec{a}t^2$$

NOTES

$$\vec{v}_f{}^2 = \vec{v}_i{}^2 + 2\vec{a}\vec{d}$$

The fourth equation $\vec{v}_f{}^2 = \vec{v}_i{}^2 + 2\vec{a}\vec{d}$ is derived by combining the equations

$$\vec{a} = \frac{\vec{v}_f - \vec{v}_i}{t} \quad \text{and} \quad \vec{d} = \vec{v}_i t + \frac{1}{2}\vec{a}t^2$$

From the first equation

$$\vec{a} = \frac{\vec{v}_f - \vec{v}_i}{t}$$

$$t = \frac{\vec{v}_f - \vec{v}_i}{\vec{a}}$$

If we substitute t in the equation $\vec{d} = \vec{v}_i t + \frac{1}{2}\vec{a}t^2$ with $\frac{\vec{v}_f - \vec{v}_i}{\vec{a}}$, we obtain

$$\vec{d} = \vec{v}_i\left(\frac{\vec{v}_f - \vec{v}_i}{\vec{a}}\right) + \frac{1}{2}\vec{a}\left(\frac{\vec{v}_f - \vec{v}_i}{\vec{a}}\right)^2$$

$$\vec{d} = \left(\frac{\vec{v}_i\vec{v}_f}{\vec{a}} - \frac{\vec{v}_i{}^2}{\vec{a}}\right) + \left(\frac{\vec{v}_f{}^2}{2\vec{a}} - \frac{2\vec{v}_f\vec{v}_i}{2\vec{a}} + \frac{\vec{v}_i{}^2}{2\vec{a}}\right)$$

$$\vec{d} = \frac{\vec{v}_f{}^2}{2\vec{a}} - \frac{\vec{v}_i{}^2}{2\vec{a}}$$

$$2\vec{a}\vec{d} = \vec{v}_f{}^2 - \vec{v}_i{}^2$$

which gives us

$$\vec{v}_f{}^2 = \vec{v}_i{}^2 + 2\vec{a}\vec{d}$$

SUMMARY

Equations	Variables				
	$\vec{v}_i$	$\vec{v}_f$	$\vec{a}$	$\vec{d}$	t
$\vec{a} = \dfrac{\vec{v}_f - \vec{v}_i}{t}$	✓	✓	✓		✓
$\vec{d} = \left(\dfrac{\vec{v}_f + \vec{v}_i}{2}\right)t$	✓	✓		✓	✓
$\vec{d} = \vec{v}_i t + \dfrac{1}{2}\vec{a}t^2$	✓		✓	✓	✓
$\vec{v}_f^{\,2} = \vec{v}_i^{\,2} + 2\vec{a}\vec{d}$	✓	✓	✓	✓	

Remember: average velocity can be calculated using

$$\vec{v}_{av} = \frac{\vec{d}}{t}$$

When we have uniformly accelerated motion, average velocity can also be calculated using

$$\vec{v}_{av} = \frac{\vec{v}_f - \vec{v}_i}{2}$$

Note that each equation has four of the possible five variables that can be used to describe uniform accelerated motion. In the mathematical analysis of uniform motion, the first thing that we must do is establish the equation that we will use. To do this, we will list all the given variables and the unknown variable. In this list there must be four variables (three known, and one unknown). From this list, you will note that one of the five variables listed in the summary is missing. The equation to use is the equation that is also missing this variable.

Example 1

An object initially travelling at a velocity of 7.0 m/s east accelerates uniformly to a velocity of 22.0 m/s east in a time of 1.7 s. Calculate the acceleration of the object.

Solution

$\vec{v}_i$	$\vec{v}_f$	$\vec{a}$	$\vec{d}$	t
7.0 m/s	22.0 m/s	?	×	1.7 s

$$\vec{a} = \frac{\vec{v}_f - \vec{v}_i}{t}$$

$$= \frac{22.0 \text{ m/s} - 7.0 \text{ m/s}}{1.7 \text{ s}}$$

$$= 8.8 \text{ m/s}^2 \text{ east}$$

Because we are not concerned about $\vec{d}$, we use the equation that does not have $\vec{d}$.

Because we are not concerned about $\vec{a}$, we use the equation that does not have $\vec{a}$.

Example 2

An object moving north accelerates uniformly from rest in a time of 2.70 s. In this time, it travels 20.0 m. What is the final velocity?

Solution

$\vec{v}_i$	$\vec{v}_f$	$\vec{a}$	$\vec{d}$	t
0	?	×	20.0 m	2.70 s

$$\vec{d} = \left(\frac{\vec{v}_f + \vec{v}_i}{2}\right)t$$

$$20.0 \text{ m} = \left(\frac{\vec{v}_f}{2}\right)(2.70 \text{ s})$$

$$\vec{v}_f = \frac{2(20.0 \text{ m})}{2.70 \text{ s}}$$
$$= 14.8 \text{ m/s north}$$

Example 3

An object accelerated uniformly from rest. If the acceleration was 2.00 m/s^2 west, what was the displacement when it reached a velocity of 1.00×10^2 km/h ?

Solution

$$\vec{v}_f = 1.00 \times 10^2 \text{ km/h} \times 10^3 \text{ m/km} \times 1 \text{ h/3 600 s}$$
$$= 27.8 \text{ m/s west}$$

$\vec{v}_i$	$\vec{v}_f$	$\vec{a}$	$\vec{d}$	t
0	27.8 m	2.00 m/s^2	?	×

$$\vec{v}_f{}^2 = \vec{v}_i{}^2 + 2\vec{a}\vec{d}$$
$$= (27.8 \text{ m/s})^2 = (0)^2 + 2(2.00 \text{ m/s}^2)(\vec{d})$$

$$\vec{d} = \frac{(27.8 \text{ m/s})^2}{2(2.00 \text{ m/s}^2)}$$

$$= 193 \text{ m west}$$

Because we are not concerned about t, we use the equation that does not have t.

PRACTICE EXERCISE

Formulae: $\qquad \vec{a} = \dfrac{\vec{v}_f - \vec{v}_i}{t} \qquad\qquad \vec{d} = \left(\dfrac{\vec{v}_f + \vec{v}_i}{2}\right)t \qquad\qquad \vec{d} = \vec{v}_i t + \dfrac{1}{2}\vec{a}t^2 \qquad\qquad \vec{v}_f^{\,2} = \vec{v}_i^{\,2} + 2\vec{a}\vec{d}$

1. An object accelerates uniformly from rest to a velocity of 12.0 m/s west in 3.40 s. Calculate the acceleration of the object.

2. An object accelerates uniformly from rest. If the final velocity of the object after 4.7 s is 15 m east, what is the displacement?

3. An object accelerates uniformly from rest at a rate of 1.9 m/s² right for 5.0 s. Find:

   a) the displacement.

   b) the final velocity.

c) the distance travelled.

d) the final speed.

4. An object initially travelling at a velocity of 2.0 m/s west accelerates uniformly at a rate of 1.3 m/s^2 west. During this time of acceleration, the displacement of the object is 15 m west. Find:

   a) the final velocity.

   b) the final speed.

5. An object accelerates uniformly from a velocity of 5.0 m/s north at a rate of 3.0 m47s^2 north. What is the velocity of the object at 2.9 s?

6. An object accelerates uniformly from rest. If it travels 26.0 m south and reaches a velocity of 11.0 m/s south, how long does the object accelerate?

7. An object accelerates uniformly from rest for 8.10 s. If in this time the displacement of the object is 20.0 m to the right, what is the acceleration?

8. An object uniformly accelerates from 15 km/h east to 65 km/h east. If the rate of acceleration is 4.0 m/s^2, what is the displacement of the object during acceleration?

9. An object uniformly accelerates from rest and reaches a velocity of 122 km/h north in 10.5 s. What was the average velocity of the object?

10. An object accelerates uniformly from rest at a rate of 2.40 m/s² west. At what time did the object reach a velocity of 12.0 m/s west?

11. While accelerating uniformly from rest, an object is displaced 19.0 m north in 7.10 s. What is the velocity at this time?

12. An object travels 8.0 m south in 3.2 s while uniformly accelerating at a rate of 0.71 m/s² south. What was the initial velocity of the object?

13. An object uniformly accelerates from 15.0 m/s west to 35.0 m/s west. What is the rate of acceleration if the displacement during this time was 43.0 m?

14. An object uniformly accelerates from a velocity of 7.0 m/s west to 19.0 m/s west. What is the average velocity of the object?

15. An object accelerates uniformly at a rate of 1.50 m/s² east for 10.0 s. If the velocity of the object reaches 25.0 m/s east at this time, what was the initial velocity?

16. An object is displaced 25.0 m north while accelerating uniformly. If a velocity of 14.0 m/s north is reached in 1.90 s, what was the initial velocity?

17. An object accelerates uniformly from rest for 5.6 s. What velocity did the object reach if its displacement was 31.0 m west?

18. An object accelerates uniformly at a rate of 0.900 m/s^2. This object reached a velocity of 25.0 m/s south while its displacement was 37.0 m south. What was the initial velocity of the object?

19. A ball, starting from rest, accelerates uniformly down an incline at a rate of 1.4 m/s^2. Find:

    a) the distance travelled by the ball in 5.0 s.

    b) the velocity of the ball at 5.0 s.

20. An object was travelling at an average velocity of 9.60 m/s to the right. If the time of travel was 2.70 s, what was the displacement of the object?

21. An object was uniformly accelerated from rest at a rate of 3.10 m/s² south. If this object reaches a velocity of 12.4 m/s south in 4.00 s, what is the displacement of the object while accelerating?

22. An object initially at rest is uniformly accelerated to a velocity of 10.0 m/s west in 2.50 s. If, the displacement of the object was 12.5 m west during this time, what was the rate of acceleration?

23. An object was displaced 19.6 m east while uniformly accelerating from rest. If the average velocity of the object was 5.00 m/s east, what was the rate of acceleration?

24. An object uniformly accelerates at a rate of 1.00 m/s² east. After 27.0 s, the object is displaced 417.2 m east. What velocity did this object reach in this time?

Lesson 5   FREELY FALLING OBJECTS

If you drop your pen, it will fall to the floor. How do we describe this motion? Does it fall to the floor with uniform velocity, or uniformly accelerated motion? Aristotle, the early Greek natural philosopher, came to the conclusion that objects fall with a uniform or constant velocity, and this velocity is proportional to the mass of the falling object.

Galileo, however, concluded that falling objects accelerate uniformly at the same rate, and this constant rate of acceleration exists independent of the mass of the object.

Galileo: Objects accelerate uniformly at the same rate as they fall

Questions

1. Why do you think Aristotle came to the conclusion that he did?

2. How did Galileo come to his conclusion about falling objects?

Activity 3

• Drop your pen and a sheet of paper from a height of 1.5 m.

Questions

1. Which object reached the floor first?

2. Did the pen and paper accelerate uniformly as they fell?

3. Does this support Galileo's conclusion?

• Now crumple the paper into a tight ball. Drop your pen and paper ball from a height of 1.5 m.

Questions

1. Which object reached the floor first?

2. Does this support Aristotle's conclusion?

Activity 4

- Design an experiment to study the motion of freely falling objects. Use objects that are heavy enough so that air friction is negligible.

- Collect data that will allow you to calculate the acceleration of different masses released from different heights.

- State your conclusion.

Activity 3 clearly demonstrates that air friction affects different objects in different ways. However, when air friction is negligible, the acceleration is nearly constant. Hopefully you observed this in Activity 4.

In 1971, Astronaut David Scott dropped a feather and a hammer simultaneously from the same height above the moon's surface.

Question

1. Which object (feather or hammer) hit the moon's surface first?

The acceleration of a freely falling object is called the acceleration due to gravity (g). Near the Earth's surface this acceleration is approximately 9.81 m/s^2. It should be noted that it varies slightly due to altitude and latitude. However, we will use 9.81 m/s^2 in our problem solving unless we are told otherwise.

$$g = 9.81 \, \text{m/s}^2$$

We can use the variable g to represent the vector quantity of $\vec{a}$ because when we discuss acceleration due to gravity on Earth, the direction is always assumed to be *down*, relative to the core of the Earth.

The acceleration due to gravity near Earth's surface is approximately 9.81 m/s^2

Acceleration due to gravity causes motion towards the Earth's surface

NOTES

Problems involving freely falling objects are some of the best examples of uniformly accelerated linear motion. Therefore, the problems that follow will be solved using the kinematic equations:

$$\vec{a} = \frac{\vec{v}_f - \vec{v}_i}{t}$$

$$\vec{d} = \left(\frac{\vec{v}_f + \vec{v}_i}{2}\right)t$$

$$\vec{d} = \vec{v}_i t + \frac{1}{2}\vec{a}t^2$$

$$\vec{v}_f^2 = \vec{v}_i^2 + 2\vec{a}\vec{d}$$

You can replace "$\vec{a}$" in these equations with "g" if you wish.

Example 1

A large steel ball is dropped from a height of 7.00 m above the floor. What is the velocity at which the object will strike the floor?

Solution

$\vec{v}_i$	$\vec{v}_f$	$\vec{a}$	$\vec{d}$	t
0	?	$9.81\,\text{m/s}^2$	7.00 m	×

$$\vec{v}_f^2 = \vec{v}_i^2 + 2\vec{a}\vec{d}$$
$$= 2\left(9.81\,\text{m/s}^2\right)(7.00\,\text{m})$$
$$\vec{v}_f = \sqrt{137\,\text{m}^2/\text{s}^2}$$
$$\vec{v}_f = 11.7\,\text{m/s down}$$

Example 2

A cement block falls from the roof of a building. If the time of fall was 5.60 s, what is the height of the building?

Solution

$\vec{v}_i$	$\vec{v}_f$	$\vec{a}$	$\vec{d}$	t
0	×	$9.81\,\text{m/s}^2$	?	5.60 s

$$\vec{d} = \vec{v}_i t + \frac{1}{2}\vec{a}t^2$$
$$= \frac{1}{2}\left(9.81\,\text{m/s}^2\right)(5.60\,\text{s})^2$$
$$= 154\,\text{m}$$

Example 3

If you drop your pen from a height of 2.50 m above the floor, how long will it take to fall?

Solution

$\vec{v}_i$	$\vec{v}_f$	$\vec{a}$	$\vec{d}$	t
0	×	9.81 m/s^2	2.50 m	?

$$\vec{d} = \vec{v}_i t + \frac{1}{2} \vec{a} t^2$$

$$t = \sqrt{\frac{2\vec{d}}{\vec{a}}}$$

$$= \sqrt{\frac{2(2.50 \text{ m})}{9.81 \text{ m/s}^2}}$$

$$= 0.714 \text{ s}$$

PRACTICE EXERCISE

Formulae: $\bar{a} = \dfrac{\bar{v}_f - \bar{v}_i}{t}$ $\bar{d} = \left(\dfrac{\bar{v}_f + \bar{v}_i}{2}\right)t$ $\bar{d} = \bar{v}_i t + \dfrac{1}{2}\bar{a}t^2$ $\bar{v}_f^{\,2} = \bar{v}_i^{\,2} + 2\bar{a}\bar{d}$

For the following questions, assume that air resistance is negligible.

1. A steel ball, initially at rest, falls from a height of 15.0 m above the ground. How fast will it be travelling when it strikes the ground?

2. An apple falls from a tree. If the time of fall was 0.50 s, from what height did the apple fall?

3. A book falls from a shelf that is 1.75 m above the floor. How long will it take the book to reach the floor?

4. If you drop a coin from a height of 9.50 m above the ground, how fast will it be travelling when it reaches the ground?

5. An object is dropped from the roof of a building. If the object takes 2.5 s to reach the ground, what was the velocity of the object at impact?

6. A rock was thrown vertically downward from a bridge over a river. If the rock was released when it was 11.2 m above the water, and it took 0.550 s for the rock to reach the water, what was the velocity of the rock when it was released?

7. An egg is thrown vertically downward from a window. If the egg is released with a velocity of 10.0 m/s and it strikes the ground at a velocity of 25.0 m/s, how long did it take the egg to reach the ground?

8. A rock was thrown vertically downward. If the rock was released with a velocity of 5.0 m/s and it hit the ground below at a velocity of 15.0 m/s, from what height was the rock released?

9. An object is thrown vertically downward. If the object hit the ground with a velocity of 10.0 m/s and it fell for 0.880 s, at what velocity was the object released?

10. A steel ball is dropped from a height of 50.0 m. How far does this ball travel during the third second of fall?

11. The following velocity-time graph represents the motion of an object that accelerates uniformly to the left.

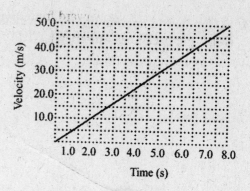

a) What is the average velocity during the 8.0 s of travel?

b) At what time does the object have an instantaneous velocity equal to the average velocity?

12. A rock is dropped from a height of 7.0 m. What is the average velocity of the rock during the fall?

13. In Question 12, how long does it take the rock to fall?

14. In Question 12, at what time is the rock actually travelling at the average velocity?
    (Hint: Go back to Question 11.)

15. You will note from Questions 13 and 14 that the average velocity occurs at the mid-time of the motion if the object is being uniformly accelerated. Using this information, determine the time of fall when an object is dropped given that the average velocity of the falling object was 12.0 m/s.

16. When an object is dropped from a height of 10.0 m above the surface of Planet X, it takes 1.20 s for the object to reach the surface. What is the acceleration of a falling object near the surface of this planet?

17. When an object is dropped from a height of 24.0 m above the surface of Planet Y, it hits the surface at a velocity of 19.6 m/s down. What is the acceleration of a falling object near the surface of this planet?

18. When an object is dropped near the surface of Planet F, it reaches a velocity of 11.0 m/s in 1.50 s. What is the acceleration of a falling object near the surface of Planet F?

19. A rock, thrown vertically downward, travels 10.0 m before hitting the ground. If it strikes the ground at a velocity of 15.0 m/s, how long did it take to reach the ground?

20. A rock that is thrown vertically downward takes 0.85 s to reach the ground. If it travels 9.2 m before reaching the ground, what is its impact velocity?

21. An object is dropped from a short distance above Planet T. If the average velocity during a fall of 40.0 m is 30.0 m/s, what is the acceleration of a falling object near the surface of Planet T?

22. When an object is dropped from a height of 20.0 m above the surface of Planet Z, it will fall 5.00 m during the 2nd second of fall. What is the acceleration of a falling object near the surface of this planet?

Lesson 6 KINEMATICS IN ONE DIMENSION

To this point, all vector quantities have been in the same direction along a line.

Now, let's consider problems in which the vector quantities may have opposite directions along a straight line.

Example 1

A ball starts up an incline with a certain velocity. The ball slows down, comes to a stop, and starts to roll back down.

In this example,

$\vec{v}_i$ is up the incline

$\vec{a}$ is down the incline

$\vec{v}_f$ is down the incline

$\vec{d}$ is up the incline

Displacement becomes zero when the ball returns to its starting point and will be down if it rolls beyond its starting point in the opposite direction.

PROBLEM SOLVING

In solving problems involving vectors in both directions along a straight line, we will continue to use the kinematic equations:

$$\vec{a} = \frac{\vec{v}_f - \vec{v}_i}{t}$$

$$\vec{d} = \left(\frac{\vec{v}_f + \vec{v}_i}{2}\right)t$$

$$\vec{d} = \vec{v}_i t + \frac{1}{2}\vec{a}t^2$$

$$\vec{v}_f{}^2 = \vec{v}_i{}^2 + 2\vec{a}\vec{d}$$

However, we will indicate the direction by using positive $(+)$ and negative $(-)$ signs. It is customary to identify a direction to the right or up as positive $(+)$, and a direction to the left or down as negative $(-)$.

Direction along a line is indicated using a positive $(+)$ and negative $(-)$ sign

NOTES

Activity 5

1. Design an experiment in which you can analyze the motion of an object that moves up an incline, reverses its direction, and moves back down.
2. Collect data that will allow you to determine the position and velocity at various times.
3. Analyze your data by drawing a position-time graph and a velocity-time graph

Data:

Position-Time Graph

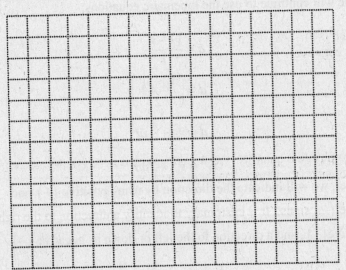

Velocity-Time Graph

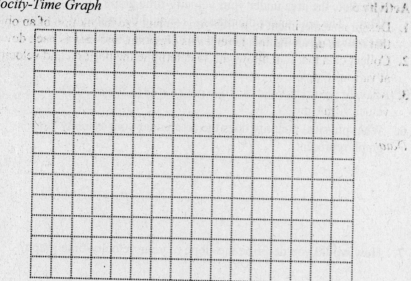

Questions

1. How would you describe the slope of your position-time graph?

2. When is the slope of your position-time graph positive, and when is it negative?

3. What physical quantity does the slope of your position-time graph represent? (Remember Activity 2.)

4. Do you think the changing slope of your position-time graph represents the changing velocity of the object as it moves up and down the incline? When is the slope equal to zero? Was the velocity of the object zero at any time?

NOTES

5. Calculate the area under your velocity-time graph.
   (Hint: The area under the time axis should be treated as negative; the area above the time axis should be treated as positive.)

6. What physical quantity does the area under your velocity-time graph represent?

7. How would you describe the slope of your velocity-time graph?

8. How would you describe the velocity of the object as it moves up and down the incline?

SUMMARY

- slope of position-time graph is the velocity
- slope of velocity-time graph is the acceleration
- area under a velocity-time graph is the displacement

Slopes may be + or −
Area may be + or −
(This is because displacement, velocity, and acceleration can be in either direction along a line.)

PRACTICE EXERCISE

1. The following position-time graph represents the motion of a steel ball rolling up an incline, coming to a stop, and returning back to its original position. Find the velocity at:

   a) 3.0 s.

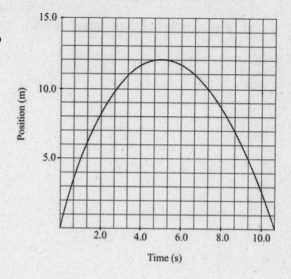

   b) 7.0 s.

2. Given the following velocity-time graph for an object moving along a line, find the acceleration of the moving object at:

   a) 4.0 s.

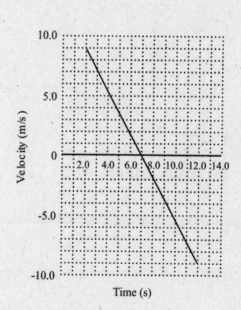

   b) 10.0 s.

3. Given the following position-time graph for an object moving north along a line, find the:

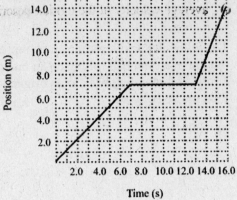

a) displacement of the object at 16.0 s.

b) velocity at 5.0 s.

c) velocity at 9.0 s.

d) velocity at 15.0 s.

e) average velocity of the motion described.

f) acceleration at between 2.0 s and 6.0 s.

4. The following is a velocity-time graph for an object moving along a line. If the initial direction of the object is east, find the:

   a) velocity at 4.0 s.

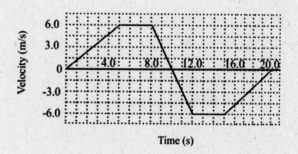

   b) velocity at 7.0 s.

c) velocity at 11.0 s.

d) acceleration at 10.0 s.

e) acceleration at 17.0 s.

f) displacement at 10.0 s.

g) average velocity during the total motion described.

5. The following is a position-time graph for an object moving along a line. If the direction of the object is south, find the:

a) velocity at 2.0 s.

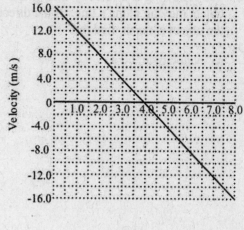

b) velocity at 8.0 s.

c) acceleration between 2.0 s and 8.0 s.

6. The following is a velocity-time graph for an object moving along a line. If the direction of the object is north, find the:

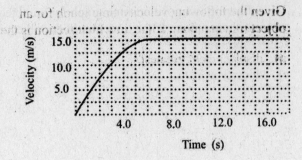

a) velocity at 7.0 s.

b) acceleration at 9.0 s.

c) displacement between 8.0 s and 18.0 s.

7. Given the following velocity-time graph for an object moving along a line, in which section is the:

   a) displacement greatest?

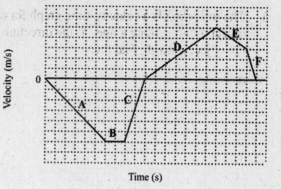

   b) velocity the greatest?

8. Given the following position-time graph for an object moving north along a line, find the:

   a) velocity at 8.0 s.

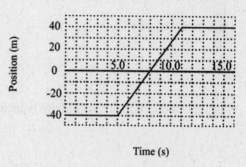

   b) velocity at 15.0 s.

   c) displacement between 4.0 s and 15.0 s.

9. Given the following position-time graphs,

A.

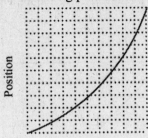

B.

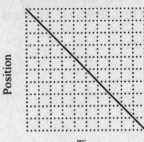

C.

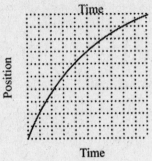

D.

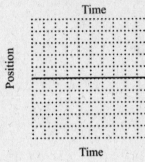

which of these graphs represents:

a) zero velocity?

b) motion in which the velocity is increasing?

c) motion in which the velocity is decreasing?

d) motion in which the velocity is constant?

10. The following is a position-time graph for an object moving along a line.

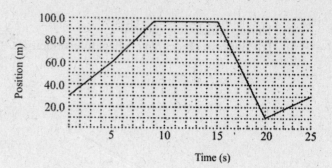

a) If the initial direction of the motion is east, find:

    i) the velocity of the object at 17.0 s.

    ii) the total distance travelled by the object from the beginning to the end of the motion described in the graph.

    iii) the displacement of the object from the beginning to the end of the motion described in the graph.

    iv) the average speed of the object during the motion described in the graph.

b) During which time interval

    i) does the object have a negative velocity?

    ii) does the object reach its highest velocity?

11. Given the following velocity-time graph for an object moving along a line,

    a) during which time interval is the object's velocity the greatest?

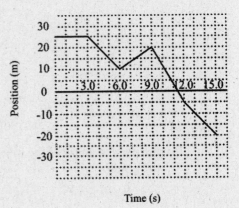

b) during which time interval is the acceleration of the object zero?

c) during which time interval is the acceleration of the object the greatest?

12. The dots below represent the position of an object every 0.10 s as it moves up an incline.

The dots below represent the position of the same object as it continues its motion back down the incline.

a) Analyze this motion by completing the following data table.

time (s)	displacement (m)	displacement during time interval (m)	average velocity during time interval (m/s)
0			
0.10			
0.20			
0.30			
0.40			
0.50			
0.60			
0.70			
0.80			
0.90			
1.00			
1.10			
1.20			
1.30			
1.40			

b) Draw a position time graph using this data table.

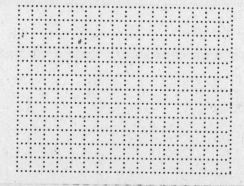

c) Draw a velocity-time graph using this data.

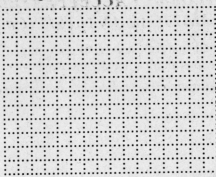

d) Find the velocity of the object using your position-time graph at:

i) 0.40 s.

ii) 1.10 s.

e) Using your velocity-time graph, find the displacement of the object after 1.40 s.

f) Using your velocity-time graph, find the acceleration of the object.

Lesson 7 UNIFORMLY ACCELERATED MOTION— MATHEMATICAL ANALYSIS (Continued)

It is important to keep in mind in mathematical analysis of uniformly accelerated motion when both directions along a line are involved.

- The direction to the right or up is positive $(+)$

- The direction to the left or down is negative $(-)$

NOTES

Example 1

A stone is thrown vertically upward with an initial velocity of 25.2 m/s. Calculate the maximum displacement (height) of this stone.

Solution

$\vec{v}_i$	$\vec{v}_f$	$\vec{a}$	$\vec{d}$	t
25.2 m/s	0	$-9.81\,\text{m/s}^2$	?	×

$$\vec{v}_f^{\,2} = \vec{v}_i^{\,2} + 2\vec{a}\vec{d}$$

$$0 = \left(25.2\,\text{m/s}\right)^2 + 2\left(-9.81\,\text{m/s}^2\right)\left(\vec{d}\right)$$

$$\vec{d} = 32.4\ \text{m} \ \ \text{up}$$

Example 2

A stone is dropped from a height of 32.4 m above the ground. Calculate the velocity of this object when it reaches the ground.

Solution

$\vec{v}_i$	$\vec{v}_f$	$\vec{a}$	$\vec{d}$	t
0	?	$-9.81\,\text{m/s}^2$	-32.4 m	×

$$\vec{v}_f^{\,2} = \vec{v}_i^{\,2} + 2\vec{a}\vec{d}$$

$$\vec{v}_f^{\,2} = 0 + 2\left(-9.81\,\text{m/s}^2\right)\left(-32.4\ \text{m}\right)$$

$$\vec{v}_f = \sqrt{2\left(-9.81\,\text{m/s}^2\right)\left(-32.4\ \text{m}\right)}$$

$$= -25.2\,\text{m/s} \ \ \text{or} \ \ 25.2\,\text{m/s} \ \text{down}$$

The initial velocity in Example 1 and the final velocity in Example 2 are equal in magnitude. This will always be true when the same displacement up and down is involved.

NOTES

Example 3

A stone is thrown vertically upward with an initial velocity of 11 m/s².
Calculate the time the stone is in the air.

Solution

$\vec{v}_i$	$\vec{v}_f$	$\vec{a}$	$\vec{d}$	t
11 m/s	−11 m/s	−9.81 m/s²	×	?

$$\vec{a} = \frac{\vec{v}_f - \vec{v}_i}{t}$$

$$t = \frac{\vec{v}_f - \vec{v}_i}{\vec{a}}$$

$$= \frac{-11\,\text{m/s} - 11\,\text{m/s}}{-9.81\,\text{m/s}^2}$$

$$= 2.2\ \text{s}$$

Although we were not given the velocity in which the stone returned, we know that when an object is thrown vertically upward, it will return with the same speed but opposite direction.

Example 4

A ball is rolled up a constant slope with an initial velocity of 12.0 m/s.
If the ball's displacement is 0.500 m up the slope after 3.60 s, what is the velocity of the ball at this time?

Solution

$\vec{v}_i$	$\vec{v}_f$	$\vec{a}$	$\vec{d}$	t
12.0 m/s	?	×	0.500 m	3.60 s

$$\vec{d} = \left(\frac{\vec{v}_f + \vec{v}_i}{2}\right) t$$

$$0.500\ \text{m} = \left(\frac{\vec{v}_f + 12.0\,\text{m/s}}{2}\right) 3.60\ \text{s}$$

$$\vec{v}_f = \frac{2(0.500\ \text{m})}{3.60\ \text{s}} - 12.0\ \text{m/s}$$

$$= -11.7\ \text{m/s}\ \ \text{OR}\ \ 1.7\ \text{m/s down}$$

88

PRACTICE EXERCISE

Formulae: $\qquad \vec{a} = \dfrac{\vec{v}_f - \vec{v}_i}{t} \qquad \vec{d} = \left(\dfrac{\vec{v}_f + \vec{v}_i}{2} \right) t \qquad \vec{d} = \vec{v}_i t + \dfrac{1}{2} \vec{a} t^2 \qquad \vec{v}_f^{\,2} = \vec{v}_i^{\,2} + 2\vec{a}\vec{d}$

For the following questions, assume that air resistance is negligible.

1. An object is thrown vertically upward with an initial velocity of 14.0 m/s. What is the displacement after 1.80 s?

2. A ball is rolled up a constant slope with an initial velocity of 9.3 m/s. What is the acceleration of the ball if its displacement is 1.9 m up the slope after 2.7 s?

3. A ball is rolled up a constant slope with an initial velocity of 11.0 m/s. After 9.3 s, the ball is rolling down the slope with a velocity of 7.3 m/s. What is the rate of acceleration of the ball on the slope?

4. A ball is rolled up a constant slope with an initial velocity of 9.4 m/s. After 3.0 s, the ball is rolling down the slope with a velocity of 7.4 m/s. How far up the slope is the ball at this time?

5. An object is thrown vertically upward with an initial velocity of 15.0 m/s. How high is the object when it is travelling down with a velocity of 8.0 m/s?

6. An object is thrown vertically downward toward the ground with an initial velocity of 5.0 m/s. This object hits the ground with a velocity of 12.0 m/s. How long did the object take to reach the ground?

7. A ball is rolled up a constant slope. After 3.6 s it reaches its maximum displacement of 2.6 m and then begins to roll back down. What was the initial velocity of the ball when it started up the slope?

8. An object is thrown vertically upward with an initial velocity of 10.0 m/s. What is the velocity of the object when it is on its way back down and is 5.0 m above the point of release?

9. An object is thrown vertically upward with a velocity of 25.0 m/s. What is the velocity of this object after 3.0 s?

10. A ball is rolled up a constant slope with an initial velocity of 2.0 m/s. After 1.5 s, the ball is 2.8 m up the incline from the point of release. What is the velocity of the ball at this time?

11. An object is thrown vertically upward. If after 3.0 s the object has a vertical displacement up of 5.0 m, what was the initial velocity?

12. A ball is rolled up a constant slope with an initial velocity of 2.2 m/s. After 2.0 s, the ball is rolling down the slope with a velocity of 1.1 m/s. What is the acceleration of the ball?

13. A ball is rolled up a constant slope with an initial velocity of 2.5 m/s. When the displacement of the ball is 1.0 m up the slope it has a velocity of 1.6 m/s down. What is the acceleration of the ball?

14. A ball rolls 2.7 m up a constant slope, coming to a stop momentarily before rolling back down. If the initial velocity of the ball was 2.0 m/s how long does it take the ball to roll up and down the slope?

15. While on Planet X, an object is thrown vertically upward with an initial velocity of 5.0 m/s. If this object returns to the point of release in 3.0 s, what is the acceleration of a freely falling object on this planet?

16. An object is thrown vertically upward from a helicopter that is hovering 30.0 m above the ground. The initial velocity of the object was 20.0 m/s.

   a) Calculate the velocity with which the object hits the ground.

   b) Calculate the time it took for the object to reach the ground.

17. While riding on an amusement park vehicle, you drop an object. The vehicle was rising vertically at a velocity of 11.0 m/s and was 5.0 m above the ground when the object was dropped. How long does it take the object to reach the ground?

18. An object is thrown vertically upward. If this object takes 5.30 s to go up and down, what height did it reach?

19. An object is dropped from a height of 25.0 m above the ground. What is the average velocity of the object as it falls to the ground?

20. An object was thrown upward from the ground with an initial velocity of 14.0 m/s. When the object reached its maximum displacement (height),

   a) find its displacement from the ground.

   b) find the time of travel.

21. An object is rolled up an incline. If the object is 2.75 m up the incline after 4.50 s and rolling back down at a velocity of 1.90 m/s, what is the acceleration of the object?

Lesson 8   KINEMATICS IN TWO DIMENSIONS

A student walks 73 m north then turns and walks 62 m east. What is the student's displacement?

Remember: displacement is a vector quantity. A vector quantity has both magnitude (size) and direction.

Vectors are represented by arrows. The direction of the arrow represents the direction of the vector, and the length of the arrow represents the magnitude of the vector.

Direction can be expressed in a number of ways. Direction can be expressed as an angle measured from the horizontal, from the vertical, or from some convenient feature like a shoreline.

In mathematics and physics, we sometimes make use of the *Rectangular Coordinate System* to measure direction (Diagram A). Note that the angles (directions) are measured counterclockwise from the positive *x*-axis. This convention is also referred to as the unit circle.

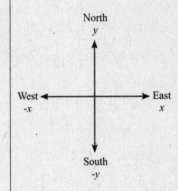

Diagram A

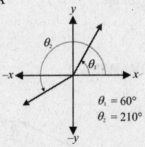

$\theta_1 = 60°$
$\theta_2 = 210°$

You will also find that direction is expressed in terms of north, east, south and west as shown in Diagrams B and C. This is a common method and is found in most physics texts.

Diagram B   Diagram C

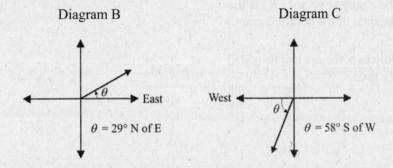

$\theta = 29°$ N of E $\theta = 58°$ S of W

The two displacements in the diagrams shown can be added graphically or analytically. In both methods, a vector diagram is drawn. In the graphical method, a careful scale vector diagram is drawn. In the analytical method, a reasonable representation is drawn.

NOTES

The vector diagrams can be drawn by drawing the vectors tail to tip (tail to tip method) or by drawing the vectors from a single point (parallelogram method).

TAIL TO TIP DRAWING

- The vector $\vec{v}_1$ is drawn.

- To the head (tip) of this first vector, $\vec{v}_1$, start the drawing of vector $\vec{v}_2$.

- Draw the resultant vector $\vec{R}$ as shown in the diagram.

- If there are more than two vectors, keep adding vectors tail to tip.

- The resultant vector $\vec{R}$ is the arrow drawn from the tail of the first vector to the tip of the last vector.

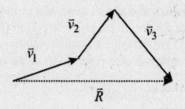

PARALLELOGRAM DRAWING

- Both vectors ($\vec{v}_1$ and $\vec{v}_2$) are drawn from a point as shown in the diagram.

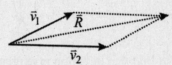

- A parallelogram is completed as shown.

- The resultant vector ($\vec{R}$) is the diagonal of the parallelogram.

- Only two vectors can be added at a time.

GRAPHICAL METHOD

The graphical method is also known as the ruler and protractor method.

- Draw a careful scale diagram using either the tail to tip or parallelogram method.

- Measure the resultant vector $\vec{R}$ and the angle θ.

- Scale 1.0 cm = 10 m

$$\vec{R} = 9.6 \text{ cm}$$
$$= 96 \text{ m}$$
$$\theta = 49.7°$$
$$\vec{R} = 96 \text{ m } 50° \text{ N of E}$$

or $\vec{R} = 96 \text{ m } 50°$ (using RCS)

(RCS = rectangular coordinate system)

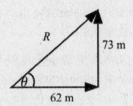

ANALYTICAL METHOD

- Draw a vector diagram of reasonable representation using either the tail to tip or parallelogram method
- If the vectors are perpendicular to each other, find the magnitude of the resultant vector $\left(\vec{R}\right)$ using the Pythagorean Theorem

$$c = \sqrt{a^2 + b^2}$$

or

$$\vec{R} = \sqrt{\left(\vec{v_1}\right)^2 + \left(\vec{v_2}\right)^2}$$

and find the direction of the resultant vector $\left(\vec{R}\right)$ using one of the trigonometric functions:

$$\sin \theta = \frac{\text{opposite}}{\text{hypotenuse}}$$

$$\cos \theta = \frac{\text{adjacent}}{\text{hypotenuse}}$$

$$\tan \theta = \frac{\text{opposite}}{\text{adjacent}}$$

Example 1

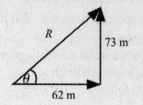

$$\vec{R} = \sqrt{(\vec{v}_1)^2 + (\vec{v}_2)^2}$$

$$= \sqrt{(62 \text{ m})^2 + (73 \text{ m})^2}$$

$$= 95.8 \text{ m}$$

$$\tan \theta = \frac{\text{opposite}}{\text{adjacent}}$$

$$= \frac{73 \text{ m}}{62 \text{ m}}$$

$$\theta = 49.7°$$

$$\vec{R} = 96 \text{ m} \quad 50° \text{ N of E}$$

$$\text{or} \quad \vec{R} = 96 \text{ m} \quad 50° \ (\text{using } RCS)$$

PRACTICE EXERCISE

NOTE: Answers are also expressed in terms of rectangular coordinate system (*RCS*).

1. Add the following displacement vectors.

   a) 3.0 m south and 4.0 m south

   b) 3.0 m south and 4.0 m north

   c) 4.0 m east and 3.0 m south

   d) 8.0 m west and 5.0 m north

e) 7.0 m east and 11.0 m north

f) 20.0 m east and 15.0 m south

g) 7.0 m south, 6.0 m east and 8.0 m north (**Hint:** add vectors that are along the same axis first:)

h) 15 m west, 12 m north and 20 m east

Lesson 9   VECTOR COMPONENTS

A student walks 75 m north then turns and walks 62 m 32° W of N. What is the student's displacement?

The vector problems to this point could be solved using Pythagorean Theorem and basic trigonometry.

- Pythagorean Theorem

$$c = \sqrt{a^2 + b^2}$$

- Trigonometry Functions

$$\sin\theta = \frac{\text{opposite}}{\text{hypotenuse}}$$

$$\cos\theta = \frac{\text{adjacent}}{\text{hypotenuse}}$$

$$\tan\theta = \frac{\text{opposite}}{\text{adjacent}}$$

$$\sin\theta = \frac{\text{opposite}}{\text{hypotenuse}} = \frac{\vec{R}_x}{\vec{R}}$$

$$\cos\theta = \frac{\text{adjacent}}{\text{hypotenuse}} = \frac{\vec{R}_y}{\vec{R}}$$

$$\tan\theta = \frac{\text{opposite}}{\text{adjacent}} = \frac{\vec{R}_y}{\vec{R}_x}$$

$$\vec{R} = \sqrt{\vec{R}_x^{\,2} + \vec{R}_y^{\,2}}$$

However, in this problem, the vectors are not perpendicular; therefore, they do not form a right angle. Although this problem may be solved using a number of methods, we will solve it by making use of the rectangular coordinate system. In this method we find the components of the vectors. The following formulae will be used:

$$\vec{R} = \sqrt{\vec{R}_x^{\,2} + \vec{R}_y^{\,2}} \qquad \vec{R}_x = \vec{R}\cos\theta$$

$$\vec{R}_y = \vec{R}\sin\theta \qquad \tan\theta = \frac{\vec{R}_y}{\vec{R}_x}$$

where $\vec{R}$ = resultant vector

$\vec{R}_x$ = resultant x component

$\vec{R}_y$ = resultant y component

Example 1

A student walks 75 m north then turns and walks 62 m 32° W of N. What is the student's displacement?

Solution

First express the directions in terms of the x-axis (rectangular coordinate system).

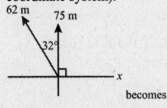

becomes

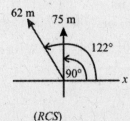

(*RCS*)

NOTES

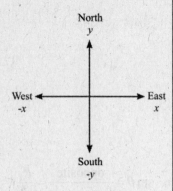

We know that θ is in the second quadrant because x is negative and y is positive, i.e.,
$\theta = 180° - 76° = 104°$

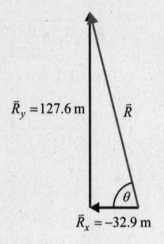

Resolve 75 m north into its x and y components $\left(\vec{R}_x \text{ and } \vec{R}_y\right)$.

$$\vec{R}_x = \vec{R}\cos\theta$$
$$= (75 \text{ m})\cos 90°$$
$$= 0$$
$$\vec{R}_y = \vec{R}\sin\theta$$
$$= (75 \text{ m})\sin 90°$$
$$= 75 \text{ m}$$

Resolve 62 m 32° W of N into its x and y components $\left(\vec{R}_x \text{ and } \vec{R}_y\right)$.

$$\vec{R}_x = \vec{R}\cos\theta$$
$$= (62 \text{ m})\cos 122°$$
$$= -32.9 \text{ m}$$
$$\vec{R}_y = \vec{R}\sin\theta$$
$$= (62 \text{ m})\sin 122°$$
$$= 52.6 \text{ m}$$

Add x components to obtain $\vec{R}_x$.

$$\vec{R}_x = \vec{R}_{1x} + \vec{R}_{2x}$$
$$= 0 + (-32.9 \text{ m})$$
$$= -32.9 \text{ m} \quad (\text{negative indicates a west direction})$$

Add y components to obtain $\vec{R}_y$.

$$\vec{R}_y = \vec{R}_{1y} + \vec{R}_{2y}$$
$$= 75 \text{ m} + 52.6 \text{ m}$$
$$= 127.6 \text{ m} \quad (\text{positive indicates a north direction})$$

Add $\vec{R}_x$ and $\vec{R}_y$ to obtain $\vec{R}$

$$\vec{R} = \sqrt{\vec{R}_x^2 + \vec{R}_y^2}$$
$$= \sqrt{(-32.9 \text{ m})^2 + (127.6 \text{ m})^2}$$
$$= 132 \text{ m or } 1.3 \times 10^2 \text{ m}$$

$$\tan\theta = \frac{\vec{R}_y}{\vec{R}_x}$$
$$= \frac{127.6 \text{ m}}{-32.9 \text{ m}}$$
$$\theta = 75.5° \quad \text{or} \quad 76°$$
$$\vec{R} = 1.3 \times 10^2 \text{ m } 76° \text{ N of W or } \vec{R} = 1.3 \times 10^2 \text{ m } 104° (RCS)$$

PRACTICE EXERCISE

Answers should also be expressed in terms of the rectangular coordinate system where possible.

1. Find the x and y components of the following displacements.

   a) 16.0 m north

   b) 16.0 m 27.0° E of N

   c) 20.0 m 52.0° W of N

   d) 10.0 m 327°

2. Add the following displacement vectors.

   a) 8.0 m east and 6.0 m east

b) 8.0 m east and 6.0 m west

c) 8.0 m east and 6.0 m north

d) 8.0 m east and 6.0 m 35° N of E

e) 12 m south and 15 m 55° E of N

f) 5.0 m 26° S of E and 7.0 m 58° W of N

g) 9.0 m 35° N of E and 7.0 m 25° S of E

Lesson 10 *VELOCITY VECTORS AND NAVIGATION*

A boat with a speed in still water of 4.5 m/s travels north across a river. The river current is 2.0 m/s east. What is the velocity of the boat relative to the shore?

We see that the velocity of the boat with respect to the shore is the sum of the velocity of the boat relative to water (4.5 m/s north) and the velocity of the river (2. m/s east).

These vectors are added in the same way in which we added displacement vectors.

- Draw a vector diagram.

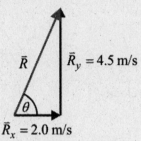

$$\vec{R}_y = 4.5 \text{ m/s}$$

$$\vec{R}_x = 2.0 \text{ m/s}$$

- Find the magnitude of $\vec{R}$ using the Pythagorean Theorem,

$$\vec{R} = \sqrt{\vec{R}_x{}^2 + \vec{R}_y{}^2}$$

$$= \sqrt{(2.0 \text{ m/s})^2 + (4.5 \text{ m/s})^2}$$

$$= 4.9 \text{ m/s}$$

- Find the direction using: $\tan\theta = \dfrac{\text{opposite}}{\text{adjacent}} = \dfrac{\vec{R}_y}{\vec{R}_x}$

$$\tan\theta = \frac{4.5 \text{ m/s}}{2.0 \text{ m/s}}$$

$$\theta = 66°$$

- $\vec{R} = 4.9 \text{ m/s} \; 66° \text{ N of E}$ or $\vec{R} = 49 \text{ m/s} \; 66° \; (RCS)$

PRACTICE EXERCISE

NOTE: Answers should also be expressed in terms of the rectangular coordinate system where possible.

1. A car is travelling in a straight line with uniform motion. The east component of this motion is 15.0 m/s, and the south component of the motion is 11.0 m/s. What is the velocity of the car?

2. A girl is moving up an escalator at a velocity of 2.0 m/s at an angle of 35.0° to the horizontal.

    a) What is the horizontal component of the girl's velocity?

    b) What is the vertical component of the girl's velocity?

3. A pilot flies her plane with a velocity of 255 km/h north. If there is a strong wind of 112 km/h blowing east, what is the velocity of the plane relative to the ground?

4. A ball is thrown into the air at an angle of 40.0° to the horizontal with an initial velocity of 25.0 m/s. Calculate:

a) the vertical component of the initial velocity.

b) the horizontal component of the initial velocity.

5. An airplane is headed due north at an airspeed of 32 m/s. A sudden wind of 12 m/s arises from the west (blowing east). What is the velocity of the plane relative to the ground while the wind is blowing?

6. A boat that can travel at a speed of 2.5 m/s in still water is on a river with a velocity of 1.0 m/s south. What is the velocity of the boat relative to the shore when:

a) the boat is headed south?

b) the boat is headed north?

c) the boat is headed west?

7. An airplane is travelling east at an airspeed of 125 m/s. If a 25.0 m/s wind is blowing south, what is the velocity of the plane relative to the ground?

8. A boat that can maintain a speed of 3.0 m on still water wants to travel north perpendicular to the river current. If the river current is 1.2 m/s east, in what direction must the boat head? (**NOTE:** The boat's resultant is to be perpendicular to river current.)

9. A boat travels directly north across a river at a velocity of 1.0 m/s. If the river flows at a velocity of 0.50 m/s east, in what direction must the boat be headed to accomplish this? (**NOTE:** Resultant is perpendicular to the river current. The 1.0 m/s is resultant.)

10. A pilot wants to fly west (i.e., the resultant is west). If the plane has an airspeed of 9.5 m/s, and there is a 25 m/s wind blowing north, in what direction must she head the plane?

11. A boat is headed north on a river that flows due east at a velocity of 5.0 m/s. If the resultant velocity of this boat is 8.7 m/s 35.0° E of N, what is the speed of the boat with respect to the water?

12. A boat with a speed in still water of 5.0 m/s is headed west across a river. The river current is 2.5 m/s south.

   a) What is the velocity of the boat relative to the shore?

   b) If the river is 2 395 m wide, how long does it take the boat to cross the river?

   c) How far downstream is the boat when it reaches the other side of the river?

13. A boat that can travel 2.5 m/s on still water is now on a river that flows due east at a velocity of 2.0 m/s. What is the velocity of this boat with reference to a point on the shore when:

a) the boat is headed east?

b) the boat is headed west?

c) the boat is headed north?

d) the boat is headed 45.0° W of N (135°)?

14. A boat that can travel 4.0 m/s on still water heads directly north across a river that is 125 m wide. If the river current is 2.1 m/s east,

a) what is the velocity of the boat with respect to the shore?

b) how long does it take the boat to reach the opposite shore?

c) how far downstream is the boat when it reaches the opposite shore?

Lesson 11   PROJECTILE MOTION

A baseball thrown by a baseball player, a football kicked by a football player, a bullet fired at a distant target, and an object dropped from a plane are all examples of projectile motion.

When an object is thrown into the air, it is a projectile. We have already dealt with projectiles when they are thrown vertically upward and when they are dropped. In this section we will deal with projectiles that are thrown horizontally through the air.

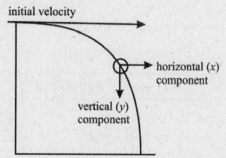

- The horizontal motion is uniform motion, and is described by the equation:

$$\vec{v} = \frac{\vec{d}}{t}$$

- The vertical motion is uniformly accelerated motion, and is described by the equations:

$$\vec{a} = \frac{\vec{v}_f - \vec{v}_i}{t}$$

$$\vec{d} = \left(\frac{\vec{v}_f + \vec{v}_i}{2}\right)t$$

$$\vec{d} = \vec{v}_i t + \frac{1}{2}\vec{a}t^2$$

$$\vec{v}_f^{\,2} = \vec{v}_i^{\,2} + 2\vec{a}\vec{d}$$

The acceleration is g

$$g = 9.81\,\text{m/s}^2$$

Example 1

An object is thrown horizontally at a velocity of 20.0 m/s from the top of a building 50.0 m tall. How far from the base of the building did the object hit the ground?

Solution

i) We are asked to find a distance, which we know is the magnitude of the horizontal component of the displacement.

$$\therefore \text{ we use } \vec{v} = \frac{\vec{d}}{t} \text{ or } \vec{d} = \vec{v}t$$

ii) Find t from the vertical component.

$\vec{v}_i$	$\vec{v}_f$	$\vec{a}$	$\vec{d}$	t
0	×	9.81 m/s^2	50.0 m	?

$$\vec{d} = \vec{v}_i t + \frac{1}{2}\vec{a}t^2$$

$$-50.0 \text{ m} = \frac{1}{2}\left(-9.81 \text{ m/s}^2\right)\left(t^2\right)$$

$$t = \sqrt{\frac{2(-50.0 \text{ m})}{-9.81 \text{ m/s}^2}}$$

$$= 3.19 \text{ s}$$

$$\vec{d} = \vec{v}t$$

$$= (20.0 \text{ m/s})(3.19 \text{ s})$$

$$= 63.9 \text{ m}$$

PRACTICE EXERCISE

For the following questions, assume that air resistance is negligible.

1. An object is thrown horizontally at a velocity of 10.0 m/s from the top of a 90.0 m building. Calculate the horizontal distance from the base of the building at which the object will hit the ground.

2. An object is thrown horizontally at a velocity of 25.0 m/s from the top of a 1.50×10^2 m building. Calculate the distance from the base of the building that the object will hit the ground.

3. An object is thrown horizontally at a velocity of 18.0 m/s from the top of a cliff. If the object hits the ground 100.0 m from the base of the cliff, how high is the cliff?

4. An object is thrown horizontally at a velocity of 20.0 m/s from the top of a cliff. If the object hit the ground 48.0 m from the base of the cliff, how high is the cliff?

5. An object is thrown horizontally from the top of a building at a velocity of 15.0 m/s. If the object takes 5.50 s to reach the ground, how high is the building?

6. An object is thrown horizontally from the top of a cliff at a velocity of 20.0 m/s. If the object takes 4.20 s to reach the ground, how far from the base of the cliff did the object hit the ground?

7. An object is thrown horizontally from the top of an 85.0 m building. If the object hits the ground 67.8 m from the base of the building, what was the horizontal velocity of the object?

NOTES

Activity 6

- Design an experiment to study the projectile motion of an object projected horizontally. (A stroboscopic multiple exposure photograph or air table with spark timer will be required.)

- Complete the following data table.

time (s)	displacement from t = 0 (m)		displacement during time interval (m)		average velocity during time interval (m/s)	
	horiz.	vert.	horiz.	vert.	horiz.	vert.
0						

- Using your horizontal velocity, draw a velocity-time graph.

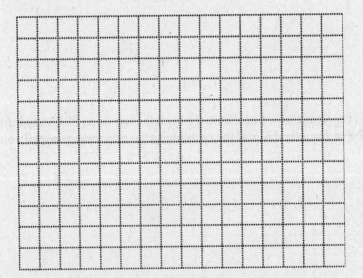

• Using your vertical velocity, draw a velocity-time graph.

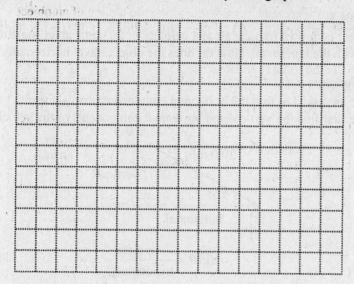

• Using your graphs, find:
   i)   the horizontal acceleration
   ii) the vertical acceleration

Lesson 12 PROJECTILE MOTION AT AN ANGLE

Example 1

An object is thrown into the air at a velocity of 20.0 m/s at an angle of 30.0° with the horizontal. How far does the object travel horizontally?

Solution:

We are asked to find the horizontal component (displacement).
We first find the vertical and horizontal components of the velocity.

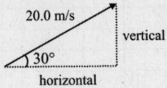

20.0 m/s

vertical

30°

horizontal

$$\sin \theta = \frac{\text{opposite}}{\text{hypotenuse}}$$

$$\sin 30° = \frac{\text{vertical}}{20.0 \text{ m/s}}$$

$$\text{vertical} = 10.0 \text{ m/s}$$

$$\cos \theta = \frac{\text{adjacent}}{\text{hypotenuse}}$$

$$\cos 30.0° = \frac{\text{horizontal}}{20.0 \text{ m/s}}$$

$$\text{horizontal} = 17.3 \text{ m/s}$$

Find t from the vertical component.

$\vec{v}_i$	$\vec{v}_f$	$\vec{a}$	$\vec{d}$	t
10.0 m/s	−10.0 m/s	−9.81 m/s^2	×	?

(Remember: An object will return to the ground at the same speed that it was thrown from the ground.)

$$\vec{a} = \frac{\vec{v}_f - \vec{v}_i}{t}$$

$$t = \frac{-10.0 \text{ m/s} - 10.0 \text{ m/s}}{-9.81 \text{ m/s}^2}$$

$$= 2.04 \text{ s}$$

Use $\vec{d} = \vec{v}t$

$$= (17.3 \text{ m/s})(2.04 \text{ s})$$

$$= 35.3 \text{ m}$$

PRACTICE EXERCISE

1. An object is thrown from the ground into the air at an angle of 40.0° from the horizontal at a velocity of 18.0 m/s. How far will this object travel horizontally?

2. An object is thrown from the ground into the air at an angle of 20.0° from the horizontal at a velocity of 15.0 m/s. How far will this object travel horizontally?

3. An object is thrown into the air with a velocity of 25.0m/s at an angle of 32.0° to the horizontal. How far will this object travel horizontally?

4. An object is thrown from the ground into the air with a velocity of 20.0 m/s at an angle of 27.0° to the horizontal. What is the maximum height reached by this object?

5. An object is thrown from the ground into the air at an angle of 30.0° to the horizontal. If this object reaches a maximum height of 5.75 m, at what velocity was it thrown?

6. An object is projected from the ground into the air at an angle of 35.0° to the horizontal. If this object is in the air for 9.26 s, at what velocity was it thrown?

7. An object is thrown from the ground into the air at a velocity of 15.7 m/s at an unknown angle to the horizontal. If this object travels 25.0 m horizontally and was in the air for 2.15 s, at what angle was this object thrown?

8. An object is thrown into the air with a velocity of 30.0 m/s at an angle of 35.0° to the horizontal. How far will this object travel horizontally?

9. A ball rolls off an incline, as shown, at a velocity of 22 m/s. How far from B will the ball hit the floor?

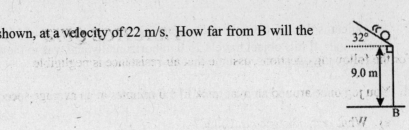

10. An object is projected from the top of a building at an angle of 28°, as shown in the diagram, at a velocity of 15 m/s. If the object hits the ground 32 m from the base of the building, how high is the building?

PRACTICE QUIZ

For the following questions, assume that air resistance is negligible.

1. You jog once around an oval track in 6.0 minutes at an average speed of 1.7 m/s.

   a) What is the distance travelled?

   b) What is the displacement?

2. A car travels at an average velocity of 95 km/h for 1.25 h north and at an average velocity of 75 km/h south for another 1.75 h.

   a) Find the average velocity of the car during the 3.00 h of travel.

   b) Find the average speed of the car during the 3.00 h of travel.

3. A bungee cord is 11.0 m long. What will the velocity of a bungee jumper be just as the cord begins to stretch?

4. If a stone is thrown vertically upward with a velocity of 9.0 m/s, what is its:

    a) displacement after 1.5 s?

    b) velocity after 1.5 s?

5. A stone is thrown vertically upward and it returns to the thrower 3.2 s later.

   a) What is the stone's maximum displacement (height)?

   b) What is the velocity of the stone when it is released by the thrower?

6. A car is travelling north on a city street. It starts from rest at a stop light and accelerates uniformly at a rate of 1.3 m/s^2 until it reaches the speed limit of 14 m/s. The car will travel at this velocity for 3.0 minutes and will then decelerate at a uniform rate of 1.6 m/s^2 until it comes to rest at the next stop light. How far apart are the two lights?

7. A student throws a ball vertically downward at a velocity of 8.0 m/s from the top of a 25 m building.

   a) How long does it take the ball to reach the ground?

   b) What is the velocity of the ball as it hits the ground?

8. A model rocket is launched vertically upward from the ground. After 4.3 s, its fuel is completely burned. Assume uniform acceleration of 3.0 m/s^2 while the fuel is burning.

   a) What is the velocity of the rocket at the instant that the fuel is completely burned?

   b) What is the rocket's maximum displacement (maximum height reached) during its motion? (Remember it will continue to rise after the fuel is consumed.)

9. A car accelerates uniformly from rest to a velocity of 101 km/h east in 8.0 s. What is the magnitude of its acceleration?

10. A car slows down uniformly from 30.0 m/s to rest in 7.20 s. How far did it travel while decelerating?

11. A ball is thrown vertically into the air with a velocity of 20.0 m/s. How long is the ball in the air?

12. A heavy object was dropped from a helicopter when the helicopter was moving vertically upward at a velocity of 3.0 m/s. Assuming the helicopter was 75 m above the ground when the object was dropped, how long will it take the object to reach the ground?

13. While travelling at 65 km/h north on a city street, you see the traffic light change to yellow and you decide to stop. If your reaction time is 0.35 s, how far do you travel before you react?

14. A car, initially at rest, accelerates uniformly for 5.0 s. If in this time the car travels 21 m east,

    a) what is the average velocity of the car?

    b) what is the velocity at the end of 5.0 s?

    c) what is the acceleration of the car?

15. A student throws a stone vertically downward with an initial velocity of 5.0 m/s from the top of a 165 m building. How far does the stone travel during its fourth second of travel?

16. The following position-time graph describes the motion of an object along a straight line. If the initial direction of the object was east,

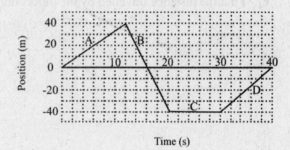

a) find the velocity during:
   i) A

   ii) B

   iii) C

b) Find the average velocity for the complete motion.

c) Find the distance travelled by the object during the complete motion.

17. The following position-time graph describes the motion of two cars, A and B, travelling north along a straight line. Find the velocity of:

a) A

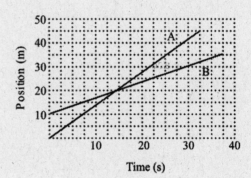

b) B

18. The following velocity-time graph describes the motion of two cars, A and B, travelling east along a straight line.

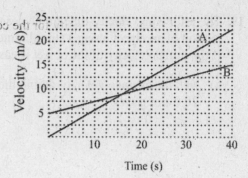

a) Find the displacement of:

i) A at 40.0 s.

ii) B at 40.0 s.

b) Find the acceleration of:

i) A

ii) B

19. The following velocity-time graph describes the
motion of an object along a straight line.
If the initial velocity of the object is east,

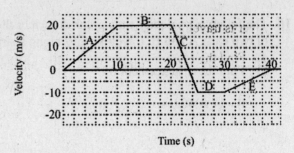

a) find the average velocity during the first
20.0 s of travel.

b) find the displacement during part C of the motion.

c) find the acceleration during:
i) A

ii) B

iii) C

20. A car is travelling at a velocity of 95 km/h 25° S of E.

    a) Find the east (x) component of this velocity.

    b) Find the south (y) component of this velocity.

21. An object is thrown into the air at a velocity of 18 m/s at an angle of 55° from the horizontal.

    a) Find the horizontal (x) component of this velocity.

    b) Find the vertical (y) component of this velocity.

22. A student walks 45 m south then turns and walks 45 m 23° S of W. Find the displacement of this student.

23. A student walks 25 m east, 35 m south, and then 15 m west. Find the displacement of this student.

24. A car is travelling in a straight line with uniform motion. The east component of this motion is 45 km/h, and the north component of the motion 55 km/h. What is the velocity of the car?

25. A pilot heads her plane south at a velocity of 875 km/h. If there is a wind of 65 km/h blowing east, what is the velocity of the plane relative to the ground?

26. A pilot wants to fly her plane directly north. The speed of the plane in still air is 305 km/h and a wind of 105 km/h is blowing east. What is the speed of the plane with respect to the ground?

PRACTICE TEST

For the following questions, assume that air resistance is negligible.

1. Which of the following graphs best represents a velocity-time graph for a falling object, initially at rest, in which air resistance can be ignored?

    A.
    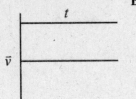
    B.
    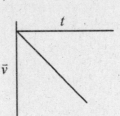

    C.
    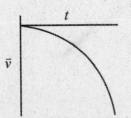
    D.
    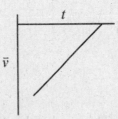

2. Which of the following graphs best represents a displacement-time graph for a falling object, initially at rest, in which air resistance can be ignored?

    A.
    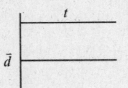
    B.
    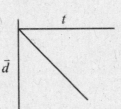

    C.
    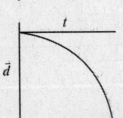
    D.

3. Which of the following graphs best represents an acceleration-time graph for a falling object in which air resistance can be ignored?

A.
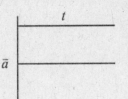

B.
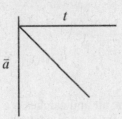

C.
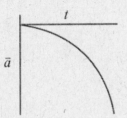

D.
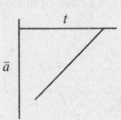

4. Which of the following graphs best represents a displacement-time graph for an object that is travelling along a straight horizontal line at a constant velocity of 10.0 m/s?

A.
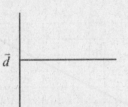

B.
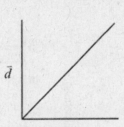

C.
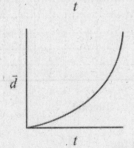

D.
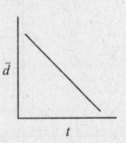

5. Given the position-time graph for an object travelling along a straight horizontal line, what is the velocity of the object?

A. 0.12 m/s   B. 0.20 m/s

C. 5.0 m/s   D. 8.3 m/s

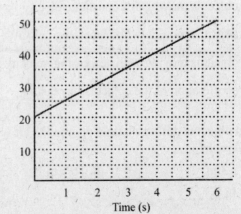

6. Uniform motion is described as motion in which

   A. the displacement remains constant

   B. the velocity remains constant

   C. the acceleration remains constant

   D. the velocity is 9.81 m/s^2

7. A ball player throws a ball straight up into the air and catches it a short time later. Which of the following velocity-time graphs best describe the motion of this ball?

   A.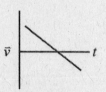

   B.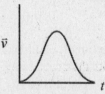

   C.

   D.

8. Given the velocity-time graph for an object undergoing free fall, what is the displacement of the object during the six seconds of motion described in the graph?

   A. 5.0 m

   B. 90 m

   C. 180 m

   D. 210 m

   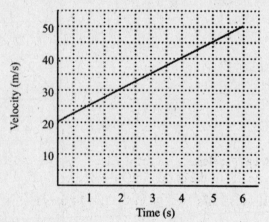

9. The motion described by the graph is best expressed as motion in which the:

   A. object is moving at a constant velocity

   B. object is moving with increasing velocity

   C. object is moving with decreasing velocity

   D. acceleration of the object is increasing

   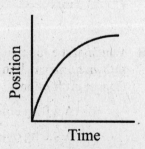

10. If an object is thrown straight up into the air with a velocity of 8.0 m/s, what is the maximum height it will reach?

    A. 3.3 m

    B. 6.5 m

    C. 44 m

    D. 84 m

11. A ball rolls 2.7 m up a constant slope before it comes to a stop. If the initial velocity of the ball was 2.0 m/s, what is the acceleration of the ball as it rolls up the slope?

    A. -0.37 m/s^2 **B.** -0.74 m/s^2

    C. -1.4 m/s^2 **D.** -9.81 m/s^2

12. A ball rolls 3.2 m up a constant slope before it comes to a stop. If the initial velocity of the ball was 2.2 m/s, how long does it take the ball to roll up the slope?

    A. 0.65 s   **B.** 2.9 s

    C. 4.2 s   **D.** 8.6 s

13. An object is thrown straight up into the air from the top of a building at a velocity of 15 m/s as shown in the diagram. If it hits the ground in 8.00 s, what is the height of the building?

    A. 1.6×10^2 m   **B.** 1.9×10^2 m

    C. 3.1×10^2 m   **D.** 4.3×10^2 m

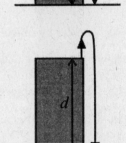

14. An object is thrown straight up into the air from the top of a building at a velocity of 12 m/s as shown in the diagram. If it hits the ground in 8.0 s, what is the speed of the object when it hits the ground?

    A. 12 m/s   **B.** 66 m/s

    C. 79 m/s   **D.** 91 m/s

15. A car accelerates uniformly from rest to a velocity of 105 km/h east in 9.0 s. What is the average velocity of the car during this acceleration?

    A. 6.38 m/s   **B.** 14.6 m/s

    C. 23.3 m/s   **D.** 52.5 m/s

16. Which of the following objects will reach the ground first if they are thrown horizontally from the top of a high cliff as shown in the diagram? (Ignore air friction.)

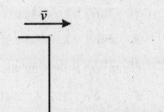

    i) A 2.0 kg object is thrown at 10.0 m/s

    ii) A 4.0 kg object is thrown at 10.0 m/s

    A. The 2.0 kg object.

    B. The 4.0 kg object.

    C. They will both reach the ground at the same time.

17. Which of the following objects will reach the ground first if they are thrown horizontally from the top of a high cliff as shown in the diagram? (Ignore air friction.)

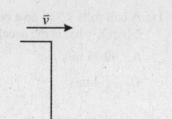

    i) A 2.0 kg object is thrown at 10.0 m/s

    ii) A 2.0 kg object is thrown at 15.0 m/s

A. The 2.0 kg object thrown at 10.0 m/s .

B. The 2.0 kg object thrown at 15.0 m/s .

C. They will both reach the ground at the same time.

18. Which of the following objects will reach the ground first if they are thrown horizontally from the top of a high cliff as shown in the diagram? (Ignore air friction.)

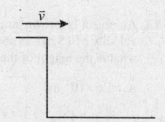

    i) A 2.0 kg object is thrown at 10.0 m/s

    ii) A 4.0 kg object is thrown at 10.0 m/s

    iii) A 4.0 kg object is thrown at 15.0 m/s

A. The 2.0 kg object thrown at 10.0 m/s .

B. The 4.0 kg object thrown at 10.0 m/s .

C. The 4.0 kg object thrown at 15.0 m/s .

D. They will all reach the ground at the same time.

19. Which of the following objects will reach the ground first if they are thrown horizontally from the top of cliffs as described? (Ignore air friction.)

    i) A 4.0 kg object is thrown from the top of a 75.0 m cliff at a velocity of 15.0 m/s

    ii) A 2.0 kg object is thrown from the top of a 50.0 m cliff at a velocity of 12.0 m/s

    iii) A 1.0 kg object is thrown from the top of a 25.0 m cliff at a velocity of 10.0 m/s

A. The 4.0 kg object.

B. The 2.0 kg object.

C. The 1.0 kg object.

D. There is not enough information to determine the answer.

Use the following information to answer the next two questions.

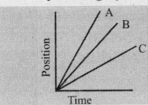

These position time graphs represent the motion of three (3) objects.

20. Which object has the greatest velocity?

 A. A   **B.** B

 C. C   **D.** They all have the same velocity.

21. Which object has the greatest acceleration?

 A. A   **B.** B

 C. C   **D.** They all have zero acceleration.

22. The following is a velocity-time graph of an object moving along a horizontal surface.

 In which section does the object experience the greatest constant acceleration?

 A. A   **B.** B

 C. C   **D.** D

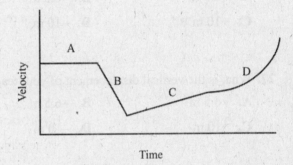

23. The following is a position-time graph of an object moving along a horizontal surface.

 In which section does the object experience the greatest acceleration?

 A. A   **B.** B

 C. C   **D.** D

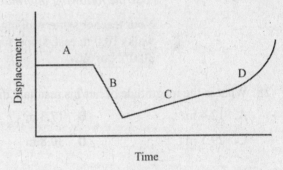

24. For an object that is thrown upward, which of the following statements is correct?

 A. The acceleration of the object is greater as it travels up.

 B. The acceleration of the object is greater as it travels down.

 C. The acceleration of the object at the top of its motion is zero.

 D. The acceleration of the object is constant as it travels up and down.

25. If an object is thrown vertically upward, which of the following is zero when it reaches its maximum height?

    i) acceleration

    ii) velocity

A. i) only

B. ii) only

C. Both i) and ii) are correct

D. Neither i) nor ii) is correct

Use the following information to answer the next two questions.

Your teacher starts walking from the corner of a vacant lot and walks 12 m 33° W of S.

26. What is the horizontal displacement of your teacher from the corner of the lot?

A. +6.5 m   **B.** −6.5 m

C. +10 m   **D.** −10 m

27. What is the vertical displacement of your teacher from the corner of the lot?

A. +6.5 m   **B.** −6.5 m

C. +10 m   **D.** −10 m

Use the following information to answer the next two questions.

Your teacher starts walking from the corner of a vacant lot and walks 10.0 m east, stops, turns, and walks an additional 20.0 m 30.0° N of W.

28. What is the magnitude of her/his resultant displacement?

A. 12.4 m   **B.** 17.3 m

C. 29.1 m   **D.** 30.8 m

29. What is the direction of her/his displacement?

A. 20° N of E   **B.** 20° N of W

C. 54° N of E   **D.** 54° N of W

Use the following information to answer the next two questions.

A pilot heads her plane with a velocity of 215 km/h east.
There is a wind blowing 85 km/h south (i.e. from the north).

30. What is the speed of the plane in reference to the ground?

    A. 130 km/h   **B.** 197 km/h

    C. 231 km/h   **D.** 300 km/h

31. What is the direction of her resultant displacement?

    A. 22° E of S   **B.** 22° S of E

    C. 68° S of E   **D.** 68° *RCS*

32. If we ignore air friction, when the speed of a ball that is thrown horizontally from the roof of a building is increased, the time that it takes to reach the ground will

    A. increase   **B.** decrease

    C. remain the same

33. If we ignore air friction, when the speed of a ball that is thrown horizontally from the roof of a building is increased, the vertical velocity with which the ball hits the ground will

    A. increase   **B.** decrease

    C. remain the same

34. If we ignore air friction, when we throw an object into the air at an angle above the horizontal, which of the following remains constant?

    i) The horizontal component of the velocity

    ii) The vertical component of the velocity

    A. i) only   **B.** ii) only

    C. both i) and ii)   **D.** neither i) nor ii)

35. An object is thrown into the air at an angle of 30° above the horizontal. If we ignore air friction, what is the vertical acceleration and the vertical velocity when the object reaches its maximum displacement?

    A. $\bar{v} = 0,\ \bar{a} = 0$ **B.** $\bar{v} = 0,\ \bar{a} = -9.81\,\text{m/s}^2$

    C. $\bar{v} = \text{maximum},\ \bar{a} = 0$ **D.** $\bar{v} = \text{maximum},\ \bar{a} = 9.81\,\text{m/s}^2$

36. An object is thrown from ground level at a velocity of 25.0 m/s at an angle of 20.0° above the horizontal. If there is a building 25.0 m away, at what height above the ground will the object hit the building?

A. 3.55 m   **B.** 3.90 m

C. 14.2 m   **D.** 14.7 m

37. Which of the following graphs best represents the displacement-time graph for the vertical motion of a projectile that is thrown horizontally?

A.

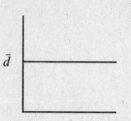

B.

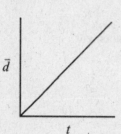

C.

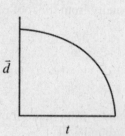

D.

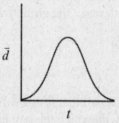

38. Which of the following graphs best represents the velocity-time graph for the horizontal motion of a projectile that is thrown into the air at an angle of 30° above the horizontal?

A.

B.

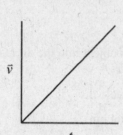

C.

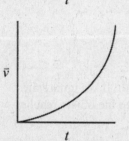

D.

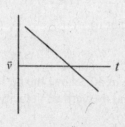

39. Which of the following graphs best represents the acceleration-time graph for the vertical motion of a projectile thrown into the air at an angle of 30° above the horizontal?

A.

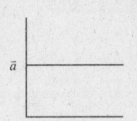

B.

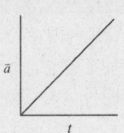

C.

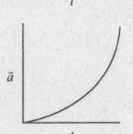

D.

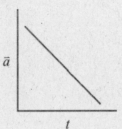

40. Given the following objects:

    i)   an object that is thrown horizontally from a height of 6.0 m above the ground

    ii)   an object that is dropped from a height of 6.0 m above the ground

Which of these objects hits the ground first?

A. i)

B. ii)

C. both will reach the ground at the same time

NOTES

DYNAMICS

When you are finished this unit, you will be able to…

- explain that a non-zero net force causes a change in velocity
- quantitatively apply Newton's first law of motion to explain an object's state of rest or uniform motion
- quantitatively apply Newton's second law of motion to explain the relationships among net force, mass and acceleration
- qualitatively apply Newton's third law of motion to explain the interaction between two objects, recognizing that two forces, equal in magnitude and opposite in direction, do not act on the same object
- quantitatively and qualitatively explain static and kinetic forces of friction acting on an object
- calculate the resultant force, or its constituents, acting on an object by adding vector components graphically and algebraically
- algebraically apply Newton's laws of motion to solve linear motion problems in horizontal, vertical and inclined planes near the surface of the Earth, ignoring air resistance
- explain that the goal of technology is to provide solutions to practical problems, that technological development includes testing and evaluating designs and prototypes on the basis of established criteria, and that the products of technology cannot solve all problems
- explain that science and technology are developed to meet societal needs and that society provides direction for scientific and technological development
- explain that scientific knowledge and theories develop through hypotheses, the collection of evidence, investigation, and the ability to provide explanations
- formulate questions about observed relationships and plan investigations of questions, ideas, problems, and issues, and identify, define, and delimit questions to investigate
- conduct investigations into relationships among observable variables and use a broad range of tools and techniques to gather and record data and information, including determining, empirically, the local value of the acceleration due to gravity, and exploring the relationship between the local value of the acceleration due to gravity and the gravitational field strength
- analyze data and apply mathematical and conceptual models to develop and assess possible solutions, including listing the limitations of mass-weight determinations at different points on Earth's surface and treating acceleration due to gravity as uniform near Earth's surface

Lesson	Page	Complete
1. Introduction to Dynamics	151	
2. Forces in Nature	160	
3. Applied Force or Tension	168	
4. Physics of an Inclined Plane	181	
5. Newton's Third Law of Motion	186	
6. Newton's Law of Universal Gravitation	189	
7. Field Explanation	195	
Practice Quiz	199	
Practice Test	209	

Lesson 1   INTRODUCTION TO DYNAMICS

In the last chapter we were studying kinematics—the description of how an object moves. In this section, we will study dynamics—the study of why objects move. We will need to define and understand balanced and unbalanced forces.

In 1665, when Sir Isaac Newton was 23 years old, he formulated three laws of motion. During this time he also formulated the Law of Universal Gravitation. In this section we will study three laws. Before we start, let us look at the concept of force.

The unit of force is the newton (N)

FORCE

Symbol: $\vec{F}$
Defined: as a push or pull
Units: newton (N)

$\vec{F}$ is the symbol for force

Forces are vector quantities in that they have direction as well as magnitude.

A newton is equal to a $kg \cdot m/s^2$

NEWTON'S FIRST LAW OF MOTION

Newton's first law of motion is the law of inertia. It states that an object will remain at constant velocity unless acted on by an unbalanced force. An object at rest has a constant velocity of zero.

Newton's First Law:

An object will remain at constant velocity unless acted on by an unbalanced force

If the vector sum of all forces acting on an object is zero, we say the forces are balanced.

Symbol for net force is $\vec{F}_{net}$

If the vector sum of the forces acting on an object is greater than zero, the forces are unbalanced and this vector sum is called the net force.

$\vec{F}_1 = 6.0\,N$ ⟶ ▭ ⟵ $\vec{F}_2 = 6.0\,N$
These forces are balanced.

$\vec{F}_1 = 6.0\,N$ ⟶ ▭ ⟵ $\vec{F}_2 = 1.0\,N$
These forces are not balanced.

Inertia is the tendency for an object to remain at a constant velocity

Newton's first law of motion is sometimes referred to as the law of inertia. Inertia is the tendency for an object to remain at constant velocity. If an object is at rest, it will tend to remain at rest; if an object is moving, it will tend to remain moving.

Let's draw on your experiences to illustrate this law. If you are in a car travelling at 50 km/h when it hits a concrete wall head-on, the car will come to a sudden stop because of the extreme force acting on it. However, if you are not wearing your seat belt, you will continue at 50 km/h until forces acting on you bring you to a stop. We wear seatbelts to keep us in the car—where we usually have a better chance of less severe injury.

If you are sitting at a stop light when someone runs into your car from behind at a velocity of 40 km/h, your car experiences a sudden force which causes it to increase its velocity. Your body will move too; however, your head, which is somewhat loosely attached to your body, will have a certain tendency to remain at rest. So as your body is suddenly thrust forward, your head remains at rest. This results in whiplash injuries. Headrests in cars are designed to help reduce these injuries.

Imagine you are on a transit bus standing in the aisle travelling at 50 km/h when the bus driver brakes hard. What will happen to you? Also, imagine you are on this same bus travelling at 30 km/h and the bus suddenly turns sharply to the right. What happens to you?

These are illustrations of Newton's First Law of Motion (Law of Inertia).

Illustrations of Newton's First Law of Motion

NEWTON'S SECOND LAW OF MOTION

Newton's second law of motion, the fundamental law of dynamics, states that the rate of change in an object's velocity (acceleration) is directly proportional to the net force, and inversely proportional to the object's mass.

$$\vec{a} \propto \vec{F}_{net}$$

$$\vec{a} \propto \frac{1}{m}$$

or

$$\vec{a} = \frac{\vec{F}_{net}}{m}$$

usually written as: $\vec{F}_{net} = m\vec{a}$

NOTE: Force is the product of mass times acceleration. Therefore, the unit of force (newton) is the product of mass units (kg) and acceleration units $\left(m/s^2\right)$.

Before we discuss this law, we need to discuss the concept of mass.

Net force is the sum of all forces acting on an object

Newton's Second Law:

The rate of change in an object's velocity is directly proportional to the net force and inversely proportional to the object's mass

Force is the product of mass times acceleration

$$N = kg{\cdot}m/s^2$$

Inertia is the tendency for
an object to remain at
constant velocity

MASS

Symbol: m

Definition: mass is a measure of an object's resistance to
acceleration. It can also be defined as the quantitative measure of
an object's inertia.

Units: kilogram (kg). Mass is a scalar quantity.

From your experiences, you know that the greater the mass of an object,
the greater its inertia. Imagine a soccer ball and a ten pin bowling ball.
Kick the soccer ball. Now, kick the bowling ball. You know that the
bowling ball will resist a change in velocity to a much greater extent than
the soccer ball. The bowling ball has more mass, more inertia, and is more
difficult to accelerate.

Activity 7

• Design an experiment to study the relationship between the net force on
an object and its acceleration.

• Decide the data which you will require.

• Draw a data table and collect the data.

Data Table

• Draw an acceleration–force graph.

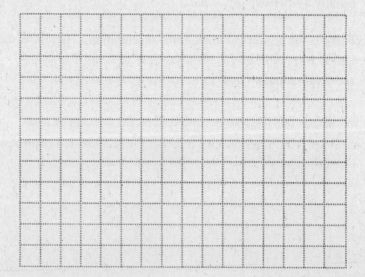

Question: Does your graph demonstrate that the acceleration of an object
varies with the net force?

Activity 8

- Design an experiment to study the relationship between the mass of an object and its acceleration.
- Decide the data which you will require.
- Draw a data table and collect the data.

Data Table:

- Draw an acceleration–mass graph.

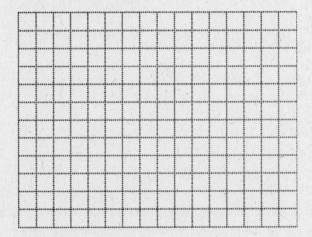

Question: Does your graph demonstrate that the acceleration of an object varies inversely with the mass of the object?

To confirm your answer to the previous question, draw a graph showing the relationship between the acceleration and $\dfrac{1}{\text{mass}}$.

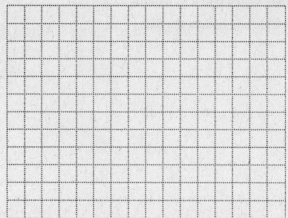

NOTE: If your experiment confirmed that the acceleration of an object varies inversely with its mass, the graph that you just drew should be a straight line graph. Is it?

Example 1

A net force of 30.0 N south acts on a 10.0 kg object.. What is the acceleration of the object?

Solution

$$\vec{F}_{net} = m\vec{a}$$

$$\vec{a} = \frac{\vec{F}_{net}}{m}$$

$$= \frac{30.0 \text{ N}}{10.0 \text{ kg}}$$

$$= 3.00 \text{ m/s}^2 \text{ south}$$

Example 2

A 22 kg object accelerates uniformly from rest to a velocity of 2.5 m/s west in 8.7 s. What is the net force acting on the car during this acceleration?

Solution

$$\vec{a} = \frac{\vec{v}_f - \vec{v}_i}{t}$$

$$= \frac{2.5 \text{ m/s}^2 - 0}{8.7 \text{ s}}$$

$$= 0.29 \text{ m/s}^2$$

$$F_{net} = m\vec{a}$$

$$= \left(22 \text{ kg}\right)\left(0.29 \text{ m/s}^2\right)$$

$$= 6.3 \text{ N west}$$

PRACTICE EXERCISE

Formula: $\bar{F}_{net} = m\bar{a}$

1. A net force of 9.0 N east is used to push a 20.0 kg object. What is the acceleration of the object?

2. A net force of 15.0 N north is used to pull an object. If the acceleration of this object is 8.0 m/s^2, what is the mass of the object?

3. A 16.0 kg object is accelerated at a rate of 2.0 m/s^2 by a net force. What is the magnitude of the net force?

4. A 12.0 kg object is accelerated by a net force of 10.2 N east. What is the acceleration of the object?

5. A 5.2 kg object is accelerating at a rate of 6.0 m/s^2. What is the magnitude of the net force acting on the object?

6. If an 18 kg object has a net force of 2.0 N south acting on it, what is the acceleration of the object?

7. A 925 kg car accelerates uniformly from rest to a velocity of 25.0 m/s south in 10.0 s. What is the net force acting on the car during this acceleration?

8. A 1.08×10^3-kg car uniformly accelerates for 12.0 s from rest. During this time the car travels 132 m north. What is the net force acting on the car during this acceleration?

9. A 1.20×10^3-kg car accelerates uniformly from 5.0 m/s east to 12 m/s east. During this acceleration the car travels 94 m. What is the net force acting on the car during this acceleration?

10. A net force of 2.5×10^3 N north acts on an object for 5.0 s. During this time an object accelerates from rest to a velocity of 48 km/h. What is the mass of this object?

11. A net force of 6.6 N east acts on a 9.0 kg object. If this object accelerates uniformly from rest to a velocity of 3.0 m/s east,

    a) how far did the object travel while accelerating?

    b) what is the time of acceleration?

Lesson 2   FORCES IN NATURE

The net force on an object is the sum of all forces acting on the object.
We can identify the various forces acting on an object with descriptive
terms.

NOTES

Force due to gravity (or weight): $\vec{F}_g$

Normal force: $\vec{F}_N$

Frictional force: $\vec{F}_f$

Applied force or tension: $\vec{T}$

Remember, we use $\vec{F}_{net}$ as
our symbol for net force

FORCE DUE TO GRAVITY (WEIGHT)

Symbol: $\vec{F}_g$

Definition: Force due to gravity
Unit: Newton (N)

Weight is a force; therefore, it is a vector quantity.

If you throw an object into the air, it will return to the Earth. If you drop
an object from some distance from the floor, it will fall to the floor.
Why is this? The Earth exerts a significant force on these objects in the
direction of the Earth. This force is due to gravity. This is what we call
weight. The weight of an object depends on:

Weight is a force

- the mass of the object
  $\vec{F}_g \propto m$

- the acceleration due to gravity
  $\vec{F}_g \propto g$

  $\vec{F}_g = mg$

Newton formulated
the Law of
Universal Gravitation

The acceleration due to gravity near the Earth's surface can be expressed
as $9.81\,\text{m/s}^2$.

Although near the Earth's surface we use $9.81\,\text{m/s}^2$ as the value of g, it is
not a constant value. This value depends on the mass of the Earth (or other
planet, etc). It also depends on the distance from the centre of the Earth.

Newton's Law of
Universal Gravitation:

$g \propto m$

$g \propto \dfrac{1}{d^2}$

$\vec{F}_g \propto m_1 m_2$

The Earth is not a perfect sphere (ball). The Earth is somewhat flatter at
the poles, and somewhat bulged at the equator. For this reason, the
acceleration due to gravity varies with the latitude. It is less at the equator
than at the poles.

$\vec{F}_g \propto \dfrac{1}{r^2}$

NOTES

Weight of an object varies from location to location

Mass of an object does not depend on location

Weight is often confused with mass. Weight is the force due to gravity and varies from location to location. Mass only depends on the amount of matter an object contains, and does not vary with the location.

NORMAL FORCE

The normal force is the perpendicular force that forces two surfaces together.

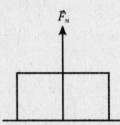 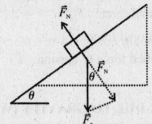

When an object is on a surface, the surface exerts an upward force on the object. This force is the normal force and acts perpendicular to the surface.

On a horizontal surface, the normal force is equal to the weight of the object.

$$\vec{F}_N = \vec{F}_g = mg$$

On an incline, the normal force is equal to the perpendicular component of the weight of the object.

$$\vec{F}_N = \vec{F}_g \cos\theta$$

FRICTIONAL FORCE

Frictional forces are forces that always oppose motion. They depend on:

- the normal force
- the nature of the two surfaces

NOTE: Frictional forces do not depend on the area of contact between the two surfaces.

The nature of the surfaces is expressed as the coefficient of friction (μ).

$$\vec{F}_f = \mu \vec{F}_N$$

There are two kinds of frictional forces:

- static frictional forces
- kinetic frictional forces

$\vec{F}_f = \mu\vec{F}_N$

Frictional forces
- static
- kinetic

Try this:

- Take a wooden block and attach a spring balance to it. Place a 1 kg mass on top of the wooden block.

- You should note that when the block starts to slide, the frictional force decreases.

When an object is at rest, the frictional force is greater than the frictional force when it is moving. We call the frictional force when the object is not moving the static frictional force. We call the frictional force when the object is moving the kinetic frictional force.

The static frictional force is greater than the kinetic frictional force.

$$\left(\vec{F}_f\right)_{static} > \left(\vec{F}_f\right)_{kinetic}$$

Question: Why is $\left(\vec{F}_f\right)_{static} > \left(\vec{F}_f\right)_{kinetic}$?

Answer: We do not have a reliable theory of frictional forces. It appears that there are intermolecular forces between the two surfaces and when there is no relative motion between the surfaces, these intermolecular forces increase.

Example 1

A 7.6 kg object is resting on a horizontal surface. What is the normal force acting on the object?

Solution

The normal force is upward and is equal to the perpendicular component of the weight.

$$\vec{F}_N = \vec{F}_g$$

$$\vec{F}_g = mg$$

$$= (7.6 \text{ kg})(9.81 \text{ m/s}^2)$$

$$= 75 \text{ N}$$

Example 2

A 7.6 kg object is at rest on an inclined plane. If the inclined plane makes an angle with the horizontal of 33°, what is the normal force acting on the object?

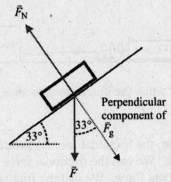

Solution

The normal force is upward and is equal to the perpendicular component of the weight.

$$\cos\theta = \frac{\text{adjacent}}{\text{hypotenuse}}$$

$$= \frac{\vec{F}_N}{\vec{F}_g}$$

$$\vec{F}_g = mg$$

$$= (7.6\ \text{kg})(9.81\ \text{m/s}^2)$$

$$= 75\ \text{N}$$

$$\vec{F}_N = \vec{F}_g \cos 33°$$

$$= (75\ \text{N})\cos 33°$$

$$= 63\ \text{N}$$

Example 3

A 7.6 kg object is pulled along a horizontal surface. If the coefficient of friction between the surfaces is 0.20, what is the force of friction?

Solution

$$\vec{F}_N = \vec{F}_g$$

$$\vec{F}_g = mg$$

$$= (7.6\ \text{kg})(9.81\ \text{m/s}^2)$$

$$= 75\ \text{N}$$

$$\vec{F}_f = \mu \vec{F}_N$$

$$= (0.20)(75\ \text{N})$$

$$= 15\ \text{N}$$

Example 4

A 7.6 kg object is pulled up an inclined plane. If the inclined plane makes an angle with the horizontal of 33°, and the coefficient of friction is 0.20, what is the force of friction?

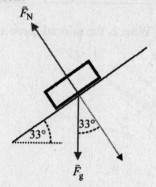

Solution

The normal force is upward and is equal to the perpendicular component of the weight.

$$\cos\theta = \frac{adjacent}{hypotenuse}$$

$$= \frac{\vec{F}_N}{\vec{F}_g}$$

$$\vec{F}_g = mg$$

$$= (7.6 \text{ kg})(9.81 \text{ m/s}^2)$$

$$= 75 \text{ N}$$

$$\vec{F}_N = \vec{F}_g \cos 33°$$

$$= (75 \text{ N})\cos 33°$$

$$= 63 \text{ N}$$

$$\vec{F}_f = \mu\vec{F}_N$$

$$= (0.20)(63 \text{ N})$$

$$= 13 \text{ N}$$

Example 5

What is the weight of a 12.0 kg object near the surface of the Earth?

Solution

$$\vec{F}_g = mg$$

$$= (12.0 \text{ kg})(9.81 \text{ m/s}^2)$$

$$= 118 \text{ N}$$

PRACTICE EXERCISE

Formula: $\quad \vec{F}_f = \mu \vec{F}_N \qquad \vec{F}_f = \mu mg \cos \theta$

1. A 14.0 kg object is resting on a horizontal surface. What is the normal force acting on the object?

2. A 9.6 kg object is pulled along a horizontal surface. If the coefficient of friction between the surfaces is 0.11, what is the force of friction?

3. A 20.0 N object is placed on a horizontal surface. A force of 3.0 N is required to keep the object moving at a constant speed, what is the coefficient of friction between the two surfaces?

4. A 16.2 kg object is at rest on an inclined plane. If the inclined plane makes an angle with the horizontal of 25.0°, what is the normal force acting on the object?

5. A 15.0 N object is pulled up an inclined plane. If the inclined plane makes an angle with the horizontal of 35.0°, and the coefficient of friction is 0.300, what is the force of friction?

6. A 6.2 kg object is pulled along a horizontal surface as shown in the diagram by a force of 22.0 N. If the acceleration of the object is $1.1 \, \text{m/s}^2$, what is the coefficient of friction between the surfaces?

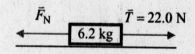

7. What is the weight of a 25.0 kg object near the surface of the Earth?

8. What is the mass of an object if it has a weight of 80.0 N near the Earth's surface?

9. What is the acceleration due to gravity near the surface of the moon if an object that has a mass of 22.0 kg has a weight of 36.0 N near the moon's surface?

10. What is the weight of a 72.0 kg object near the surface of the Earth?

11. What is the mass of an object if it has a weight of 127 N near the Earth's surface?

Lesson 3   APPLIED FORCE OR TENSION

A force applied through a rope (etc.) is referred to as a tension or applied force. However this force can be exerted by pushing or pulling the object directly.

The net force on an object is the sum of all forces acting on the object. To determine the net force on an object we identify all the force acting on the object. It can be useful to draw a free body diagram to determine the net force.

FREE BODY DIAGRAMS

Free body diagrams are diagrams that show all the forces acting on the object.

Example 1

An object is pulled at constant velocity along a horizontal surface. The applied force is through a rope which makes an angle of 30.0° to the horizontal.

Solution

Free body diagram:

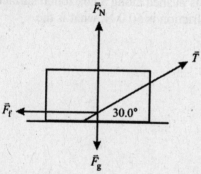

Example 2

An elevator with a mass of 9.00×10^2 kg is accelerating downward at a rate of 1.30 m/s^2. What is the tension in the cable?

Solution
- Draw a free body diagram.

- Find $\vec{F}_g$

$$\vec{F}_g = mg$$

$$= \left(9.00 \times 10^2 \text{ kg}\right)\left(9.81 \text{ m/s}^2\right)$$

$$= 8.83 \times 10^3 \text{ N}$$

- Find $\vec{F}_{net}$

$$\vec{F}_{net} = m\vec{a}$$

$$= \left(9.00 \times 10^2 \text{ kg}\right)\left(1.30 \text{ m/s}^2\right)$$

$$= 1.17 \times 10^3 \text{ N}$$

- Find $\vec{T}$

Subtract because $\vec{F}_g$ and $\vec{T}$ are in opposite directions

$$\vec{F}_{net} = \vec{F}_g - \vec{T}$$

$$\vec{T} = \vec{F}_g - \vec{F}_{net}$$

$$= \left(8.83 \times 10^3 \text{ N}\right) - \left(1.17 \times 10^3 \text{ N}\right)$$

$$= 7.66 \times 10^3 \text{ N}$$

Example 3

An object that has a mass of 25.0 kg is pushed along a horizontal surface by a force of 95.0 N. If the force of friction is 50.0 N, what is the acceleration of the object?

Solution

- Draw a free body diagram.

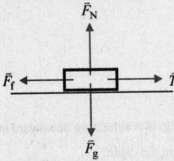

The object accelerates horizontally. Therefore, we are only concerned with the horizontal forces.

- Find $\vec{F}_{net}$.

$$\vec{F}_{net} = \vec{T} - \vec{F}_f$$

$$= 95.0 \text{ N} - 50.0 \text{ N}$$

$$= 45.0 \text{ N}$$

- Find acceleration

$$\vec{F}_{net} = m\vec{a}$$

$$a = \frac{45.0 \text{ N}}{25.0 \text{ kg}}$$

$$= 1.8 \text{ m/s}^2$$

Example 4

A 3.0 kg object is thrown vertically upward with a force of 55 N. What is the acceleration of the object while the force is applied to it?

Solution

- Draw a free body diagram.

- Find $\vec{F}_g$.

$$\vec{F}_g = mg$$

$$= (3.0 \text{ kg})(9.81 \text{ m/s}^2)$$

$$= 29.4 \text{ N}$$

- Find $\vec{F}_{net}$

$$\vec{F}_{net} = \vec{T} - \vec{F}_g$$

$$= 55.0 \text{ N} - 29.4 \text{ N}$$

$$= 25.6 \text{ N}$$

- Find acceleration

$$\vec{F}_{net} = m\vec{a}$$

$$\vec{a} = \frac{25.6 \text{ N}}{3.0 \text{ kg}}$$

$$= 8.5 \text{ m/s}^2$$

Example 5

An object that has a mass of 45.0 kg is pulled along a horizontal surface by a rope that makes an angle of 32.0° with the horizontal. If the force of friction is 50.0 N and the tension in the rope is 95.0 N, what is the acceleration of the object?

Solution

- Draw a free body diagram.

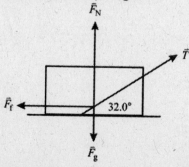

- Because the object accelerates horizontally, we must find the net horizontal force.

Find the horizontal component of $\vec{T}$.

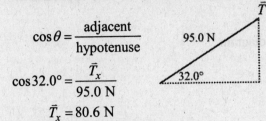

$$\cos\theta = \frac{\text{adjacent}}{\text{hypotenuse}}$$

$$\cos 32.0° = \frac{\vec{T}_x}{95.0 \text{ N}}$$

$$\vec{T}_x = 80.6 \text{ N}$$

- Find net horizontal force.

$$\vec{F}_{net} = \vec{T}_x - \vec{F}_f$$

$$= 80.6 \text{ N} - 50.0 \text{ N}$$

$$= 30.6 \text{ N}$$

- Find acceleration

$$\vec{F}_{net} = m\vec{a}$$

$$\vec{a} = \frac{30.6 \text{ N}}{45.0 \text{ kg}}$$

$$= 0.679 \text{ m/s}^2$$

Example 6

A 75.0 kg student stands on a bathroom scale on an elevator that is accelerating upward at a rate of 1.00 m/s^2. What is the reading in Newton's on the scale?

(NOTE: Scale reading will be the applied force, $\vec{T}$.)

Solution
- Draw a free body diagram.

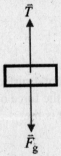

- Find $\vec{F}_{net}$.

$$\vec{F}_{net} = m\vec{a}$$

$$= (75.0 \text{ kg})(1.00 \text{ m/s}^2)$$

$$= 75 \text{ N}$$

170

- Find $\vec{F}_g$.

$$\vec{F}_g = m\vec{g}$$

$$= (75.0 \text{ kg})(9.81 \text{ m/s}^2)$$

$$= 736 \text{ N}$$

- Find $\vec{T}$ (scale reading).

$$\vec{F}_{net} = \vec{T} - \vec{F}_g$$

$$\vec{T} = \vec{F}_{net} + \vec{F}_g$$

$$= 75 \text{ N} + 736 \text{ N}$$

$$= 811 \text{ N}$$

PRACTICE EXERCISE

Formulae: $\vec{F}_{net} = m\vec{a}$ $\vec{F}_f = \mu \vec{F}_N$ $\vec{F}_f = \mu mg \cos \theta$ $\vec{F}_g = mg$

1. An 11.0 kg object is thrown vertically into the air with an applied force of 145 N. What is the initial acceleration of the object?

2. A 12.0 kg object is pushed with a horizontal force of 6.0 N east across a horizontal table. If the force of friction between the two surfaces is 2.0 N, what is the acceleration of the object?

3. A 15.0 kg object is thrown vertically into the air. If the initial acceleration of the object is 8.80 m/s^2, what is the applied force?

172

4. A 20.0 kg object is pulled horizontally along a level floor with an applied force of 27.0 N. If this object is accelerating at a rate of 0.80 m/s^2, what is the magnitude of the force of friction?

5. An object is pulled west along a horizontal frictionless surface with a steady horizontal force of 12.0 N. If the object accelerates from rest to a velocity of 4.0 m/s while moving 5.0 m, what is the mass of the object?

6. A 6.3 kg object is thrown upward with an acceleration of 0.45 m/s^2. What is the magnitude of the force applied to the object?

7. What is the tension in the cable of an 1.20×10^3 kg elevator that is:

   a) accelerating downward at a rate of 1.05 m/s^2 ?

   b) accelerating upward at a rate of 1.05 m/s^2 ?

   c) moving downward at a constant velocity of 1.10 m/s ?

8. An object that has a mass of 36.0 kg is pushed along a horizontal surface with a force of 85.0 N. If the force of friction is 72.0 N, what is the magnitude of the acceleration of the object?

9. A horizontal force of 90.0 N is required to push a 75.0 kg object along a horizontal surface at a constant speed. What is the magnitude of the force of friction?

10. A 1.0 kg object is given a push along a horizontal surface. If the velocity of the object when it is released is 0.50 m/s west, and the object slides 0.25 m before coming to a stop, what is the magnitude of the force of friction?

11. A 1.0×10^2 N box slides north along a horizontal surface propelled by a 2.5×10^2 N horizontal force. If the force of friction on the box is 1.4×10^2 N, what is the acceleration of the box?

12. A 7.0 kg object rests on a horizontal frictionless surface. What is the magnitude of the horizontal force that is required to accelerate it at the rate of $2.3 \, \text{m/s}^2$?

13. You are travelling in your car at a velocity of 24.0 m/s east when you slam on your brakes. The force of friction on your car tires is 1.80×10^4 N. If the mass of you and your car is 1.50×10^3 kg, how far do you skid before coming to a stop?

14. A 1.2×10^3 kg car is travelling at a velocity of 20.0 m/s east when its brakes are lock. Assuming a force of friction of 2.5×10^4 N, what is the velocity of the car after 0.50 s?

15. A 1.0 kg box on a horizontal frictionless surface is accelerated by attaching a 1.5 kg mass as shown in the diagram. What is the acceleration of the box? (Remember: both boxes are accelerated.)

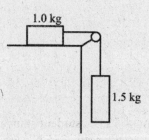

16. Two masses of 1.5 kg and 2.0 kg are hung on a frictionless pulley as shown in the diagram. What is the acceleration of:

    a) the 1.5 kg mass?

    b) the 2.0 kg mass?

17. A 125 N box is pulled east along a horizontal surface with a force of 60.0 N acting at an angle of 42.0° as shown in the diagram. If the force of friction on the box is 15.0 N, what is the acceleration?

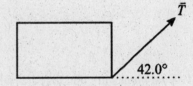

18. A 725 N student stands on a bathroom scale while riding in an elevator. The student observes that the scale reads 775 N as the elevator begins to rise. Find the acceleration of the elevator as it begins to rise. (Remember: the scale reading is the applied force, $\bar{T}$.)

19. A hockey puck with a mass of 0.48 kg is shot north along the ice with an initial velocity of 3.0 m/s. If, after travelling 8.0 m, the puck comes to rest, what is the force of friction on the puck?

20. An 8.0 kg object is pulled vertically upward by a rope. If the tension in the rope is constant at 95 N, what is the velocity of the object after 1.1 s? (Assume the object was initially at rest.)

21. Two blocks are tied together with a string as shown in the diagram. If a force of 20.0 N is applied to the 2.0 kg block as shown,

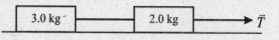

a) what is the acceleration of the blocks if the surface is frictionless?

b) what is the tension in the string joining the two blocks?

22. Repeat the previous problem when the coefficient of friction between the blocks and the horizontal surface is 0.21.

23. Two students are dragging a 25.0 kg object along the hall as shown in the diagram. If the force of friction acting on the object is 5.0 N, what is the acceleration of the object? (include the direction)

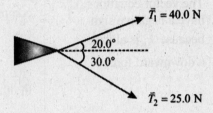

Lesson 4   PHYSICS OF AN INCLINED PLANE

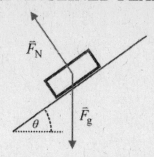

You will remember that the normal force is dependent on the weight.

$$\vec{F}_N = -\vec{F}_g \cos\theta \quad \text{or} \quad \vec{F}_N = -\left(m\vec{g}\cos\theta\right)$$

If you look carefully at this equation, you will see that is really one of the component equations.

$$\vec{R}_x = \vec{R}\cos\theta$$
$$\vec{R} = \vec{R}\sin\theta$$

In other words, the normal force is a component of the weight.

When we deal with an inclined plane, it is convenient to establish the inclined plane as the x axis. This means that a line drawn perpendicular (normal) to the inclined plane is the y axis.

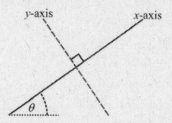

Question: Why does an object slide down a frictionless inclined plane?
or
What is the force that causes an object to accelerate down a frictionless inclined plane?

Answer: Gravitational force causes the acceleration.

The force of gravity always acts toward the centre of the Earth—straight down as shown in the diagram.

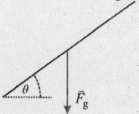

However, this force, $\vec{F}_g$, has an x component (a component that is acting along the inclined plane). It is this force that causes the object to slide down the frictionless inclined plane.

The vector equations have a negative sign because $\vec{F}_g$ is always a downward force.

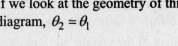

If we look at the geometry of this diagram, $\theta_2 = \theta_1$

Note:

$$\theta_1 + x = 90°$$

But:

$$\theta_2 + x \text{ also } = 90°$$
$$\therefore \qquad \theta_2 = \theta_1$$

You will also note that θ_2 is measured from the y axis—the perpendicular. Remember that one of the conditions of using your component equations is that the angle is to be expressed from the x axis. If we are to express the angle in the component equations from the y axis, the component equations switch. That is, rather than using

$$\vec{R}_x = \vec{R} \cos \theta$$
$$\vec{R} = \vec{R} \sin \theta$$

we use

$$\vec{R}_x = \vec{R} \sin \theta$$
$$\vec{R} = \vec{R} \cos \theta$$

Note that the x component of the force due to gravity in the diagram above is the opposite side of the triangle.

$$\sin \theta = \frac{\text{opposite}}{\text{hypotenuse}}$$

$$\therefore \text{ opposite} = (\text{hypotenuse})(\sin \theta)$$

or $\left(\vec{F}_g\right)_x = \vec{F}_g \sin \theta$

Going back to the equation

$$\vec{F}_N = -\vec{F}_g \cos \theta \quad \text{or} \quad \vec{F}_N = -(m\vec{g} \cos \theta)$$

$\vec{F}_N$ is the y component of the force due to gravity. In the diagram above, the y component of the force due to gravity is the adjacent side of the triangle.

$$\cos \theta = \frac{\text{adjacent}}{\text{hypotenuse}}$$
$$\therefore \text{ adjacent} = (\text{hypotenuse})(\cos \theta)$$

or $\left(\vec{F}_g\right)_y = \vec{F}_g \cos \theta$

$$\left(\vec{F}_g\right)_y = -\vec{F}_N$$

$$\vec{F}_N = -\vec{F}_g \cos \theta$$

$$\vec{F}_N = -(m\vec{g} \cos \theta)$$

Example 1

A 175 N box is sliding down a frictionless 35.0° incline. Find the parallel component of the weight that causes the box to slide. That is, find $\left(\vec{F}_g \right)_x$.

Solution

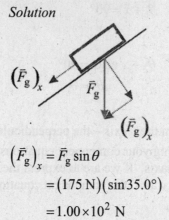

$$\left(\vec{F}_g \right)_x = \vec{F}_g \sin \theta$$
$$= (175 \text{ N})(\sin 35.0°)$$
$$= 1.00 \times 10^2 \text{ N}$$

Example 2

A 19.2 kg box is sliding down a frictionless incline. If the incline makes an angle of 30.0° with the horizontal, what is the acceleration along the incline?

Solution

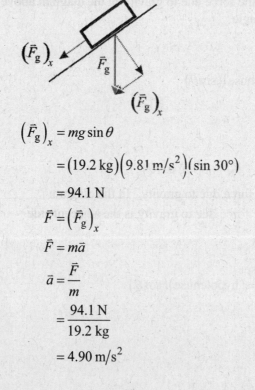

$$\left(\vec{F}_g \right)_x = mg \sin \theta$$
$$= (19.2 \text{ kg})(9.81 \text{ m/s}^2)(\sin 30°)$$
$$= 94.1 \text{ N}$$
$$\vec{F} = \left(\vec{F}_g \right)_x$$
$$\vec{F} = m\vec{a}$$
$$\vec{a} = \frac{\vec{F}}{m}$$
$$= \frac{94.1 \text{ N}}{19.2 \text{ kg}}$$
$$= 4.90 \text{ m/s}^2$$

PRACTICE EXERCISE

1. A 445 N box is sliding down a frictionless 25.0° inclined plane. Find the parallel component of the weight, $\left(\bar{F}_g\right)_x$, that causes the box to slide.

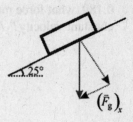

2. A 325 N box is sliding down a frictionless inclined plane. If the incline makes an angle of 30.0° with the horizontal, what is the acceleration along the incline?

3. A 275 N box is sliding down a 35.0° incline. If the force of friction along the incline is 96.0 N, what is the acceleration of the box?

4. A 435 N box is sliding down a 40.0° incline. If the acceleration of the box is 0.250 m/s^2, what is the force of friction on the box?

5. A student pulls a 125 N object up a 23.0° inclined plane as shown in the diagram. If the coefficient of friction between the object and the incline is 0.180, what force must the student pull with for the object to move at a constant velocity? Assume the applied force is parallel to the incline.

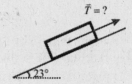

6. Two blocks are tied together with a string as shown in the diagram. If both the pulley and the incline are frictionless,

   a) what is the acceleration of the 1.0 kg block up the incline?

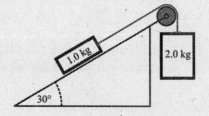

   b) what is the tension in the string joining the two blocks?

7. Repeat the above problem if the pulley is still frictionless but the coefficient of friction between the incline and the 1.0 kg block is 0.25.

Lesson 5 NEWTON'S THIRD LAW OF MOTION

Newton's third law of motion states that when an object exerts a force on a second object, that the second object exerts an equal and opposite force on the first. We often see this law stated in terms of action and reaction forces.

For every action (force) there is an equal, but opposite reaction (force).

$$\vec{F}_1 = -\vec{F}_2$$

For example, if you push on your desk, the desk pushes back with an equal amount of force. Birds can fly because when they push down with their wings, the air pushes up and provides lift. In the image below, we see that a car's tires exert force in the opposite direction to which the car travels.

Newton's Third Law:
For every action (force) there is an equal but opposite reaction (force)

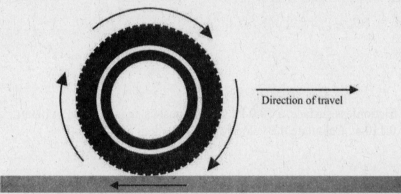

Direction of travel

Direction of force applied by wheel

The wheel exerts force upon the road; the road exerts an equal and opposite force upon the wheel. The force exerted by the wheel is not enough to move the road (obviously). The force exerted by the road upon the wheel is enough to propel the car down the road.

Example 1
While standing on a horizontal frictionless surface, two students push against each other. One student has a mass of 35 kg and the other 45 kg. If the acceleration of the 35 kg student is 0.75 m/s^2 south, what is the acceleration of the 45 kg student?

Solution

$$\vec{F}_1 = -\vec{F}_2$$
$$m_1\vec{a}_1 = -m_2\vec{a}_2$$
$$(35 \text{ kg})(0.75 \text{ m/s}^2) = -(45 \text{ kg})\vec{a}_2$$
$$\vec{a}_2 = 0.58 \text{ m/s}^2 \text{ north}$$

PRACTICE EXERCISE

1. While standing on a horizontal frictionless surface, two students, A and B, push against each other. Student A has a mass of 38 kg and during the push is accelerating east at a rate of $0.60 \, \text{m/s}^2$.

   If student B is accelerating west during the push at a rate of $0.75 \, \text{m/s}^2$, what is her mass?

2. While standing on a horizontal frictionless surface, a 50.0 kg student pushes against a wall with an **average force of 125 N east for 0.110 s**. Calculate the velocity of this student at 0.110 s.

3. A 9.8×10^3 kg rocket is travelling east along a horizontal frictionless rail at a velocity of 11 m/s. The rocket is then accelerated uniformly to a velocity of 22 m/s in a time of 0.75 s by the expulsion of hot gases. What is the average force at which the gases are expelled by the rocket?

4. While standing on a horizontal frictionless surface, a 45 kg student throws a 3.0 kg object to her right. During the throw the object was accelerated horizontally through a distance of 0.60 m from rest to a velocity of 9.6 m/s . Calculate the velocity of the student when the object is released.

5. A force of 14.0 N is applied to a block as shown in the diagram. If the coefficient of friction between the blocks and the horizontal surface is 0.35,

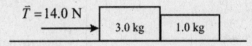

   a) what is the acceleration of the two blocks?

   b) what is the force that the 3.0 kg block exerts on the 1.0 kg block?

Lesson 6 Newton's Law of Universal Gravitation

NOTES

Newton formulated the Law of Universal Gravitation

According to popular folklore, one day when Newton was sitting under an apple tree thinking about the motion of the moon around the Earth, an apple broke free from its branch and fell to the ground.

Newton understood that the force that caused the apple to fall was the attractive force of the Earth on the apple—gravity. This small event started him wondering if it was also the Earth's gravity that was responsible for the moon's motion around the Earth. Does the Earth's gravity extend that far into space? Newton hypothesized that it did, and that this force was responsible for the moon's motion. He formulated the Law of Universal Gravitation. It is this law that explains the motion of the moon around the Earth, and the motion of the planets around the sun.

Newton's Law of Universal Gravitation:

$$\vec{F}_g \propto \frac{m_1 m_2}{r^2}$$

Newton's Law of Universal Gravitation states:

- the gravitational force between two masses is directly proportional to the product of their masses.

$$\vec{F}_g \propto m_1 m_2$$

- the gravitational force between two masses varies inversely to the square of the distance between the centres of the masses.

$$\vec{F}_g \propto \frac{1}{r^2}$$

$$\vec{F}_g \propto \frac{1}{r^2}$$

By combining these two statements, we get

$$\vec{F}_g \propto \frac{m_1 m_2}{r^2} \qquad \text{or} \qquad \vec{F}_g = \frac{G m_1 m_2}{r^2}$$

G is called the gravitational constant, and has been determined to be

$$6.67 \times 10^{-11} \frac{\text{N} \cdot \text{m}^2}{\text{kg}^2}.$$

Cavendish measured the value of G

CAVENDISH EXPERIMENT

In 1798, Cavendish measured the value of G using a torsion balance.

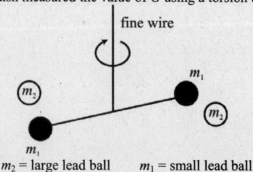

m_2 = large lead ball m_1 = small lead ball

Cavendish equated the angle of rotation with force. By measuring the angle of rotation, he determined the force. Knowing the masses and the distance between them, he was able to calculate G.

Now using Newton's Law of Universal Gravitation and the value of G, we can calculate the mass of the Earth. This mass is calculated to be 5.98×10^{24} kg.

The mass of the Earth is calculated to be 5.98×10^{24} kg

Example 1

Calculate the gravitational force between two objects when they are 7.50×10^{-1} m apart. Each object has a mass of 5.00×10^{1} kg.

Solution

$$\vec{F}_g = \frac{Gm_1 m_2}{r^2}$$

$$= \frac{\left(6.67 \times 10^{-11} \, \frac{\text{N} \cdot \text{m}^2}{\text{kg}^2}\right)\left(5.00 \times 10^{1} \, \text{kg}\right)\left(5.00 \times 10^{1} \, \text{kg}\right)}{\left(7.50 \times 10^{-1} \text{m}\right)^2}$$

$$= 2.96 \times 10^{-7} \, \text{N}$$

Example 2

Calculate the gravitational force on a 6.0×10^{2} kg spacecraft that is 1.6×10^{4} km above Earth's surface.

Solution

$$\vec{F}_g = \frac{Gm_1 m_2}{r^2}$$

$$= \frac{\left(6.67 \times 10^{-11} \, \frac{\text{N} \cdot \text{m}^2}{\text{kg}^2}\right)\left(5.98 \times 10^{24} \, \text{kg}\right)\left(6.0 \times 10^{2} \, \text{kg}\right)}{\left(1.6 \times 10^{7} \text{m} + 6.37 \times 10^{6} \text{m}\right)^2}$$

$$= 4.8 \times 10^{2} \, \text{N}$$

NOTE: The radius of Earth must be added to the distance above Earth.

PRACTICE EXERCISES

Formula: $\vec{F}_g = \dfrac{Gm_1 m_2}{r^2}$

1. Two students are sitting 1.50 m apart. One student has a mass of 70.0 kg and the other has a mass of 52.0 kg. What is the gravitational force between them?

2. What gravitational force does the moon produce on Earth if the centres of Earth and the moon are 3.88×10^8 m apart and the moon has a mass of 7.34×10^{22} kg ?

3. If the gravitational force between two objects of equal mass is 2.30×10^{-8} N when the objects are 10.0 m apart, what is the mass of each object?

4. Calculate the gravitational force on a 6.50×10^2 kg spacecraft that is 4.15×10^6 m above the Earth's surface.

5. The gravitational force between two objects that are 2.1×10^{-1} m apart is 3.2×10^{-6} N. If the mass of one object is 5.5×10^1 kg, what is the mass of the other object?

6. If two objects, each with a mass of 2.0×10^2 kg, produce a gravitational force between them of 3.7×10^{-6} N, what is the distance between them?

7. What is the gravitational force on a 70.0 kg person on the Earth's surface?

8. What is the gravitational force on a 35.0 kg object resting on the Earth's surface? (Use your answer to Question 7 to reduce the calculations.)

9. What is the gravitational force on a 70.0 kg object that is 6.37×10^6 m above the Earth's surface? (Use your answer to Question 7 to reduce the calculations.)

10. What is the gravitational force on a 70.0 kg object that is 3.18×10^6 m above the Earth's surface? NOTE: this is one-half the radius of the Earth. (Use your answer to Question 7 to reduce the calculations.)

11. Three objects each with a mass of 10.0 kg are placed in a straight line 5.00×10^{-1} m apart as shown in the diagram. What is the net gravitational force on the centre object due to the other two objects?

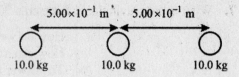

5.00×10^{-1} m $\quad$ 5.00×10^{-1} m

10.0 kg $\qquad$ 10.0 kg $\qquad$ 10.0 kg

12. Three objects A, B, and C, are placed 5.00×10^{-1} m apart along a straight line as shown in the diagram. If A and B have equal masses of 10.0 kg and C has a mass of 15.0 kg, what is the net gravitational force on B due to A and C?

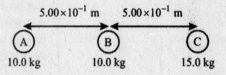

5.00×10^{-1} m $\quad$ 5.00×10^{-1} m

A $\qquad$ B $\qquad$ C

10.0 kg $\qquad$ 10.0 kg $\qquad$ 15.0 kg

13. The gravitational force between two small masses, A and B, when placed a short distance apart, is 3.24×10^{-7} N. What is the gravitational force between these objects if the masses of both A and B are doubled and the distance between them is tripled?

Lesson 7 FIELD EXPLANATION

How do we explain gravitational forces—forces between two masses? How can a force exist between two objects that are not in contact? To answer these questions, scientists invented the concept of fields. The fields are invisible. A mass is surrounded by a gravitational field. Although the Earth and the moon are not in physical contact, their gravitational fields do interact.

Fields are defined as spheres of influence

Fields are defined as spheres of influence. Fields can be classified as scalar or vector. Scalar fields, like scalar quantities, do not have direction, but have magnitude only. Examples of scalar fields are sound fields and heat fields. If you are standing near a camp fire, you are in the sphere of influence of the heat from the fire. You can measure the intensity of the heat at different points (i.e., you can measure the temperature). Temperature is a scalar quantity, and is described by the collection of these points. Therefore, the heat field is said to be a scalar field.

Vector fields, like vector quantities, have direction as well as magnitude. A gravitational field is an example of a vector field. A gravitational field is a force field, and because a force is a vector quantity, a force field is a vector field.

GRAVITATIONAL FIELD STRENGTH

Symbol g

Note: This is the same symbol that we used for acceleration due to gravity. This is because gravitational field strength is the same as acceleration due to gravity.

Definition: Gravitational force per mass

gravitational force (weight)

Gravitational Field Strength: $g = \dfrac{\vec{F}_g}{m}$

$$g = \dfrac{\vec{F}_g}{m}$$

mass

Units: N/kg

N/kg is the same as m/s^2

If we return to the definition of gravitational field strength, we have:

$$g = \dfrac{\vec{F}_g}{m}$$

You will note that if you transpose this equation, you get

$$\vec{F}_g = mg$$

We see from this equation that the weight of an object depends on the object's mass and the gravitational field strength. The gravitational field strength near Earth's surface is taken as $9.81\,m/s^2$ or N/kg.

Example 1

What is the weight of a 12.0 kg object near the surface of the Earth?

Solution

$$\vec{F}_g = mg$$

$$= (12.0\,\text{kg})(9.81\,\text{m/s}^2)$$

$$= 118\,\text{N}$$

PRACTICE EXERCISE

Formula: $\vec{F}_g = mg$

1. What is the weight of a 25.0 kg object near the Earth's surface?

2. What is the mass of an object if it has a weight of 80.0 N near the Earth's surface?

3. What is the acceleration due to gravity near the surface of the moon if an object that has a mass of 22.0 kg has a weight of 36.0 N near the moon's surface?

4. What is the weight of a 72.0 kg object near the Earth's surface?

5. What is the mass of an object if it has a weight of 127 N near the Earth's surface?

PRACTICE QUIZ

1. An average net force of 16.0 N acts on an object for 2.00×10^{-1} s, causing it to accelerate from rest to 3.50 m/s^2. What is the mass of the object?

2. A 0.500 kg object is thrown vertically upward with an average applied force of 8.20 N by a student. This force is applied through a displacement of 1.50 m.

   a) What is the average net force acting on the object?

   b) What is the velocity of the object when it leaves the student's hand? Assume the initial velocity of the object is zero.

3. What is the tension in the cable of a 1.20×10^3 kg elevator that is:

a) accelerating downward at a rate of 1.05 m/s^2 ?

b) accelerating upward at a rate of 1.05 m/s^2 ?

c) moving downward at a constant velocity of 1.10 m/s ?

4. A horizontal force of 90.0 N is required to push a 75.0 kg object along a horizontal surface at a constant speed. What is the magnitude of the force of friction?

5. An astronaut has a weight of 1.95×10^3 N when she is on the surface of a hypothetical planet that has a mass of 25 times and a radius of 2.5 times that of Earth. What is her mass when she is on Earth?

6. An object (mass = 525 kg) is 3.00×10^6 m above the Earth's surface. The object is falling toward the Earth because of the Earth's gravitational force on it. What is the gravitational field strength at this distance?

7. On the surface of Planet T, which has a mass of 7.90×10^{25} kg, an object has a weight of 112 N and a mass of 75.0 kg. What is the radius of this planet?

8. An 85 N object is pulled along a horizontal surface by a force of 32 N as shown in the diagram. The frictional force acting on this object is 14 N.

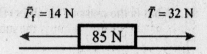

$\vec{F}_f = 14$ N $\vec{T} = 32$ N

85 N

   a) What is the acceleration of the object?

   b) What is the coefficient of friction between the surfaces?

9. A 2.5 kg object is pulled along a horizontal surface at a constant velocity of 2.0 m/s by a force of 3.0 N as shown in the diagram. What is the coefficient of friction between the surfaces?

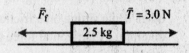

$\vec{F}_f$ $\vec{T} = 3.0$ N

2.5 kg

10. A 1.20×10^3 kg car is travelling at a speed of 22.5 m/s when the brakes are applied. If the car comes to a stop in 112 m, what is the braking force? (Assume uniform deceleration.)

11. What is the mass of an object that has a weight near the surface of the Earth of 50.0 N?

12. A hockey puck is shot along the ice at a velocity of 11 m/s and it slides 25 m before it comes to a stop. What is the coefficient of friction between the puck and the ice?

13. Two blocks $\left(m_1 = 6.8 \text{ kg}, m_2 = 5.2 \text{ kg}\right)$ are in contact with each other while sitting on a frictionless surface as shown in the diagram. A horizontal force of 85 N is applied to m_1.

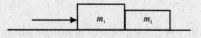

a) What is the acceleration of the system?

b) What is the force that m_1 exerts on m_2?

14. Two blocks $(m_1 = 5.0 \text{ kg}, m_2 = 9.0 \text{ kg})$ are attached by a light rope as shown in the diagram. If these two blocks are pulled along a frictionless surface by a force of 42 N, what is the tension in the rope between the blocks?

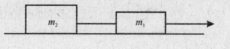

15. Two blocks $(m_1 = 4.0 \text{ kg}, m_2 = 7.5 \text{ kg})$ are attached by a light cord and pulled along a horizontal surface by a force of 53 N as shown in the diagram. If the coefficient of friction between the blocks and the surface is 0.30, what is the tension in the rope between the two blocks?

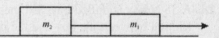

16. What is the tension in the cable of a 1.5×10^3 kg elevator that is:

a) accelerating downward at a rate of 0.50 m/s?

b) moving downward at a constant velocity of 1.0 m/s?

17. A 25.0 kg block slides down a 30.0° incline at a constant speed. What is the coefficient of friction between the block and the incline?

18. A 55 N box is pulled up a 35° incline by a force of 46 N. If the coefficient of friction between the box and the incline is 0.18,

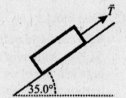

a) what is the normal force?

b) what is the force of friction?

c) what is the acceleration of the box?

19. A 7.6 kg object is pulled up an incline. If the incline makes an angle of 33° with the horizontal, and the coefficient of friction is 0.20, what is the force of friction acting on the object?

20. A 42 N block is pulled along a horizontal surface by a force of 28 N as shown in the diagram. What is the normal force on the block?

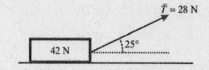

21. Three equally sized balls (masses = 0.35 kg) are placed at the corners of a right angle triangle as shown in the diagram. What is the net gravitational force on B due to the presence of the other two balls?

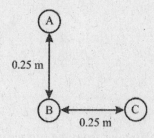

22. On the surface of Planet T, which has a mass of 7.90×10^{25}, an object has a weight of 112 N and a mass of 75.0 kg. What is the radius of this planet?

23. An object (mass = 525 kg) is 3.0×10^3 km above the Earth's surface. This object is falling toward the Earth because of the Earth's gravitational force on it. What is the rate of acceleration when it is at this distance? $\left(m_E = 5.98 \times 10^{24} \text{ kg}, r_E = 6.37 \times 10^6 \text{ m} \right)$

24. How far from the surface of the Earth is the gravitational field strength 6.13×10^{-1} N/kg ? $\left(m_E = 5.98 \times 10^{24} \text{ kg}, r_E = 6.37 \times 10^6 \text{ m} \right)$

25. Calculate the gravitational field strength at a point in space where the weight of an object is 7.22×10^2 N and its mass is 1.10×10^2 kg.

26. If an object has a weight of 7.00×10^2 N on the surface of the Earth, what is its weight at a distance of 6.37×10^6 m above the Earth's surface? $\left(m_E = 5.98 \times 10^{24} \text{ kg}, r_E = 6.37 \times 10^6 \text{ m} \right)$

PRACTICE TEST

1. The coefficient of friction, μ, can best be described as the ratio of

A) $\dfrac{\text{weight}}{\text{force of friction}}$

B) $\dfrac{\text{normal force}}{\text{force of friction}}$

C) $\dfrac{\text{force of friction}}{\text{weight}}$

D) $\dfrac{\text{force of friction}}{\text{normal force}}$

2. According to Newton's Second Law of Motion, which of the following graphs best shows the relationship between the acceleration $(\bar{a})$ of an object and the mass of the object?

A)

B)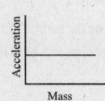

C)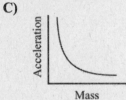

D)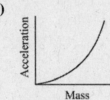

3. According to Newton's Second Law of Motion, which of the following graphs best represents the relationship between the net force acting on an object and the acceleration of the object?

A)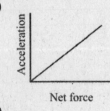

B)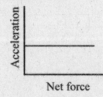

C)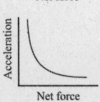

D)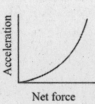

4. A 625 N student (as weighed in the physics lab) wants to see how his weight is affected by his riding on an elevator. Suppose this student is standing on a scale that reads in Newton's and is moving up at a constant velocity. The scale will read at a value

A) less than 625 N

B) greater than 625 N

C) equal to 625 N

5. A 625 N student (as weighed in the physics lab) wants to see how his weight is affected by his riding on an elevator. Suppose this student is standing on a scale that reads in Newton's and is accelerating downward. The scale will read at a value

A) less than 625 N

B) greater than 625 N

C) equal to 625 N

6. If there is no net force acting on an object, it is

    i)   at rest

    ii) moving at constant velocity

    iii) moving with constant acceleration.

Which of the above can be correct?

A. i) only   **B.** i) and ii) only

C. i) and iii) only   **D.** i), ii), and iii)

7. In studying the relationship between the acceleration and the net force on an object, a student obtained the following graph. What did the graph tell her about the relationship?

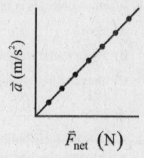

$\vec{a}$ (m/s^2)

$\vec{F}_{net}$ (N)

A. $\vec{a} \propto \vec{F}_{net}$ **B.** $\vec{a} \propto \dfrac{1}{\vec{F}_{net}}$

C. $\vec{F}_{net} \propto \dfrac{1}{\vec{a}}$ **D.** $\vec{a} \propto \vec{F}_{net}{}^2$

8. In studying the relationship between the acceleration and the mass of an object, a student obtained the following graph. What did this graph tell her about the relationship?

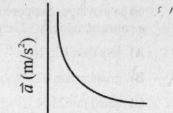

m (kg)

A. $\vec{a} \propto m$

B. $\vec{a} \propto m^2$

C. $\vec{a} \propto \dfrac{1}{m}$

D. $m \propto \dfrac{1}{\vec{a}}$

9. A 75 kg student stands on a bathroom scale while riding in an elevator. What can you infer about the motion of the elevator if the scale reading is 775 N?

A. The elevator is going down at a constant velocity.

B. The elevator is going up at a constant velocity.

C. The elevator is accelerating downward.

D. The elevator is accelerating upward.

10. Which of the following statements is true about mass? (g on the moon is 1.6 m/s^2)

A. The mass of an object is greater on the moon than it is on Earth.

B. The mass of an object is less on the moon than it is on Earth.

C. The mass of an object is the same on the moon as it is on Earth.

11. When an object is at rest on a horizontal frictionless surface, the normal force on the object is

A) zero

B) equal to the weight of the object

C) the net force acting on the object

12. A 6.0 N object is pulled at constant velocity along a horizontal surface as shown in the diagram by a horizontal force of 2.0 N. What is the force of friction acting on the object?

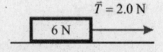

$\vec{T} = 2.0 \text{ N}$

A) zero

B) 2.0 N

C) 4.0 N

D) 6.0 N

13. A 3.0 kg object is pulled along a horizontal surface as shown in the diagram by a horizontal force of 2.0 N. If the object is accelerating at a rate of 1.2 m/s^2, what is the force of friction acting on the object?

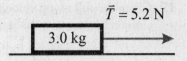

$\vec{T} = 5.2 \text{ N}$

3.0 kg

A) 1.6 N   **B)** 2.0 N

C) 3.6 N   **D)** 29 N

14. A 6.0 N object is moving at a constant velocity along a horizontal frictionless surface. What is the coefficient of friction between the object and the surface?

A) zero

B) 6.0

C) There is not enough information to calculate, but it is less than 6.0 and greater than zero.

D) There is not enough information to calculate, but it is greater than 6.0.

15. If an object has a weight of 15 N on earth, what is the weight on Planet F $\left(g = 27 \text{ m/s}^2\right)$?

A. 15 N   **B.** greater than 15 N

C. Less than 15 N

16. When two objects $\left(m_1 = 4.5 \text{ kg}, m_2 = 9.0 \text{ kg}\right)$ are dropped from the same height, which of the following statements is true about their velocities when they hit the ground? (Assume air resistance can be ignored.)

A. m_2 has twice the velocity of m_1.

B. m_2 is travelling faster than m_1, but not twice as fast.

C. m_2 is travelling slower than m_1.

D. m_2 and m_1 are travelling at the same velocity.

17. Given the following velocity-time graph for an object moving in a straight line along a horizontal surface, a physics student tells his friend that

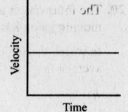

   i)   there is no net force acting on the object

   ii) the surface must be frictionless

   Which of the above is/are correct, if any?

   A) only i) is correct

   B) only ii) is correct

   C) both i) and ii) are correct

   D) neither i) nor ii) is correct

18. Given the following acceleration-time graph for an object moving in a straight line along a horizontal surface, a physics student tells her friend that

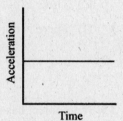

   i)   there is no net force acting on the object

   ii) the surface must be frictionless

   Which of the above is/are correct, if any?

   A) only i) is correct

   B) only ii) is correct

   C) both i) and ii) are correct

   D) neither i) nor ii) are correct

19. The following is a velocity-time graph of an object moving along a horizontal surface.

   In which section does the object experience the largest constant net force?

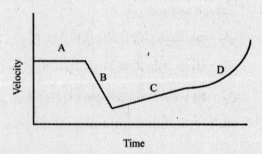

   A) A   **B)** B

   C) C   **D)** D

20. The following is a displacement-time graph of an object moving along a horizontal surface.

    In which section does the object experience the largest average net force?

    A) A

    B) B

    C) C

    D) D

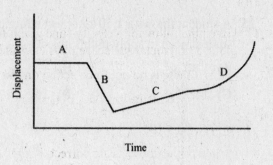

21. A, B, and C are three objects with identical masses at rest on a horizontal surface. On which of the above objects is/are the normal force the greatest?

    A) A

    B) B

    C) C

    D) The normal force on all three is the same.

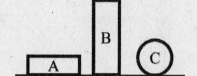

22. An object which is travelling east hits a wall with a force of 12 N. What force does the wall exert on the object?

    A. 12 N east

    B. A force less than 12 N east

    C. 12 N west

    D. A force less than 12 N west

23. A 5.0 N object is tied to a string and moves downward at a constant velocity.

    A physics teacher suggests three possible answers. Which of the following suggestions is true?

    A) The tension in the string is zero.

    B) The tension in the string is 5.0 N

    C) The tension in the string is less than 5.0 N, but not zero

24. Two forces, $\vec{T}_1$ and $\vec{T}_2$, are exerted on a 2.0 kg object as shown in the diagram. If $\vec{T}_1 = 17$ N and the acceleration of the object is 1.6 m/s^2, what is the magnitude of $\vec{T}_2$?

    A) 1.6 N

    B) 3.2 N

    C) 14 N

    D) 20 N

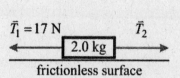

25. A student throws a 1.50 kg object straight up into the air at a rate of 1.20 m/s^2. What force does the student need to apply to this object?

A) 1.80 N   **B)** 12.9 N

C) 14.7 N   **D)** 16.5 N

26. Mass is defined in terms of

   A. inertia   **B.** weight

   C. acceleration   **D.** gravity

27. If we know the net force acting on an object and the acceleration of the object, it is possible for us to find the

   A. velocity of the object   **B.** force of friction on the object

   C. applied force on the object   **D.** mass of the object

28. $\vec{F}_1$ is the force that the Earth exerts on the moon, and $\vec{F}_2$ is the force that the moon exerts on the Earth. Which of the following statements about the magnitude of these forces is true?

   A. $\vec{F}_1 > \vec{F}_2$ **B.** $\vec{F}_2 > \vec{F}_1$

   C. $\vec{F}_1 = \vec{F}_2$ **D.** $\vec{F}_1 + \vec{F}_2 = 0$

29. If an object has a weight of 2.0 N at the surface of the Earth, what is the weight at a distance of one Earth radius above the Earth's surface?

   A. 0.50 N   **B.** 1.0 N

   C. 2.0 N   **D.** 4.0 N

30. Which of the following graphs best represent the relationship between the gravitational field strength (g) due to the Earth and the distance (r) from the centre of the Earth?

A.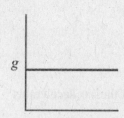

B.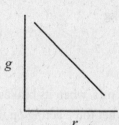

C.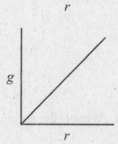

D.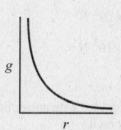

31. If object A has a mass of 1 100 kg and object B has a mass of 2 200 kg, which of the following statements is/are true?

    i)   On earth, object B has twice the weight of object A.

    ii) On the moon, object B experiences twice the gravitational force that object A experiences.

    iii) Near the surface of Earth, object B experiences twice the acceleration due to gravity that object A experiences as they toward the surface of the Earth.

  A. i) only   **B.** i) and ii) only

  C. ii) and iii) only   **D.** i), ii) and iii)

32. A student is pulling a 95.0 kg block along a horizontal surface with a force of 105 N as shown in the diagram. If the force of friction on the block is 48.0 N, what is the acceleration of the block?

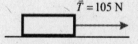

  A. $0.505 \, \text{m/s}^{2}{}^{2}$ **B.** $0.600 \, \text{m/s}^{2}$

  C. $1.11 \, \text{m/s}^{2}$ **D.** $1.61 \, \text{m/s}^{2}$

33. A 3.0 kg block is resting on a frictionless horizontal surface. If another block $(m = 7.5 \text{ kg})$ is attached to the first block as shown in the diagram, what is the acceleration of the 3.0 kg block?

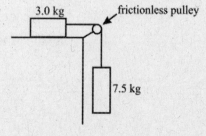

  A. $2.8 \, \text{m/s}^{2}$ **B.** $4.2 \, \text{m/s}^{2}$

  C. $7.0 \, \text{m/s}^{2}$ **D.** $9.8 \, \text{m/s}^{2}$

34. If the force of gravity on an object is 12.0 N, what is its mass? (Assume the object is near the surface of the Earth.)

    A. 0.82 N   **B.** 1.22 kg

    C. 12.0 N   **D.** 118 kg

35. A 1.2×10^3 kg car is travelling at 22 m/s when its brakes are applied. If the car decelerates uniformly to rest in 9.0 s, what is the net force acting on the car?

    A. 2.4 N   **B.** 1.7×10^2 N

    C. 5.0×10^2 N   **D.** 2.9×10^3 N

36. A 3.0 kg object is thrown vertically upward with an applied force of 55 N. What is the acceleration of the object while the force is acting on it?

    A. $8.5 \, \text{m/s}^2$ **B.** $9.8 \, \text{m/s}^2$

    C. $18 \, \text{m/s}^2$ **D.** $23 \, \text{m/s}^2$

NOTES

CIRCULAR MOTION, WORK, AND ENERGY

When you are finished this unit, you will be able to…

- describe uniform circular motion as a special case of two-dimensional motion
- explain, qualitatively and quantitatively, that the acceleration in uniform circular motion is directed toward the centre of the circle
- explain, quantitatively, the relationships among speed, frequency, period and radius for circular motion
- explain, qualitatively, uniform circular motion in terms of Newton's laws of motion
- explain, quantitatively, planetary and natural and artificial satellite motion, using circular motion to approximate elliptical orbits
- predict the mass of a celestial body from the orbital data of a satellite in uniform circular motion around the celestial body
- explain, qualitatively, how Kepler's laws were used in the development of Newton's Universal Law of Gravitation
- determine, quantitatively, the relationships among the kinetic, gravitational potential, and total mechanical energies of a mass at any point between maximum potential energy and maximum kinetic energy
- define mechanical energy as the sum of kinetic and potential energy
- analyze, quantitatively, kinematics and dynamics problems that relate to the conservation of mechanical energy in an isolated system
- recall work as a measure of the mechanical energy transferred and power as the rate of doing work
- describe power qualitatively and quantitatively
- describe, quantitatively, the change in mechanical energy in a system that is not isolated
- explain that concepts, models, and theories are often used in interpreting and explaining observations and in predicting future observations
- explain that the products of technology are devices, systems and processes that meet given needs; however, these products cannot solve all problems
- evaluate whether Canadian society supports scientific research and technological development to facilitate a sustainable society, economy, and environment
- explain that the process of scientific investigation includes analyzing the evidence and providing explanations based upon scientific theories and concepts
- explain how science and technology are developed to meet societal needs and expand human capability
- explain that the goal of technology is to provide solutions to practical problems, and analyze the principles and applications of circular motion in daily situations

Lesson 1   UNIFORM CIRCULAR MOTION

NOTES

We will extend our study of kinematics and dynamics by studying circular motion. Let us begin by looking at uniform circular motion.

There are many examples of uniform circular motion. This motion can be illustrated by tying a mass to a string and whirling it in a circle on the floor at a constant speed—note that we said speed, and not velocity.

We have described linear motion and how Newton's laws of motion apply to it. Now, let's describe uniform circular motion and how Newton's laws of motion are applied to it.

The speed of an object that is moving with uniform circular motion is given by

$$v = \frac{d}{t}$$

$$v = \frac{2\pi r}{T}$$

where $2\pi r$ = circumference of the circle
    T = period of motion (time of one revolution)

or
$v = 2\pi rf$

Remember: $T = \dfrac{1}{f}$, therefore $v = \dfrac{2\pi r}{\dfrac{1}{f}}$ or $v = 2\pi rf$

The formulae $v = \dfrac{2\pi r}{T}$ and $v = 2\pi rf$ are special cases of $v = \dfrac{d}{t}$

These formulae are just special cases of $v = \dfrac{d}{t}$.

Although the speed of this mass is uniform, its velocity is not (remember velocity is a vector quantity—it has direction). If the direction changes, the velocity changes. If the velocity changes, the object must be accelerating. This acceleration is called the centripetal acceleration, and is found using

$$\vec{a}_{c} = \frac{v^2}{r}$$

where $\vec{a}_{c}$ = centripetal acceleration
    v = speed
    r = radius of circle

This equation is derived using the reference circle.

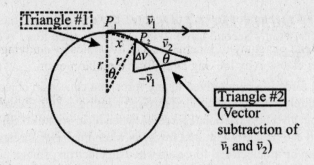

Triangle #2
(Vector subtraction of $\vec{v}_1$ and $\vec{v}_2$)

To subtract $\vec{v}_1$ from $\vec{v}_2$, reverse the direction of $\vec{v}_1$, giving $-\vec{v}_1$. Then, add the vector to $\vec{v}_2$.

$$\vec{v}_2 + \left(-\vec{v}_1\right) = \vec{v}_2 - \vec{v}_1$$

P is an object that is travelling at a constant speed v in a circle with radius r. At $t = 0$, the object is at P_1 travelling at a velocity of $\vec{v}_1$. Some short time later $\left(\Delta t\right)$, the object is at P_2 travelling at a velocity of $\vec{v}_2$. The acceleration of this object is:

$$\vec{a} = \frac{\vec{v}_2 - \vec{v}_1}{\Delta t} \qquad \text{or} \qquad \vec{a} = \frac{\Delta \vec{v}}{\Delta t}$$

Triangles 1 and 2 are similar; therefore:

$$\frac{\Delta v}{v} = \frac{x}{r} \qquad \text{or} \qquad \Delta v = \frac{vx}{r}$$

But $\quad x = v\Delta t \qquad$ (true when θ is small)

(this is the same as $d = vt$)

therefore

$$\Delta v = \frac{v\left(v\Delta t\right)}{r}$$

Now $\quad a = \dfrac{\Delta v}{\Delta t}$

therefore

$$\vec{a}_c = \frac{\dfrac{v^2 \Delta t}{r}}{\Delta t} \qquad \text{or} \qquad \vec{a}_c = \frac{v^2}{r}$$

Note that the centripetal acceleration is always directed toward the centre of the circle. This is really the meaning of centripetal—centre-seeking.

Also note that the velocity is always directed along the tangent of the circle. That is, it is perpendicular to the acceleration.

Centripetal acceleration is always directed toward the centre of the circular path

Velocity is always directed along the tangent of the circle

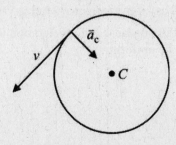

Centripetal force is a name given to any force that causes an object to move in a circle

If an object is accelerated toward the centre, there must be a force toward the centre (Newton's Second Law). This centre-directed force is called the centripetal force.

Centripetal force is a name given to any force that causes an object to move in a circle. It can be supplied through a string as in the example given. It can also be a frictional force, as when a car rounds a curve on the highway. It can be a gravitational force, as when the moon circles the Earth. It can be an electrical force, as when an electron orbits a proton.

Circular motion is really a special case of two-dimensional motion (projectile motion). In circular motion, the force vector is always perpendicular to the velocity vector.

From Newton's Second Law of Motion:

$$\vec{F} = m\vec{a}$$

$$\vec{F}_c = m\vec{a}_c$$

$$\vec{F}_c = \frac{m\vec{v}^2}{r}$$

This formula can also be expressed as

$$\vec{F}_c = \frac{4\pi^2 rm}{T^2}$$

The formula is derived as follows.

$$\vec{F}_c = \frac{mv^2}{r}$$

But $\quad v = \dfrac{d}{t} \quad$ or $\quad \dfrac{2\pi r}{T}$

Therefore

$$v^2 = \frac{4\pi^2 r^2}{T^2}$$

$$\vec{F}_c = \frac{m\left(\dfrac{4\pi^2 r^2}{T^2}\right)}{r}$$

$$\vec{F}_c = \frac{4\pi^2 rm}{T^2}$$

In uniform circular motion, because the acceleration is uniform, the force that causes it must also be uniform.

Before we move on, let's discuss another force—centrifugal force. Whereas centripetal means centre-seeking, centrifugal means centre-fleeing. The centrifugal force is real in the sense that it, along with the centripetal force, forms an action–reaction pair of forces.

Consider a string attached to a mass which is rotated in a horizontal circular trajectory. The force exerted by the string on the mass (centripetal force) is equal and opposite to the force exerted by the mass on the string (centrifugal force).

The centrifugal force is apparent or fictitious when an object is observed in an accelerating frame of reference.

When we study motion, the motion of an object is always in reference to something else. This something else is called the frame of reference. In many cases the Earth is our frame of reference. For example, when we say that a car is travelling at a velocity of $25\,\text{m/s}$ south, this is in reference to the fixed environment around it—the Earth. Frames of reference are classified as:

- non-accelerating frames of reference (or inertial frames of reference)
- accelerating frames of reference (or non-inertial frames of reference)

You should note that when an object moves in a circle at a constant speed, this object is an accelerating frame of reference. Any accelerating object can be regarded as an accelerating frame of reference, while any object moving at a constant velocity can be regarded as a non-accelerating frame of reference. In any accelerating frame of reference, there appears to be some force acting that really is not.

Consider the motion of a front-seat passenger if the car in which he or she is riding makes a sharp turn to the left. The car becomes an accelerating frame of reference and, in this frame, the passenger is apparently forced toward the car door.

What is really happening is the result of the passenger's inertia. The passenger tends to keep moving in the same direction while the car turning left has the effect of moving the car door into the passenger's inertial path.

Centripetal means
centre-seeking
Centrifugal means
centre-fleeing

Frames of Reference:
Accelerating (non-inertial)
Non-accelerating (inertial)

NOTES

Activity 9

- Design an experiment from which you can analyze uniform circular motion.
- Suggestion: Set up a system as shown below:

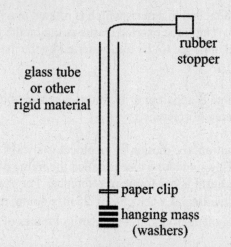

glass tube
or other
rigid material

rubber
stopper

paper clip

hanging mass
(washers)

- Twirl this apparatus above your head at a constant speed in a way that maintains an equilibrium between the rotating mass (stopper) and the hanging mass (washers). This can be tricky—be patient.
- Vary the hanging mass, keeping the radius constant.
- Measure the period by timing ten rotations.

Complete the following data table:

Mass of stopper (kg)	Radius (m)	Hanging Mass (kg)	Weight of Hanging Mass (N)	Time of 10 Rotations (s)	Time of 1 Rotation (s)	Calculate the speed (m/s) using	
						$\vec{F}_c = \dfrac{mv^2}{r}$	$v = \dfrac{2\pi r}{T}$

- Draw a graph of centripetal force vs. speed. (Which column of the data table is the centripetal force?)

In this activity, the hanging mass is the manipulated variable and $\vec{F}_c$ should be plotted on the x-axis

The calculated speed is the responding variable, plotted on the y-axis

NOTES

Questions

1. How would you describe the slope of your graph?

   A. constant   **B.** increasing
   C. decreasing   **D.** none of these

2. What does the formula $\vec{F}_c = \dfrac{mv^2}{r}$ suggest about the slope of your graph?

   A. constant   **B.** increasing
   C. decreasing   **D.** none of these

- Draw another graph of, F_c vs. v^2.

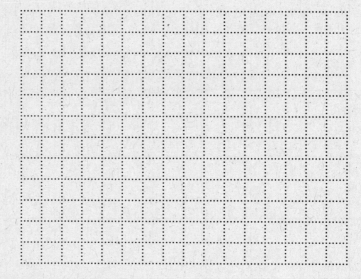

Questions

3. How would you describe the slope of the graph?

   A. constant   **B.** increasing
   C. decreasing   **D.** none of these

4. What does the formula $\vec{F}_c = \dfrac{mv^2}{r}$ suggest about the slope of this graph?

   A. constant   **B.** increasing
   C. decreasing   **D.** none of these

This experiment can be repeated by keeping the hanging mass constant and changing:
- the radius
- the mass of the rubber stopper

Example 1

Calculate the centripetal force acting on a 1.5 kg object whirling at a speed of 2.3 m/s in a horizontal circle of radius 0.60 m.

Solution

$$\vec{F}_c = \frac{mv^2}{r}$$

$$= \frac{(1.5\,\text{kg})(2.3\,\text{m/s})^2}{0.60\,\text{m}}$$

$$= 13\,\text{N}$$

Example 2

A car travelling at 14 m/s goes around an unbanked curve in the road that has a radius of 96 m. What is the centripetal acceleration?

Solution

$$\vec{a}_c = \frac{v^2}{r}$$

$$= \frac{(14\,\text{m/s})^2}{96\,\text{m}}$$

$$= 2.0\,\text{m/s}^2$$

Example 3

A plane makes a complete circle with a radius of 3 622 m in 2.10 min. What is the speed of the plane?

Solution

$$v = \frac{2\pi r}{T}$$

$$= \frac{(2\pi)(3\,622\,\text{m})}{(2.10\,\text{min})(60\,\text{s/min})}$$

$$= 181\,\text{m/s}$$

PRACTICE EXERCISE

Formulae: $\quad v = \dfrac{2\pi r}{T} \qquad \vec{a}_c = \dfrac{v^2}{r} \qquad \vec{F}_c = \dfrac{mv^2}{r} \qquad \vec{F}_c = \dfrac{4\pi^2 rm}{T^2}$

1. Calculate the centripetal force acting on a 925 kg car as it rounds an unbanked curve with a radius of 75 m at a speed of 22 m/s.

2. A small plane makes a complete circle with a radius of 3 282 m in 2.0 min. What is the centripetal acceleration of the plane?

3. A car with a mass of 822 kg rounds an unbanked curve in the road at a speed of 28.0 m/s. If the radius of the curve is 105 m, what is the average centripetal force exerted on the car?

4. An amusement park ride has a radius of 2.8 m. If the time of one revolution of a rider is 0.98 s, what is the speed of the rider?

5. An electron $\left(m = 9.11 \times 10^{-31} \text{ kg}\right)$ moves in a circle with a radius of 2.00×10^{-2} m. If the force acting on the electron is 4.60×10^{-14} N, what is the speed of the electron?

6. A 925 kg car rounds an unbanked curve at a speed of 25 m/s. If the radius of the curve is 72 m, what is the minimum coefficient of friction between the car and the road required so that the car does not skid?

7. A 2.7×10^3 kg satellite orbits the earth at a distance of 1.8×10^7 m from the Earth's centre at a speed of 4.7×10^3 m/s. What is the force acting on the satellite by the Earth?

8. An athlete whirls a 3.7 kg shotput in a horizontal circle with a radius of 0.90 m. If the period of rotation is 0.30 s,

   a) what is the speed of the shotput when released?

   b) what is the centripetal force acting on the shotput while it is rotated?

   c) how far would the shotput travel horizontally if it is released 1.2 m above the level ground?

9. Calculate the (a) speed and (b) acceleration of a point on the circumference of a $33\frac{1}{3}$ phonograph record. The diameter of the record is 30.0 cm. (NOTE: $33\frac{1}{3}$ is the frequency that it turns in revolutions/ minute.)

10. A string requires a 135 N force in order to break it. A 2.00 kg mass is tied to this string and whirled in a horizontal circle with a radius of 1.10 m. What is the maximum speed that the mass can be whirled without breaking the string?

11. A 932 kg car is travelling around an unbanked curve that has a radius of 82 m. What is the maximum speed that this car can round this curve without skidding:

   a) if the coefficient of friction is 0.95 on a dry asphalt surface?

   b) if the coefficient of friction is 0.40 on a wet asphalt surface?

   c) Explain why it is a good idea to reduce your speed when driving a car on wet roads.

12. A 0.150 kg mass, attached to a string, is twirled in a horizontal circle (radius = 0.800 m) at a rate of 99.5 RPM (revolutions per minute). Assuming the string is also horizontal, what is the speed of the mass?

13. A student does an experiment as suggested in Activity 9 and obtains the following data:

Mass of stopper (kg)	Radius of Path (m)	Hanging Mass (washers) (kg)	Weight of Hanging Mass (N)	Speed of Motion (m/s)	Period (s)
0.0400	0.350	0.0100	0.0981		
0.0400	0.350	0.0200	0.196		
0.0400	0.350	0.0400	0.392		
0.0400	0.350	0.0600	0.589		
0.0400	0.350	0.0800	0.785		

a) Complete the above data table by calculating the speed and period.

b) Draw a graph of centripetal force vs. speed. (Which column above is the centripetal force?)

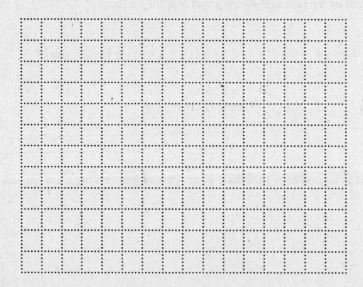

c) How would you describe the slope of your graph?

    A. constant   **B.** increasing
    C. decreasing   **D.** none of these

d) What does the formula $\vec{F}_c = \dfrac{mv^2}{r}$ suggest about the slope of your graph?

A. constant   **B.** increasing
C. decreasing   **D.** none of these

e) Draw another graph, of $\vec{F}_c$ vs. v^2.

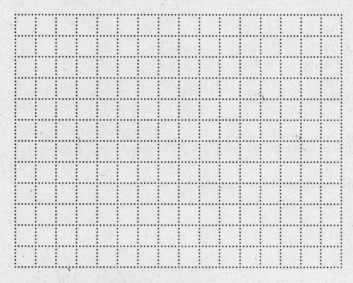

f) How would you describe the slope of this graph?

A. constant   **B.** increasing
C. decreasing   **D.** none of these

g) What does the formula $\vec{F}_c = \dfrac{mv^2}{r}$ suggest about the slope of this graph?

A. constant   **B.** increasing
C. decreasing   **D.** none of these

14. A student does an experiment as suggested in Activity 9, but this time she keeps the speed (period) constant and changes the radius. She obtains the following data:

Mass of stopper (kg)	Radius of Circular Path (m)	Hanging Mass (kg)	Weight of Hanging Mass (N)	Speed of Motion (m/s)
0.040 0	0.250	0.060 1	0.590	
0.040 0	0.350	0.042 9	0.421	
0.040 0	0.450	0.033 4	0.328	
0.040 0	0.550	0.027 3	0.268	
0.040 0	0.650	0.023 1	0.227	
0.040 0	0.800	0.016 7	0.164	
0.040 0	1.00	0.015 0	0.147	
0.040 0	1.20	0.012 5	0.123	

a) Complete the above data table by calculating the speed using $\vec{F}_c = \dfrac{mv^2}{r}$.

b) Draw a graph of centripetal force vs. radius.

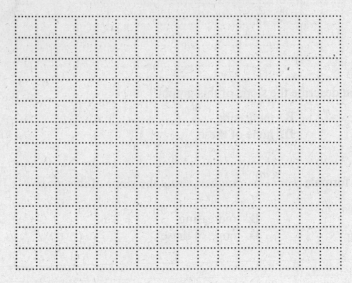

c) How would you describe the slope of your graph?

    A. constant   **B.** increasing
    C. decreasing   **D.** none of these

d) What does the formula $\vec{F}_c = \dfrac{mv^2}{r}$ suggest about the slope of your graph?

    A. constant   **B.** increasing
    C. decreasing   **D.** none of these

e) Draw another graph, of $\bar{F}_c$ vs. v^2.

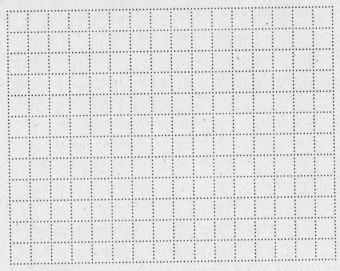

f) How would you describe the slope of this graph?

  A. constant   **B.** increasing
  C. decreasing   **D.** none of these

g) What does the formula $\bar{F}_c = \dfrac{mv^2}{r}$ suggest about the slope of this graph?

  A. constant   **B.** increasing
  C. decreasing   **D.** none of these

15. A student does an experiment as suggested in Activity 9, but this time he keeps the hanging mass (washers) constant and changes the mass of the stopper. He obtains the following data:

Mass of stopper (kg)	Radius of Path (m)	Hanging Mass (kg)	Weight of Hanging Mass (N)	Period (s)	Speed (m/s)
6.25×10^{-3}	0.350	0.100	0.0981	0.296	
2.50×10^{-2}	0.350	0.100	0.0981	0.593	
5.00×10^{-2}	0.350	0.100	0.0981	0.839	
7.50×10^{-2}	0.350	0.100	0.0981	1.03	
1.00×10^{-1}	0.350	0.100	0.0981	1.19	
1.25×10^{-1}	0.350	0.100	0.0981	1.33	

a) Complete the above data table by calculating the speed.

b) Draw a graph of speed vs. period.

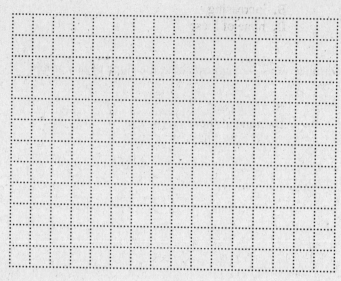

c) How would you describe the slope of your graph?

    A. constant   **B.** increasing

    C. decreasing   **D.** none of these

d) What does the formula $v = \dfrac{2\pi r}{T}$ suggest about the slope of your graph?

    A. constant   **B.** increasing

    C. decreasing   **D.** none of these

e) Draw another graph, of speed vs. frequency.

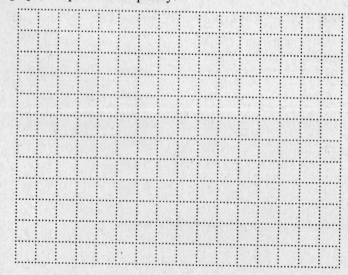

f) How would you describe the slope of this graph?

A. constant   **B.** increasing
C. decreasing   **D.** none of these

g) What does the formula $v = \dfrac{2\pi r}{T}$ suggest about the slope of this graph?

A. constant   **B.** increasing
C. decreasing   **D.** none of these

Lesson 2 VERTICAL CIRCULAR MOTION

NOTES

Now let's consider the motion of an object moving in a vertical circle. In such motion the centripetal force may vary from point to point. Remember that the centripetal force is the net force acting toward the centre. To understand why the force changes from point to point, let's look at a mass whirled in a vertical circle at the end of a string.

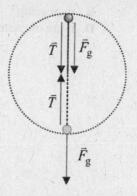

At the top position, the centripetal force (net force) is the sum of the tension and the weight, both directed downward.

$$\vec{F}_c = \vec{T} + \vec{F}_g \qquad \text{where } \vec{T} \text{ and } \vec{F}_g \text{ are negative}$$

At the bottom position, again, the centripetal force (net force) is the sum of the tension and the weight. Now, however, the tension is directed upwards while the weight (as always) is directed downward.

$$\vec{F}_c = \vec{T} + \vec{F}_g \qquad \text{where } \vec{T} \text{ is positive and } \vec{F}_g \text{ is negative}$$

There are three important things to note about this sort of motion.

- $\vec{F}_c$ is always directed toward the centre of the circular path.
- The tension in the string is greatest as the object moves through the bottom of the circle.
- The tension in the string is least as the object moves through the top of the circle.

Problems involving vertical circles often involve the calculation of the minimum speed at the top of the circle so that the object does not leave the circle, that is to say, fall. In such cases, the tension (T) in the string is zero. Therefore,

$$\vec{F}_c = \vec{F}_g$$

$$\frac{mv^2}{v} = mg$$

or $\qquad v = \sqrt{rg}$

If $\vec{F}_c = \vec{F}_g$, then we are dealing with problems involving minimum speed, and we can use $v = \sqrt{rg}$

Example 1

An object is swung in a vertical circle with a radius of 0.75 m. What is the minimum speed of the object at the top of the motion for the object to remain in its circular motion?

Solution

$$\vec{F}_c = \vec{T} + \vec{F}_g \qquad \vec{T} = 0$$

$$\vec{F}_c = \vec{F}_g$$

$$\frac{mv^2}{r} = mg$$

$$v = \sqrt{rg}$$

$$= \sqrt{(0.75\ \text{m})(9.81\ \text{m/s}^2)}$$

$$= 2.7\ \text{m/s}$$

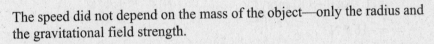

In these problems, $\vec{F}_c = \vec{F}_g$. In other words, $\vec{F}_c$ is the net force

The speed did not depend on the mass of the object—only the radius and the gravitational field strength.

Example 2

A string requires a 135 N force in order to break. A 2.00 kg mass is tied to this string and whirled in a vertical circle with a radius of 1.10 m. What is the maximum speed that this mass can be whirled without breaking the string?

In solving problems with vertical circular motion, draw a free body diagram

Solution

$$\vec{F}_g = mg$$

$$= (2.00\ \text{kg})(-9.81\ \text{m/s}^2)$$

$$= -19.6\ \text{N}$$

$$\vec{F}_c = \vec{T} + \vec{F}_g$$

$$= (135\ \text{N}) + (-19.6\ \text{N})$$

$$= 115.4\ \text{N}$$

$$\vec{F}_c = \frac{mv^2}{r}$$

$$v = \sqrt{\frac{\vec{F}_c r}{m}}$$

$$= \sqrt{\frac{(115.4\ \text{N})(1.10\ \text{m})}{2.00\ \text{kg}}}$$

$$= 7.97\ \text{m/s}$$

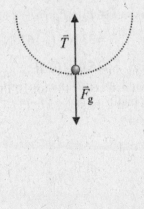

Remember that $\vec{F}_c$ is always directed toward the centre of the circle

The force is –17 N because the tension is directed downward

Example 3

A 1.7 kg object is swung from the end of a 0.60 m string in a vertical circle. If the time of one revolution is 1.1 s, what is the tension in the string (assume uniform speed):

a) when it is at the top?

Solution

$$\vec{F}_c = \frac{4\pi^2 rm}{T^2}$$

$$= \frac{\left(4\pi^2\right)(0.60\ m)(1.7\ kg)}{(1.1\ s)^2}$$

$$= -33\ N$$

$$\vec{F}_g = mg$$

$$= (1.7\ kg)\left(-9.81\ m/s^2\right)$$

$$= -16.7\ N$$

$$\vec{F}_c = \vec{T} + \vec{F}_g$$

$$T = \vec{F}_c - \vec{F}_g$$

$$= -33\ N - (-16.7\ N)$$

$$= -17\ N$$

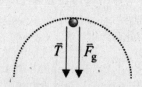

b) when it is at the bottom?

Solution

$$\vec{F}_c = \vec{T} + \vec{F}_g$$

$$\vec{T} = \vec{F}_c - \vec{F}_g$$

$$= 33\ N - (-16.7\ N)$$

$$= 5.0 \times 10^1\ N$$

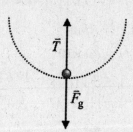

Example 4

A 826 kg car travelling at a speed of 14.0 m/s goes over a hill as shown in the diagram. If the radius of this curve is 61.0 m, what is the force exerted on the road by the car at the crest of the hill?

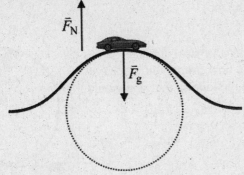

Solution

$$\vec{F}_g = mg$$

$$= (826 \text{ kg})\left(-9.81 \text{ m/s}^2\right)$$

$$= -8.10 \times 10^3 \text{ N}$$

$$\vec{F}_c = \frac{mv^2}{r}$$

$$= \frac{(826 \text{ kg})\left(14.0 \text{ m/s}^2\right)}{61.0 \text{ m}}$$

$$= -2.65 \times 10^3 \text{ N}$$

$$\vec{F}_c = \vec{F}_g + \vec{F}_N$$

$$\vec{F}_N = \vec{F}_c - \vec{F}_g$$

$$= -2.65 \times 10^3 \text{ N} - \left(-8.10 \times 10^3 \text{ N}\right)$$

$$= 5.45 \times 10^3 \text{ N}$$

Remember that $\vec{F}_c$ is always directed toward the centre of the circle

PRACTICE EXERCISE

- In solving problems with vertical circular motion, draw a free body diagram
- If $\vec{F}_c = \vec{F}_g$, we can use the formula $v = \sqrt{rg}$. These are problems involving minimum speed.
- In these problems, $\vec{F}_c = \vec{F}_{net}$

1. You are riding your bike on a track that forms a vertical circular loop as shown. If the diameter of the loop is 10.0 m, how fast would you have to be travelling when you reached the top of the loop so that you would not fall?

2. You are rotating a bucket of water in a vertical circle. Assuming that the radius of the rotation of the water is 0.95 m, what is the minimum velocity of the bucket at the top of its swing required to keep the water in the bucket?

3. A student has a weight of 655 N. While riding on a roller coaster, this same student has an apparent weight of 1.96×10^3 N at the bottom of the dip that has a radius of 18.0 m. What is the speed of the roller coaster?

4. An amusement park ride spins in a vertical circle. If the diameter of this circle is 5.80 m, what minimum speed must the ride travel so that a 75.0 kg student will remain against the wall when he is in the high position?

5. A string requires a 186 N force in order to break. A 1.50 kg mass is tied to this string and whirled in a vertical circle with a radius of 1.90 m. What is the maximum speed that this mass can be whirled without breaking the string?

6. A 2.2 kg object is whirled in a vertical circle whose radius is 1.0 m. If the time of one revolution is 0.97 s, what is the tension in the string (assume uniform speed):

   a) when it is at the top?

   b) when it is at the bottom?

7. A wheel-shaped space station with a radius of 48 m produces artificial gravity by rotating. How fast must this station rotate so that the crew members have the same apparent weight in this station as they have on Earth?

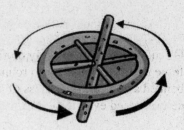

8. A 915 kg car goes over a hill as shown in the diagram. If the radius of this curve is 43 m, how fast must the car travel so that it exerts no force on the road at the crest?

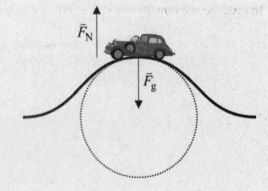

9. A 2.5 kg ball is tied to a 0.75 m string and whirled in a vertical circle (assume a constant speed of 12 m/s).

   a) Why is the tension in the string greater at its low point than at its high point?

   b) Calculate the tension in the string at its

      i) low point

      ii) high point

Lesson 3   BANKED CURVES

Often highways do not rely on friction alone to provide the centripetal force necessary for a car to round a curve safely. These curves are often banked and a car, regardless of its mass, can round this curve safely at a certain speed even if the roadway is frictionless.

A useful formula for calculating the banking angle for a certain speed is:

$$\tan \theta = \frac{v^2}{rg}$$

In order to see how this formula is derived, draw a free body diagram.

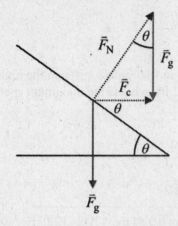

The sum of these two forces $\left(\vec{F}_N + \vec{F}_g \right)$ is equal to the centripetal force:

$$\tan \theta = \frac{\text{opposite}}{\text{adjacent}}$$

$$= \frac{\vec{F}_c}{\vec{F}_g}$$

$$= \frac{\dfrac{mv^2}{r}}{mg}$$

$$= \frac{v^2}{rg}$$

$$\tan \theta = \frac{v^2}{rg}$$

NOTES

$$\tan \theta = \frac{v^2}{rg}$$

$\tan^{-1}(0.10) \approx 5.7°$, but when using a calculator, we include all of the digits in the calculation before rounding only the final answer

Example 1

Calculate the angle at which a frictionless curve must be banked if a car is to round it safely at a speed of 22 m/s (79 km/h). The radius of the curve is 475 m.

Solution

$$\tan\theta = \frac{v^2}{rg}$$

$$= \frac{(22 \text{ m/s})^2}{(475 \text{ m})(9.81 \text{ m/s}^2)}$$

$$\approx 0.10$$

$$\theta \approx 5.9°$$

Example 2

A car is rounding a 515 m frictionless curve in the highway. If the curve is banked at an angle of 12.0°, what is the maximum speed of the car?

Solution

$$\tan\theta = \frac{v^2}{rg}$$

or $\quad v = \sqrt{rg \tan\theta}$

$$= \sqrt{(515 \text{ m})(9.81 \text{ m/s}^2)(\tan 12.0°)}$$

$$= 32.8 \text{ m/s} \qquad \text{or} \qquad 118 \text{ km/h}$$

PRACTICE EXERCISE

Formula: $\tan\theta = \dfrac{v^2}{rg}$

1. What is the maximum speed of a car rounding a 125 m curve in the highway under very icy conditions if the banking angle is 20.0°?

2. A 745 m curve on a racetrack is to be banked for cars travelling at 90 m/s. At what angle should it be banked if it is going to be used under very icy conditions?

3. An airplane travelling at a speed of 115 m/s makes a complete horizontal turn in 1.20×10^2 s. What is the banking angle?

4. A car rounds a very icy curve on the highway which is banked at an angle of 18° while travelling at a speed of 28 m/s (100 km/h). What is the minimum radius of the curve?

5. An airplane flying at a speed of 205 m/s makes a complete horizontal turn while banking at 29.0°. What is the radius of the turn?

Lesson 4   MOTION IN THE HEAVENS

When we study uniform circular motion, we are reminded of the motion of the moon around the Earth, and the motion of the planets around the sun as well as other motion in the heavens. It should be noted that the motion mentioned above takes place in slightly elliptical paths, but it can be described as uniform circular motion.

Before we look at orbital motion mathematically, let's look at some history. Remember, orbital motion is just the uniform circular motion of satellites, planets and moons—motion in the heavens.

Man has long been curious about the night sky and the motion of the objects in it. The first major theory about this motion was developed by Aristotle and later supported by Hipparchus, early Greek philosophers. This theory was further developed by Ptolemy, a Greek astronomer, in about 140 A.D. According to this early theory, the sun and other stars revolved around the Earth in circles. The planets also revolved around the Earth, but in more complex orbits. The main consideration in this early theory was that the Earth was the centre of the universe. These early Greek philosophers also made an attempt to explain the mechanism of this motion.

In 1543 Copernicus proposed a heliocentric theory. The main consideration in this theory was that the planets revolved around the sun.

Tycho Brahe made naked eye observations of the planets in the late 1500s. His assistant, Johann Kepler, used this data to modify the Copernian theory. Kepler was able to describe the motion of the planets with three statements. These statements are known as Kepler's Laws.

KEPLER'S LAWS

• Law of Elliptical Orbits: Each planet moves in an elliptical orbit, with the sun as one of the focal points.

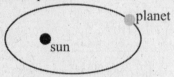

Kepler's laws describe the motion of the planets

• Law of Equal Areas: During equal time intervals, a straight line drawn from the sun to the planet will sweep out equal areas.

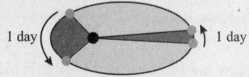

NOTES

$T^2 \propto r^3$

or

$\dfrac{T^2}{r^3} = K$

From the Law of Elliptical Orbits and the Law of Equal Areas, Kepler described the shape of planetary orbits and the speed change in those orbits.

- Law of Periods: The period of revolution is related to its radius of revolution (distance to the sun) by

$$T^2 \propto r^3 \qquad \text{or} \qquad \frac{T^2}{r^3} = K$$

  where T = period of one revolution of the planet

  r = radius of one revolution of the planet

  K = Kepler's constant

These laws summarize a mathematical model that was used to predict the position of a planet. Kepler was able to describe how planets move. The question remained—why did they move? What are the dynamics of this motion? The early Greeks thought the heavens were a gigantic celestial machine. Kepler predicted that it was a magnetic force from the sun that caused this motion.

It was Newton who explained why planets move by formulating his law of universal gravitation by using Kepler's laws and his own laws of motion.

Example 1

Knowing that the Earth's orbital radius is 1.49×10^{11} m and its period of revolution is 1.00 year, calculate the period of revolution of Jupiter, which has an orbital radius of 7.78×10^{11} m.

Solution

$$\frac{T_E^{\,2}}{r_E^{\,3}} = \frac{T_J^{\,2}}{r_J^{\,3}}$$

$$\frac{(1.00 \text{ year})^2}{\left(1.49 \times 10^{11} \text{ m}\right)^3} = \frac{T_J^{\,2}}{\left(7.78 \times 10^{11}\right)^3}$$

$$T_J = \sqrt{\frac{\left(7.78 \times 10^{11}\right)^3}{\left(1.49 \times 10^{11} \text{ m}\right)^3}}$$

$$T_J = 11.9 \text{ years}$$

Example 2

Calculate Kepler's Constant in reference to the moon, knowing that its orbital radius is 3.84×10^8 m and that its period of revolution around the Earth is 2.36×10^6 s (27.3 days).

Solution

$$K = \frac{T^2}{r^3}$$

$$= \frac{\left(2.36 \times 10^6 \text{ s}\right)^2}{\left(3.84 \times 10^8 \text{ m}\right)^3}$$

$$= 9.84 \times 10^{-14} \text{ s}^2 / \text{m}^3$$

The orbital radii of the planets are also expressed in astronomical units (AU), where the Earth's orbital radius is the standard at 1 AU. The orbital period of the planets are also expressed in years, where the Earth's orbital period is 1 year.

Therefore,

$$K = \frac{T^2}{r^3} = \frac{\left(1 \text{ y}\right)^2}{\left(1 \text{ AU}\right)^3} = \frac{1 \text{ y}^2}{\text{AU}^3}$$

for our solar system only.

PRACTICE EXERCISE

Formulae: $\dfrac{T^2}{r^3} = K$ $\qquad \dfrac{T_1^2}{r_1^3} = \dfrac{T_2^2}{r_2^3}$

1. Knowing that the Earth's orbital radius is 1.49×10^{11} m, and that its period of revolution around the sun is 1.00 year, calculate the period of revolution of the planet Mercury whose orbital radius is 5.79×10^{10} m.

2. Using Kepler's constant (calculated in Example 2), calculate the orbital radius of an artificial satellite whose period of revolution around the earth is 1.43×10^4 s (3.96 h).

3. You wish to place a geosynchronous satellite (a satellite that remains in the same position above the Earth). Using Kepler's constant (found in Example 2), calculate the distance above the Earth's surface that this satellite must be placed. (Hint: find its orbital radius, and subtract the Earth's radius of 6.37×10^6 m.)

4. If a satellite of the sun has an orbital radius of twice that of the Earth, how does its period of revolution compare with that of the Earth?

Lesson 5 A RETURN TO NEWTON'S LAW OF UNIVERSAL GRAVITATION

Let's consider briefly the formulation of the law of universal gravitation. Newton's second law of motion explained that if a planet is moving in a circular path, it has centripetal acceleration and there must be a centripetal force acting on it. Newton, using Kepler's law of areas, showed that this force must be caused by the sun.

By considering his second law of motion and Kepler's law of periods, Newton mathematically demonstrated that this force is inversely proportional to the square of the distance from the sun to the planet.

$$\vec{F}_g \propto \frac{1}{r^2}$$

Newton's second law:

$$\vec{F}_{net} = m\vec{a} \qquad \text{or} \qquad \vec{F}_c = \frac{m4\pi^2 r}{T^2}$$

Kepler's law of periods:

$$T^2 = Kr^3$$

Combination:

$$\vec{F}_c = \frac{m4\pi^2 r}{Kr^3} \qquad \text{or} \qquad \vec{F}_c = \frac{m4\pi^2}{Kr^2}$$

Since: $\dfrac{m4\pi^2}{K} = $ constant for a planet

it follows: $\vec{F}_c \propto \dfrac{1}{r^2}$

This is the inverse square law.

Newton demonstrated the usefulness of this law by calculating the centripetal acceleration of the moon.

Known:

• Centre of Earth to centre of moon $= 3.8 \times 10^8$ m

• Radius of Earth $= 6.4 \times 10^6$ m

Ratio: $\dfrac{3.8 \times 10^8 \text{ m}}{6.4 \times 10^6 \text{ m}} = 60$

From the inverse square law, the force on an object at the Earth's surface (like an apple) would be $(60)^2$ times the force on the moon. From the second law of motion, the acceleration would also be $(60)^2$ times larger.

NOTES

Thus the centripetal acceleration of the moon should be

$$\left(9.81 \text{ m/s}^2\right)\left(\frac{1}{(60)^2}\right) = 2.7 \times 10^{-3} \text{ m/s}^2$$

If we compare this to the observed value for the centripetal acceleration of the moon, the values agree closely.

Forces only exist between two objects

Newton's third law of motion states that forces only exist between two objects. Newton concluded from this that the force of gravity between two objects is directly proportional to the product of their masses.

$$\vec{F}_g \propto m_1 m_2$$

By combining this with the inverse square law,

$$\vec{F}_g \propto \frac{1}{r^2}$$

we get $\quad \vec{F}_g \propto \frac{m_1 m_2}{r^2} \quad$ or $\quad \vec{F}_g = \frac{G m_1 m_2}{r^2}$

G is called Newton's gravitational constant, and has been determined to be

$$6.67 \times 10^{-11} \frac{\text{N} \cdot \text{m}^2}{\text{kg}^2}$$

NEWTON'S LAW OF UNIVERSAL GRAVITATION

Newton's law of universal gravitation states two things.

Newton's law of universal gravitation:

$\vec{F}_g \propto m_1 m_2$, and

$\vec{F}_g \propto \dfrac{1}{r^2}$

$\vec{F}_g = \dfrac{G m_1 m_2}{r^2}$

- That the gravitational force between two masses is directly proportional to the product of their masses.
- That the gravitational force between two masses varies inversely to the square of the distance between the centres of the masses.

SATELLITES IN ORBITS (ORBITAL MOTION)

In addition to the moon, there are many satellites in circular orbits around the Earth. Of course, the motion of these satellites is uniform circular motion and is described by the equations derived for uniform circular motion. In this motion, the force that keeps the satellites in orbit is the gravitational pull of the earth.

$$\vec{F}_c = \vec{F}_g$$

$$\frac{m_s v^2}{r} = G \frac{m_E m_s}{r^2}$$

$$v^2 = \frac{G m_E}{r}$$

or $\quad v = \sqrt{\dfrac{G m_E}{r}}$

We see from this equation that the speed of the satellite orbiting the Earth only depends on the radius of the orbit.

NOTE: the speed does not depend on the mass of the satellite.

The period of the satellite also depends on the radius of the orbit.

Remember: $v = \dfrac{2\pi r}{T}$

Therefore

$$\frac{2\pi r}{T} = \sqrt{\frac{Gm_E}{r}}$$

or

$$\frac{4\pi^2 r^2}{T^2} = \frac{Gm_E}{r}$$

Transposing:

$$T^2 = \frac{4\pi^2 r^3}{Gm_E}$$

or

$$T = \sqrt{\frac{4\pi^2 r^3}{Gm_E}}$$

which can also be written as: $\quad T = \dfrac{2\pi r^{3/2}}{\sqrt{Gm_E}}$

This expression is Kepler's third law, which expresses the relationship between the period of an orbiting satellite and the radius of the orbit. Kepler's third law is usually expressed as:

$$\frac{T^2}{r^3} = K \qquad \text{where } K \text{ is called Kepler's constant.}$$

For a satellite of Earth:

$$K = \frac{4\pi^2}{\sqrt{Gm_E}} \qquad m_E = \text{mass of Earth}$$

For a satellite of the sun:

$$K = \frac{4\pi^2}{\sqrt{Gm_s}} \qquad m_s = \text{mass of sun}$$

Newton suggested back in the 1600s that an object could be put into a low-level orbit around the Earth if it was launched from a high enough point at sufficient speed.

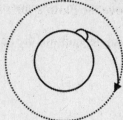

What is this speed? In our calculations, we will ignore air friction.

$$v = \sqrt{\frac{Gm_E}{r}}$$

$$= \frac{\left(6.67 \times 10^{-11}\ \frac{N \cdot m^2}{kg^2}\right)\left(5.98 \times 10^{24}\ kg\right)}{6.37 \times 10^6\ m}$$

$$= 7.91 \times 10^3\ m/s$$

We could have arrived at this same value using:

$$\vec{F}_c = \vec{F}_g$$

$$\frac{mv^2}{r} = mg$$

$$v = \sqrt{gr}$$

$$= \sqrt{\left(9.81\ N/kg\right)\left(6.37 \times 10^6\right)}$$

$$= 7.91 \times 10^3\ m/s$$

A satellite of the Earth, including the moon, is constantly falling toward the Earth as it moves around the Earth. In a falling elevator, you would appear to be weightless. In an artificial satellite orbiting the Earth, you would experience the same sensation of weightlessness.

Example 1

Calculate the speed of an artificial satellite in an orbit around the Earth with a radius of 6.9×10^6 m .

Solution

$$v = \sqrt{\frac{Gm_E}{r}}$$

$$= \frac{\left(6.67 \times 10^{-11}\ \frac{N \cdot m^2}{kg^2}\right)\left(5.98 \times 10^{24}\ kg\right)}{6.9 \times 10^6\ m}$$

$$= 7.6 \times 10^3\ m/s$$

Example 2

Geosynchronous satellites are used for communications. They are satellites that do not change position with respect to the Earth. What is the height of such a satellite above the Earth's surface?

The period of a geosynchronous satellite must be the same as Earth's period.

Solution

$$T = 1 \text{ day, or } 8.64 \times 10^4 \text{ s}$$

$$T = \frac{2\pi r^{3/2}}{\sqrt{Gm_E}}$$

$$r^{3/2} = \frac{T\sqrt{Gm_E}}{2\pi}$$

$$= \frac{\left(8.64 \times 10^4 \text{ s}\right)\sqrt{\left(6.67 \times 10^{-11}\dfrac{\text{N} \bullet \text{m}^2}{\text{kg}^2}\right)\left(5.98 \times 10^{24} \text{ kg}\right)}}{2\pi}$$

$$\left(r^{3/2}\right)^{2/3} = \left(2.75 \times 10^{11} \text{ m}\right)^{2/3}$$

$$r = \left(\sqrt[3]{2.75 \times 10^{11} \text{ m}}\right)^2$$

$$r = 4.23 \times 10^7 \text{ m}$$

$$\text{height} = r - r_E$$

$$= 4.23 \times 10^7 \text{ m} - 6.37 \times 10^6 \text{ m}$$

$$= 3.59 \times 10^7 \text{ m}$$

To resolve the fractional exponent $\dfrac{2}{3}$, take the cube root of the number and then square it

PRACTICE EXERCISE

Formulae: $v = \sqrt{\dfrac{Gm_E}{r}}$ $\qquad T = \dfrac{2\pi r^{3/2}}{\sqrt{Gm_E}}$

NOTE: $m_E = 5.98 \times 10^{24}$ kg , $r_E = 6.37 \times 10^6$ m

1. Calculate the speed of the moon in its orbit around the Earth.
   (Radius of moon's orbit $= 3.85 \times 10^8$ m , moon's mass $= 7.4 \times 10^{22}$ kg)

2. Calculate the speed of a satellite orbiting the earth at a height of 4.4×10^5 m above the Earth's surface. (Hint: remember to add the Earth's radius of 6.37×10^6 m .)

3. Calculate the orbital speed of a satellite 5.0×10^6 m above the surface of Jupiter.
   $\left(r_J = 7.18 \times 10^7 \text{ m}, m_J = 1.90 \times 10^{27} \text{ kg} \right)$

4. Calculate the speed of Earth in its orbit around the sun.
   (Radius of Earth's orbit $= 1.49 \times 10^{11}$ m, $m_s = 1.98 \times 10^{30}$ kg)

5. Calculate the time of one revolution (length of a year) on Mars.
   (Radius of Earth's orbit $= 1.49 \times 10^{11}$ m , radius of Mars' orbit $= 2.3 \times 10^{11}$ m)

6. Io (one of Jupiter's moons) orbits Jupiter every 1.77 days. If the orbital radius of Io is 4.22×10^8 m ,

   a) what is the mass of Jupiter?

   b) what is the orbital speed of Io?

7. At what height above the Earth must a geosynchronous satellite (a satellite that remains in the same position above the Earth) be placed? (Hint: Find its orbital radius, and subtract the Earth's radius of 6.37×10^6 m.)

8. The Hubble telescope orbits the Earth every 96.5 minutes. If the orbital radius of the telescope is 6.97×10^6 m, what is the speed of the telescope?

9. Given that the Earth's orbit has a radius of 1.49×10^{11} m, calculate the mass of the sun. (Hint: the period of the Earth around the sun is 1.00 year.)

10. A satellite orbits the Earth (radius of the orbit $= 7.05 \times 10^6$ m).

   a) Calculate the speed of the satellite.

   b) Calculate the period of the motion.

   c) Calculate the gravitational field strength at the orbit.

Lesson 6   Work

Law of Conservation of
Energy: energy cannot be
created nor destroyed, but
can be changed from one
form to another

Work = Force ×

      Displacement

$W = \vec{F}\vec{d}$

CONSERVATION OF ENERGY

The Law of Conservation of Mechanical Energy states that in an isolated
system (no friction) mechanical energy is conserved. The Law of
Conservation of Mechanical Energy is part of a more fundamental law:
the Law of Conservation of Energy. The Law of Conservation of Energy
states that energy cannot be created nor destroyed, but it can be changed
from one form to another.

Let's start by looking at these forms of energy; but first we will study work
and energy.

WORK

Work is defined as the transfer of energy. Energy is transferred when a
force acts on an object resulting in its displacement. Mathematically, work
is defined as the product of force and displacement.

Work = Force × Displacement

$$W = \vec{F}\vec{d}$$

It is important to note the language that is used in physics to describe work.
In physics, we talk about the amount of work that is done on an object.
If I am standing holding a 30.0 kg object, I am using energy; therefore,
I am doing work. However, this work is not done on the object; it is done
on my muscles by a force acting to contract these muscles. In this course
we will talk of doing work on an object. If the object does not move
through some displacement, there is no work done on the object. In the
same way, if there is no force acting on the object, there is no work done.

We do work on an object in order to overcome an opposing force (force of
gravity, friction, etc.) on the object, or we do work to accelerate an object.

Work
     Symbol: W
    Definition: Transfer of energy or, mathematically, the product of
                force and displacement.
     Formula: $W = \vec{F}\vec{d}$
       Unit: N•m which is called a joule (J).

There are several important things to note about work and force.

When an object is lifted at a constant velocity, work is done against gravity. The formula $W = \vec{F}\vec{d}$ can be written as:

$$W = mgh$$

where m = mass

g = acceleration due to gravity

h = height (vertical displacement)

In deriving this formula, $W = mgh$:

$$W = \vec{F}\vec{d} \quad \text{(definition of work)}$$

but $\quad F = mg \quad$ (force due to gravity)

therefore:

$$W = mgd$$

or $\quad W = mgh$

where h = vertical displacement

The force used in the formula $W = \vec{F}\vec{d}$ is often the applied force. It can also be the net force or the friction, as the problem requires.

Although work is the product of two vector quantities, it is a scalar quantity.

When the force is not in the same direction as the displacement, we must use the component of the force that is in the direction of the displacement. (Refer to Example 4 on the following pages.)

Work can be negative. If the force on an object is in the opposite direction to the motion, the work done on the object is negative. (Refer to Example 5.)

Example 1

A 15.0 kg object is lifted at constant velocity from the floor to height of 1.50 m. How much work is done on the object?

Solution

$W = mgh$

$\quad = (15.0\,\text{kg})\left(9.81\,\text{m/s}^2\right)(1.50\,\text{m})$

$\quad = 221\,\text{J}$

Example 2

A 10.0 kg object is moved horizontally 5.00 m across a level floor using a horizontal force of 3.00 N. How much work is done on the object?

Solution

$$W = \vec{F}\vec{d}$$
$$= (3.00 \text{ N})(5.00 \text{ m})$$
$$= 15.0 \text{ J}$$

Example 3

A 3.0 kg object is held 1.2 m above the floor for 15 s. How much work is done on the object?

Solution

0. There is no work done on the object itself. The energy of the object does not change, because there is no displacement.

Example 4

A 50.0 kg box is pulled 11.0 m along a level surface by a rope. If the rope makes an angle with the surface of 35.0°, and the force exerted through the rope is 90.0 N, how much work is done on the box?

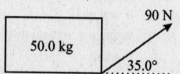

Solution

Since the object moves horizontally, we must find the horizontal component of the force.

$$\cos\theta = \frac{\text{adjacent}}{\text{hypotenuse}}$$
$$\text{adj} = \cos\theta \, (\text{hyp})$$
$$= (\cos 35.0°)(90.0 \text{ N})$$
$$= 73.7 \text{ N}$$
$$W = \vec{F}\vec{d}$$
$$= (73.7 \text{ N})(11.0 \text{ m})$$
$$= 811 \text{ J}$$

Example 5

A 1 385-kg car travelling at 61 km/h is brought to a stop while skidding 42 m. What is the work done on the car by the frictional forces?

Solution

Convert 61 km/h to m/s.

$$\vec{v}_f^{\,2} = \vec{v}_i^{\,2} + 2\vec{a}\vec{d}$$

$$0 = (16.9 \text{ m/s})^2 + (2)(\vec{a})(42 \text{ m})$$

$$\vec{a} = -3.42 \text{ m/s}^2$$

$$\vec{F} = m\vec{a}$$

$$= (1\,385 \text{ kg})\left(-3.42 \text{ m/s}^2\right)$$

$$= -4.73 \times 10^3 \text{ N}$$

$$W = \vec{F}\vec{d}$$

$$= \left(-4.73 \times 10^3 \text{ N}\right)(42 \text{ m})$$

$$= -2.0 \times 10^5 \text{ J}$$

Note that the answer is negative because the force and the displacement are in opposite directions.

PRACTICE EXERCISE

Formulae: $\quad W = \vec{F}\vec{d} \qquad W = mgh$

1. A 20.0 N object is lifted at a constant velocity from the floor to a height of 1.50 m. How much work is done on the object?

2. A 15.0 N object is moved horizontally 3.00 m across a level floor using a horizontal force of 6.00 N. How much work is done on this object?

3. A 2.20 N object is held 2.20 m above the floor for 10.0 s. How much work is done on the object?

4. A 10.0 kg object is accelerated horizontally from rest to a velocity of 11.0 m/s in 5.00 s by a horizontal force. How much work is done on this object if it accelerates along a frictionless surface?

5. A 90.0 N box is pulled 10.0 m along a level surface by a rope. If the rope makes an angle of 20.0° with the surface, and the force exerted through the rope is 75.0 N, how much work is done on the box?

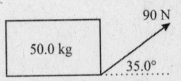

6. A 60.0 kg student runs at a constant velocity up a flight of stairs. If the vertical distance of the stairs is 3.2 m, what is the work done against gravity?

7. A 20.0 kg box is pulled horizontally 9.0 m along a level frictionless surface at a constant velocity. How much work is done on the box?

8. An 80.0 kg box is pushed at a constant velocity along a frictionless incline as shown in the diagram. How much work is done on the box in moving it from the bottom to the top of the incline?

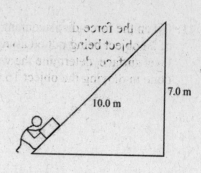

10.0 m

7.0 m

9. A 25.0 kg object is accelerated from rest through a distance of 6.0 m in 4.0 s across a level floor. If the force due to friction between the object and the floor is 3.8 N, what is the work done in moving the object?

10. A 1 165 kg car travelling at 55 km/h is brought to a stop while skidding 38 m. Calculate the work done on the car by the frictional forces.

11. Given the force-displacement graph
    of an object being pulled along a
    level surface, determine the work
    done in moving the object 16.0 m.

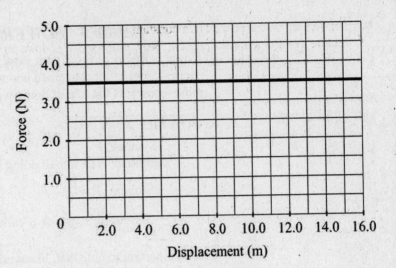

12. Given the force-displacement graph
    of an object moving along a
    horizontal surface, determine the
    work done in moving the object
    16.0 m.

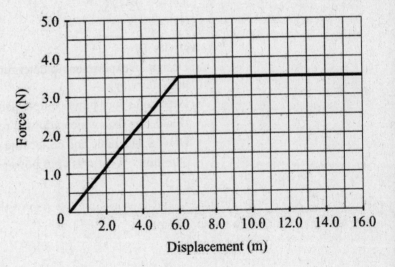

269

Lesson 7 POWER

Power is defined as the rate of doing work

$$P = \frac{W}{t}$$

746 W = 1 horsepower (hp)

$$P = Fv$$

Power is often confused with work. You will note that when we discussed work, we were not concerned about time. Power is concerned about time—power is the rate of doing work.

POWER

Symbol: P

Definition: The rate of doing work, or the rate of using energy

Formula: $P = \dfrac{W}{t}$

Units: J/s, which is called a watt (W)

It is important to note that, like work, power is a scalar quantity. A useful way of describing force can also be described as follows.

$$P = Fv$$

The formula $P = Fv$ is derived using the following equations.

$$P = \frac{W}{t} = \frac{Fd}{t}$$

but

$$\frac{d}{t} = v$$

$$\therefore P = Fv$$

Activity 10

- Design an experiment to determine your power output. (Suggestion: run up a stairway).
- Determine your power output using your design.
- Decide the data which you will require.
- Draw a data table and collect the data.
- Question: What was your power output?

Example 1

A 60.0 kg student runs at a constant velocity up the incline shown in 4.5 s. Calculate the power output by the student.

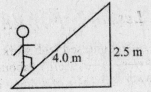

Solution

Find the work first. Since the work is against gravity, we use:

$W = mgh$

$= (60.0 \text{ kg})(9.81 \text{ m/s}^2)(2.5 \text{ m})$

$= 1.47 \times 10^3 \text{ J}$

$P = \dfrac{W}{t}$

$= \dfrac{1.47 \times 10^3 \text{ J}}{4.5 \text{ s}}$

$= 3.3 \times 10^2 \text{ W}$

Example 2

A 1.00×10^3 kg car accelerates from rest to a speed of 15 m/s in 4.00 s. Calculate the power output of the car in this time interval.

Solution

$a = \dfrac{v_f - v_i}{t}$

$= \dfrac{15.0 \text{ m/s}}{4.00 \text{ s}}$

$= 3.75 \text{ m/s}^2$

$F = ma$

$= (1.00 \times 10^3 \text{ kg})(3.75 \text{ m/s}^2)$

$= 3.75 \times 10^3 \text{ N}$

$d = \left(\dfrac{v_f + v_i}{2} \right) t$

$= \left(\dfrac{15.0 \text{ m/s}}{2} \right)(4.00 \text{ s})$

$= 30.0 \text{ m}$

$W = Fd$

$= (3.75 \times 10^3 \text{ N})(30.0 \text{ m})$

$= 1.13 \times 10^5 \text{ J}$

NOTES

$$P = \frac{W}{t}$$

$$= \frac{1.13 \times 10^5 \text{ J}}{4.00 \text{ s}}$$

$$= 2.81 \times 10^4 \text{ W}$$

PRACTICE EXERCISE 9

Formulae: $P = \dfrac{W}{t}$ $\qquad\qquad P = Fv$

1. A 45.0 kg student runs at a constant velocity up the incline described in the diagram. If the power output of the student is 1.50×10^3 W, how long does it take the student to run the 9.0 m along the incline?

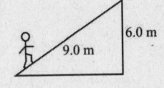

2. A student lifts a 20.0 kg object vertically 2.50 m at a constant velocity in 2.00 s. Calculate the power output of the student.

3. A 2.00 kg object is accelerated uniformly from rest to 3.00 m/s while moving 1.5 m across a level frictionless surface. Calculate the power output.

4. An 8.5×10^2 kg elevator (including occupants) is pulled up at a constant velocity of 1.00 m/s by an electric motor. Calculate the power output of the motor.

5. A 5.0 kg object is accelerated uniformly from rest to 6.0 m/s while moving 2.0 m across a level surface. If the force of friction is 4.0 N, calculate the power output.

Lesson 8 ENERGY

Energy is defined as the ability to do work. There are many forms of energy: mechanical energy, thermal energy, electrical energy, nuclear energy, etc. One form of energy can be converted to other forms. For example, mechanical energy can be converted to electrical energy using an electric generator. It should be noted that when energy is changed to different forms, work is done. Work can therefore be defined as the transfer of energy.

$$W = \Delta E$$

Let's have a look at mechanical energy. Mechanical energy is the energy that an object possesses because of its position, or because of its motion. Mechanical energy has two components: potential energy and kinetic energy. Potential energy is the energy of an object due to its position. It is also referred to as stored energy. Kinetic energy is the energy of an object due to its motion. When one energy form is converted to another, work is done. Again, work is the transfer of energy.

POTENTIAL ENERGY

This boulder has potential energy due to its position. It has the potential to fall onto the student below, and to do work on the student (changing his or her shape). We call this gravitational potential energy or potential due to gravity.

When an archer pulls the string of her bow, she is doing work on the bow. If she places an arrow in this bow, the bow has the potential of doing work on the arrow. This is spring or elastic potential energy.

When work is done against gravity, the bow, or the spring, this work is stored in the system as potential energy.

The potential energy of an object depends on:

1) the force acting on the object. If we are talking about gravitational potential energy, the potential energy depends on the gravitational force on the object.
    (Remember: $F_g = mg$)

Work can be defined as the transfer of energy

$$W = \Delta E$$

Mechanical energy
• potential energy
• kinetic energy

Potential energy is energy due to position

Potential energy can be considered stored energy

The spring constant is a measure of the spring's stiffness (elasticity)

We use the symbol x for displacement of a spring rather than d

For gravitational potential energy,

$E_p = mgh$

For elastic potential energy,

$E_p = \frac{1}{2}kx^2$

2) the displacement (change in position) of the object.
Potential energy = Force × Displacement

$E_p = Fd$

which can become

$E_p = mgh$

if we are discussing gravitational potential energy, and

$E_p = \frac{1}{2}kx^2$

if we are discussing elastic potential energy.

POTENTIAL ENERGY

Symbol: E_p

Definition: Energy due to position, or stored energy.

Formulae: $E_p = \vec{F}\vec{d}$

or in the special (but common) case of gravitational potential energy

$E_p = mgh$;

and in the case of elastic potential energy

$E_p = \frac{1}{2}kx^2$

where k = spring constant

x = diplacement

Units: Same as work, joule (J).

Energy is a scalar quantity.

We will discuss the equation

$E_p = \frac{1}{2}kx^2$

in the next unit when we learn about oscillary motion of a mass-spring system. However, this equation is a form of the equation

$E_p = \vec{F}\vec{d}$.

We will derive this equation starting with $E_p = \vec{F}\vec{d}$ in the next unit.

We will also show the relationship between the elastic potential energy and the kinetic energy in a mass-spring system in the next unit.

In the rest of this section we will limit the problems to problems involving gravitational potential energy and elastic potential energy where we can use the equation $E_p = \vec{F}\vec{d}$.

Example 1

A 15.0 kg object is lifted from the floor to a vertical height of 2.5 m. What is the gravitational potential energy of the object with respect to the floor?

Solution

$$E_p = mgh$$

$$= (15.0 \text{ kg})(9.81 \text{ m/s}^2)(2.50 \text{ m})$$

$$= 368 \text{ J}$$

Gravitational potential energy is usually expressed in relation to some point. In this problem, the floor is our point of reference.

Example 2

An archer pulls on the bow string with an average force of 12.0 N while drawing the arrow back a distance of 2.0×10^{-1} m. Calculate the potential energy of the bow-arrow system.

Solution

$$E_p = Fd$$

$$= (12.0 \text{ N})(2.00 \times 10^{-1} \text{ m})$$

$$= 2.40 \text{ J}$$

PRACTICE EXERCISE

Formulae: $E_p = Fd$ $E_p = mgh$

1. A 25.0 N object is held 2.10 m above the ground. What is the potential energy of the object with respect to the ground?

2. An uncompressed spring is 20.0 cm in length. What is the potential energy of this spring when an average force of 65.0 N compresses it to a length of 13.5 cm?

3. A 2.75 kg box is at the top of a frictionless incline as shown in the diagram. What is the potential energy of the box with respect to the bottom of the incline?

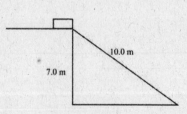

10.0 m

7.0 m

4. The bob of a pendulum has a mass of 2.0 kg. This bob is pulled sideways so that it is 0.75 m above the table top. What is the potential energy of the bob with respect to the equilibrium position?

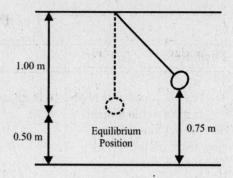

1.00 m

0.50 m

Equilibrium
Position

0.75 m

5. A 2.00×10^2 kg 2.00×10^2 kg object is pushed to the top of an incline as shown in the diagram. If the force applied along the incline is 6.00×10^2 N, what is the potential energy of the object when it is at the top of the incline with respect to the bottom of the incline?

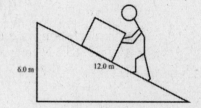

6.0 m

12.0 m

Lesson 9 KINETIC ENERGY

NOTES

When an object is thrown, a force is applied and this force acts through some distance; therefore, work is done.

$$W = \vec{F}\vec{d}$$

The work "kinetic" is derived from the Greek term for the word "motion"

Now when the object is released, it has a speed; it has kinetic energy. Kinetic energy is energy of motion. The work done in throwing this object becomes kinetic energy, assuming that the system is isolated and no work must be done to overcome friction. Kinetic energy is calculated using the formula $E_k = \frac{1}{2}mv^2$.

DERIVATION

We will derive this equation using an object accelerating uniformly from rest to a final velocity of $\vec{v}_f$. Note: by definition, the kinetic energy of an object at rest is zero. We will derive this equation using dynamics and kinematics.

$$\vec{v}_f^{\,2} = \vec{v}_i^{\,2} + 2\vec{a}\vec{d}$$

but $\vec{v}_i = 0$

therefore

$$\vec{v}_f^{\,2} = 2\vec{a}\vec{d}$$

but $\vec{a} = \dfrac{\vec{F}_{net}}{m}$

therefore

$$\vec{v}_f^{\,2} = 2\left(\dfrac{\vec{F}_{net}}{m}\right)\vec{d}$$

or $\vec{F}_{net}\vec{d} = \dfrac{1}{2}m\vec{v}^2$

Kinetic energy is energy due to the motion of an object

$E_k = \dfrac{1}{2}mv^2$

But $\vec{F}_{net}\vec{d}$ is kinetic energy (E_k). Work done by the net force becomes energy of motion—kinetic energy.

$$E_k = \frac{1}{2}mv^2$$

KINETIC ENERGY

Symbol: E_k

Definition: Energy of motion

Formula: $E_k = \dfrac{1}{2}mv^2$

Units: joule (J)

Example 1

A 60.0 kg student is running at a uniform speed of 2.70 m/s . What is the kinetic energy of the student?

Solution

$$E_k = \frac{1}{2}mv^2$$
$$= \frac{1}{2}(60.0 \text{ kg})(2.70 \text{ m/s})^2$$
$$= 219 \text{ J}$$

Example 2

The kinetic energy of a 2.1 kg object is 1.00×10^3 J . What is the speed of this object?

Solution

$$E_k = \frac{1}{2}mv^2$$
$$v = \sqrt{\frac{2E_k}{m}}$$
$$= \sqrt{\frac{2(1.00 \times 10^3 \text{ J})}{2.10 \text{ kg}}}$$
$$= 31 \text{ m/s}$$

PRACTICE EXERCISE

Formula: $E_k = \frac{1}{2}mv^2$

1. A 3.0 kg object is travelling at a constant speed of 7.5 m/s. What is the kinetic energy of this object?

2. The kinetic energy of a 20.0 N object is 5.00×10^2 J. What is the speed of this object?

3. A 10.0 N object is accelerated uniformly from rest at a rate of 2.5 m/s^2. What is the kinetic energy of this object after it has accelerated a distance of 15.0 m?

4. An 8.0 kg object is dropped from a height of 7.0 m. What is the kinetic energy of this object as it hits the ground? Assume that air resistance is negligible.

5. A 10.0 N object has kinetic energy of 3.00×10^2 J. What is the speed of the object?

6. What is the kinetic energy of a 5.0 kg object when an average net force of 8.7 N accelerates it uniformly from rest for 0.12 s?

Lesson 10 WORK-ENERGY THEOREM FOR NET FORCE

Work = Force ×
    Displacement

$\vec{F}\vec{d} = \Delta E_k$

When $\vec{F}$ = net force

or

$\vec{F}\vec{d} = \dfrac{1}{2}m\left(\vec{v}_f^2 - \vec{v}_i^2\right)$

What work is done on a 10.0 kg object to accelerate it from rest to 2.25 m/s along a 5.00 m horizontal frictionless surface?

Solution

$\vec{v}_i$	$\vec{v}_f$	$\vec{a}$	$\vec{d}$	t
0	2.25 m/s	?	5.00 m	×

$$\vec{v}_f^2 = \vec{v}_i^2 + 2\vec{a}\vec{d}$$

$$(2.25 \text{ m/s})^2 = 2(\vec{a})(5.00 \text{ m})$$

$$\vec{a} = \frac{(2.25 \text{ m/s})^2}{2(5.00 \text{ m})}$$

$$= 0.506 \text{ m/s}^2$$

$$\vec{F}_{net} = m\vec{a}$$

$$= (10.0 \text{ kg})(0.506 \text{ m/s}^2)$$

$$= 5.06 \text{ N}$$

$$\text{Work} = \vec{F}_{net}\vec{d}$$

$$= (5.06 \text{ N})(5.00 \text{ m})$$

$$= 25.3 \text{ J}$$

There is nothing wrong with solving the above problem this way; but there is an alternative method—the work-energy theorem method.

The work-energy theorem for net force states that the work done by the net force on an object is equal to the change in the object's kinetic energy.

DERIVATION

$$\vec{v}_f^2 = \vec{v}_i^2 + 2\vec{a}\vec{d}$$

but $\vec{a} = \dfrac{\vec{F}_{net}}{m}$

therefore

$$\vec{v}_f^2 = \vec{v}_i^2 + 2\frac{\vec{F}_{net}\vec{d}}{m}$$

or $\vec{F}_{net}\vec{d} = \dfrac{1}{2}m\left(\vec{v}_f^2 - \vec{v}_i^2\right)$

or   or $W = \Delta E_k$

Note that the force in this equation is the net force. We can refer to the net force as the accelerating force. When we accelerate an object, we change the kinetic energy of the object.

The work-energy theorem for net force gives us a framework to solve some motion problems.

Now we will do the previous problem using the work-energy theorem.

$$W = \Delta E_k$$
$$= \frac{1}{2}m\left(\vec{v}_f^{\,2} - \vec{v}_i^{\,2}\right)$$
$$= \frac{1}{2}(10.0 \text{ kg})\left((2.25 \text{ m/s})^2 - 0\right)$$
$$= 25.3 \text{ J}$$

Any problem that you can solve using the work-energy theorem for net force can be solved by using the method that you are already familiar with. The work-energy theorem for net force provides an alternative method that is often simpler.

The work-energy theorem for net force is only one form of the work-energy theorem. However, it is the most useful for purposes of solving motion problems.

When work is done on an object in lifting it at a constant velocity, the work done is equal to the change in the object's gravitational potential energy.
$$W = \Delta E_p \ \text{(gravitational)}$$

When work is done on an object to overcome friction, the work done is equal to the change in the thermal energy.
$$W = \Delta E_p \ \text{(thermal)}$$

When work is done on an object to compress or stretch a spring, the work done is equal to the change in the spring's elastic potential energy.
$$W = \Delta E_p \ \text{(elastic)}$$

Example 1

An archer exerts an average horizontal force of 55.0 N on her bow-arrow system by pulling the string back 0.350 m. If the arrow has a mass of 0.350 kg, what is the horizontal velocity of the arrow as it hits the target 10.0 m away? (Note: 55.0 N is the net force on the arrow.)

Solution

$$\vec{F}_{net}\vec{d} = \frac{1}{2}m\left(\vec{v}_f^{\,2} - \vec{v}_i^{\,2}\right)$$

$$(55.0 \text{ N})(0.350 \text{ m}) = \frac{1}{2}(0.350 \text{ kg})\left(\vec{v}_f^{\,2} - 0\right)$$

$$\vec{v}_f = \sqrt{\frac{2(55.0 \text{ N})(0.350 \text{ m})}{0.350 \text{ kg}}}$$

$$= 10.5 \text{ m/s}$$

Example 2

If a 985 kg car is travelling at a velocity of 12.0 m/s, how much work is required to stop it?

Solution

$$W = \Delta E_k$$

$$= \frac{1}{2}m\left(\vec{v}_f^2 - \vec{v}_i^2\right)$$

$$= \frac{1}{2}(985\ \text{kg})\left(0 - (12.0\ \text{m/s})^2\right)$$

$$= -7.09 \times 10^4\ \text{J}$$

The work is negative if the force on an object is in the opposite direction to the motion.

Example 3

A 0.85 kg puck is sliding at a velocity of 5.0 m/s along a horizontal surface on which the only force acting on the puck is friction. If 8.0 m farther along the surface the puck has a speed of 2.0 m/s, what is the force of friction? (Note: The force of friction is the only force. Therefore it is the net force.)

Solution

$$\vec{F}_{net}\vec{d} = \frac{1}{2}m\left(\vec{v}_f^2 - \vec{v}_i^2\right)$$

$$\vec{F}_{net}\,(8.0\ \text{m}) = \frac{1}{2}(0.85\ \text{kg})\left((2.0\ \text{m/s})^2 - (5.0\ \text{m/s})^2\right)$$

$$\vec{F}_{net} = -1.1\ \text{N}$$

The answer to this example question works out to a negative force because the force of friction is in the opposite direction to the motion.

Example 4

A student throws a 5.0 N object vertically into the air with an average force of 9.0 N. If this force is exerted through a distance of 0.45 m, what is the speed of the object as it leaves the student's hand?

Solution

First, find the net force by drawing a free body diagram.

$\vec{T}$ | 9.0 N $\vec{F}_{net} = \vec{T} - \vec{F}_g$

$\vec{F}_g$ | 5.0 N $= 9.0\ \text{N} - 5.0\ \text{N}$

$= 4.0\ \text{N}$

Now, we need to find the mass.

$$\vec{F}_g = mg$$

$$m = \frac{5.0 \text{ N}}{9.81 \text{ m/s}^2}$$

$$= 0.51 \text{ kg}$$

Finally, we can solve for the final speed of the object.

$$\vec{F}_{net}\vec{d} = \frac{1}{2}m\left(\vec{v}_f^2 - \vec{v}_i^2\right)$$

$$(4.0 \text{ N})(0.45 \text{ m}) = \frac{1}{2}(0.51 \text{ kg})\left(\vec{v}_f^2 - 0\right)$$

$$\vec{v}_f = \sqrt{\frac{2(4.0 \text{ N})(0.45 \text{ m})}{0.51 \text{ kg}}}$$

$$= 2.7 \text{ m/s}$$

PRACTICE EXERCISE

Formulae: $\qquad W = \Delta E_k \qquad\qquad W = \vec{F}_{net}\vec{d} \qquad\qquad E_k = \frac{1}{2}mv^2 \qquad\qquad \vec{F}_{net}\vec{d} = \frac{1}{2}m\left(\vec{v}_f{}^2 - \vec{v}_i{}^2\right)$

Although there are other methods to solve these problems, use the work-energy theorem for net force.

1. A spring exerts an average horizontal force of 23.0 N on a 0.12 kg pebble while acting through a displacement of 5.0×10^{-2} m. What is the speed of the pebble as it leaves the spring?

2. A force of friction of 3.2 N acts on a 1.1 kg puck while it is sliding along a horizontal surface. If the initial velocity of the puck was 7.5 m/s, how far will the puck travel before coming to rest?

3. How much work is required to accelerate a 1.10×10^3 kg car from rest to 5.00 km/h along a level frictionless surface?

4. A bullet leaves the barrel of a gun that is 0.70 m long with a speed of 1.0×10^3 m/s . If the mass of the bullet is 4.5×10^{-3} kg, calculate the average net force necessary to accelerate the bullet from rest.

5. A 4.0 N box slides along a frictionless surface while travelling at a speed of 2.1 m/s . This object hits an ideal spring (no energy is lost to the spring) as shown in the diagram compressing it 2.3×10^{-2} m . What is the average net force acting on the spring?

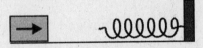

6. A 2.8 N box slides along a frictionless surface while travelling at a speed of 1.8 m/s . This object hits an ideal spring (no energy is lost to the spring) as shown in the diagram. If the average net force acting on the spring is 26 N, what is the compression of the spring?

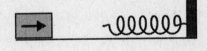

7. A student throws a 1.0 kg rock vertically into the air with an average force of 18 N. If this force was exerted through a displacement of 0.30 m, what was the speed of the rock as it left the student's hand? Is the 18 N force the applied force or the net force? (NOTE: Draw a free body diagram to help solve this problem.)

8. A student throws a 1.1 kg rock vertically into the air, accelerating it through a displacement of 0.36 m. If the rock leaves the student's hand at a speed of 4.2 m/s, what was the average force exerted by the student on the rock while accelerating it? (HINT: Are we asked to find the applied force or the net force? Draw a free body diagram to help solve this problem.)

9. A 0.65 kg puck is sliding along a horizontal surface at a speed of 2.0 m/s. If the puck comes to a stop in 5.5 m, what is the force of friction acting along the surface? (NOTE: The force of friction is the net force on the puck.)

10. A 15 kg box is pulled along a horizontal frictionless surface by a horizontal force of 35 N. If the box accelerates uniformly from rest, how fast is it travelling after travelling 3.5 m?

11. A system containing a frictionless, mass less pulley is described in the diagram. If this system is released, at what speed does the 12.0 kg object hit the floor? (HINT: Does the 12.0 kg object undergo freefall? Why or why not?)

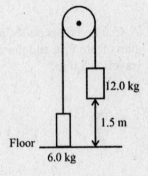

12.0 kg

1.5 m

Floor

6.0 kg

12. A 1.50×10^2 N force is pulling a 50.0 kg box along a horizontal surface. The force acts at an angle of 25.0° as shown in the diagram. If this force moves the box through a horizontal displacement of 12.0 m, and the coefficient of friction is 0.250, what is the speed of the box, assuming it started from rest?

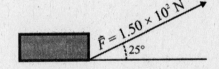

$\vec{F} = 1.50 \times 10^2$ N

25°

13. The battery of your calculator can provide energy at the rate of 0.0 290 J/s for 275 h. If this energy could be used to accelerate a 0.145 kg baseball from rest, what speed would the ball reach?

14. A 45.0 kg box is pulled across a horizontal surface by a constant horizontal force of 192 N. If the box starts from rest, and the coefficient of friction is 0.35, what is the final speed of the box when it has travelled 8.0 m?

Lesson 11   LAW OF CONSERVATION OF MECHANICAL ENERGY

The kinetic energy of an object due to its motion and the potential energy due to its position can be referred to as mechanical energy. If the only forces acting on an object are conservative forces, the mechanical energy of the object does not change—this is known as the law of conservation of mechanical energy.

When only conservative forces act on an object, kinetic energy is converted to potential energy or vice versa. If an object is thrown into the air, the object has kinetic energy (energy of motion) as it leaves the hand; however, eventually this object will reach its highest point where it will come to a stop. At this point, all of its energy is potential energy. The kinetic energy was changed to potential energy, and as the object returns to the hand, the potential is converted back to kinetic. However, the sum of the kinetic and potential energies is constant throughout this motion. The mechanical energy remains constant.

The law of conservation of mechanical energy states that in a frictionless system (isolated system) mechanical energy is conserved.

This law can be explained in symbols as:

$$\Delta E_k + \Delta E_p = 0$$

or

$$\Delta E_k = -\Delta E_p$$

$$\frac{1}{2}m\left(v_f^2 - v_i^2\right) = -mg\Delta h$$

gain in E_k = loss in E_p

$$\Delta h = h_f - h_i$$

Δh may be negative

If there is friction, then some mechanical energy is converted to thermal energy. Friction is not a conservative force.

This law provides a framework in which to solve some motion problems.

A force is conservative if the work done in moving an object from one point to another against the net force does not depend on the path taken

Gravitational and elastic forces are conservative

Frictional forces are non-conservative

The law of conservation of mechanical energy:
in a frictionless or isolated system, mechanical energy is conserved

$$\Delta h = h_f - h_i$$

NOTES

Activity 11

- Design an experiment that will demonstrate the law of conservation of mechanical energy.
- Collect the necessary data.
- Do the mathematical calculations necessary to show that mechanical energy is conserved.
- Suggestion: Use a pendulum system and photogates to determine the speed of the pendulum bob at positions 2 and 3. Release the pendulum bob from position 1.

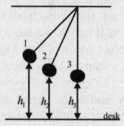

- Data table:

Position	Mass (kg)	Speed (m/s)	Height (m)	E_k (J)	E_p (J)	Mechanical Energy (J)
1						
2						
3						

Is the mechanical energy the same at all three positions?

- Conclusion:

Example 1

A heavy object is dropped from a vertical distance of 12.0 m above the ground. What is the speed of the object as it hits the ground?

Solution

$$\Delta E_k + \Delta E_p = 0$$

or

$$\Delta E_k = -\Delta E_p$$

$$\frac{1}{2}m\left(v_f^2 - v_i^2\right) = -mg\Delta h$$

$$\frac{1}{2}\left(v_f^2 - vi^2\right) = -g\left(h_f - h_i\right)$$

$$\frac{1}{2}\left(v_f^2 - 0\right) = -\left(9.81\,\text{m/s}^2\right)\left(0 - 12.0\,\text{m}\right)$$

$$v = \sqrt{-\left(9.81\,\text{m/s}^2\right)\left(-12.0\,\text{m}\right)(2)}$$

$$= 15.3\,\text{m/s}$$

Example 2

A heavy object is thrown vertically down from the top of a 1.00×10^2 m building with a velocity of 10.0 m/s down. What is the speed as it reaches the ground?

Solution

$$\Delta E_k + \Delta E_p = 0$$

or

$$\Delta E_k = -\Delta E_p$$

$$\frac{1}{2}m\left(v_f^2 - v_i^2\right) = -mg\Delta h$$

$$\frac{1}{2}\left(v_f^2 - v_i^2\right) = -g\left(h_f - h_i\right)$$

$$\frac{1}{2}\left(v_f^2 - (10.0\,\text{m/s})^2\right) = -\left(9.81\,\text{m/s}^2\right)\left(-1.00 \times 10^2\,\text{m}\right)$$

$$v_f = \sqrt{-\left(9.81\,\text{m/s}^2\right)\left(-1.00 \times 10^2\,\text{m}\right)(2) + (10\,\text{m/s})^2}$$

$$= 45.4\,\text{m/s}$$

Example 3

A roller coaster car starts from rest at point A. What is the speed of this car at point B if the track is frictionless?

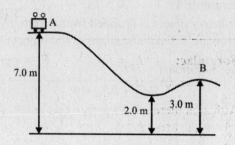

Solution

$$\Delta E_k + \Delta E_p = 0$$

$$\frac{1}{2}mv_f^2 - \frac{1}{2}mv_i^2 + mg\Delta h = 0$$

$$\frac{1}{2}v_f^2 - \frac{1}{2}v_i^2 + g\Delta h = 0$$

$$v_f = \sqrt{v_i^2 - 2g\Delta h}$$

$$= \sqrt{-2\left(9.81\ \text{m/s}^2\right)\left(-4.0\ \text{m}\right)}$$

$$= 8.9\ \text{m/s}$$

PRACTICE EXERCISE

Formulae: $E_p = Fd$ $E_p = mgh$ $E_k = \dfrac{1}{2}mv^2$

Although there are other methods to solve these problems, use the law of conservation of mechanical energy.

1. A heavy object is dropped and reaches the floor at a speed of $3.2\,\text{m/s}$. From what height was it dropped?

2. A heavy object is dropped from a vertical height of $8.0\,\text{m}$ above the ground. What is the speed of this object as it hits the ground?

3. A heavy object is dropped from the top of a building. If this object hits the ground with a speed of $37.0\,\text{m/s}$, how tall was the building?

4. A heavy object is thrown vertically down from the top of a 1.3×10^2 m building at a velocity of 11.0 m/s. What is its velocity as it hits the ground?

5. A heavy box slides down a frictionless incline as shown in the diagram. If the box starts from rest at the top of the incline, what is its speed at the bottom?

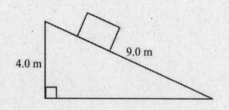

6. A heavy box slides down a frictionless incline as shown in the diagram. If the box starts from rest at the top of the incline, what is its speed at the bottom?

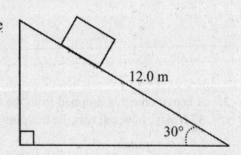

7. A roller coaster car starts from rest at point A. What is the speed of this car at point B if the track is frictionless?

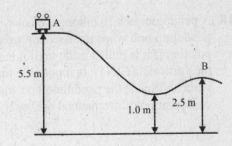

8. A roller coaster car starts from rest at point A. What is the speed of this car at point C if the track is frictionless?

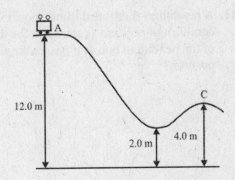

9. A student is running at a speed of 3.5 m/s and grabs a long rope that is hanging vertically from a tree. How high can the student swing?

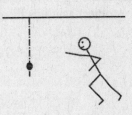

299

10. A pendulum is 1.20 m long. What is the speed of the pendulum bob when it passes through its equilibrium position if it is pulled aside until it makes a 25.0° angle to the vertical? (HINT: Is it possible to determine the vertical drop of the pendulum bob and then use the law of conservation of mechanical energy?)

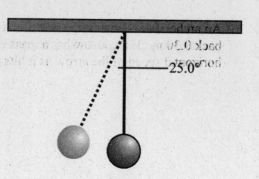

11. A pendulum is dropped from a position 0.25 m above the equilibrium position as shown in the diagram. What is the speed of the pendulum bob as it passes through the equilibrium position?

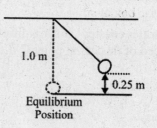

12. A 2.5 kg object is dropped from a height of 10.0 m above the ground. Calculate the speed of the object as it hits the ground.

13. An archer exerts an average horizontal force of 12 N on his bow-arrow system by pulling the string back 0.30 m. If the arrow has a mass of 0.45 kg, and at the target is 5.0 m away, what is the horizontal speed of the arrow as it hits the target?

14. A 1.0 kg box slides without friction around the loop-the-loop apparatus as shown in the diagram. If the object starts from rest at point A, and the radius of the loop is 0.75 m, what is the speed of the box at point B?

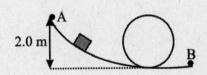

15. A 0.40 kg pendulum bob is swinging back and forth as shown in the diagram. When the pendulum bob is at position A, its gravitational potential energy is 0.20 J relative to position B.

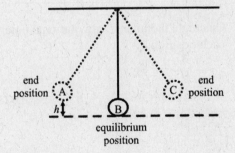

   a) What is the vertical displacement, h, as described in the diagram?

   b) What is the kinetic energy of the bob at position B?

c) What is the mechanical energy of the bob when it is halfway between B and C?

d) What is the speed of the bob at position B?

16. A student does an experiment as suggested in Activity 11. The student collects the following data:

Position	Mass (kg)	Speed (m/s)	Height (m)	E_k (J)	E_p (J)	Mechanical Energy (J)
1	0.250	0	0.300			
2	0.250	1.40	0.200			
3	0.250	1.98	0.100			

Calculate the kinetic, gravitational potential and mechanical energy of the pendulum bob at each position.

17. A 15.0 kg box slides down an incline as shown in the diagram. If the box starts from rest at the top of the incline and has a speed of 6.0 m/s at the bottom, how much work was done to overcome friction?

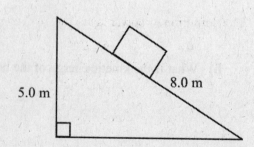

5.0 m

8.0 m

REVIEW SUMMARY

In this unit we studied:
- circular motion
- work, energy and power

Uniform circular motion can be described by the following equations:

$$v = 2\pi r f$$

$$v = \frac{2\pi r}{T}$$

$$\vec{a}_c = \frac{v^2}{r}$$

$$\vec{F}_c = \frac{mv^2}{r}$$

Orbital motion is circular motion. To describe the motion of the planets or satellites, we use the following equations:

Kepler's third law:

$$\frac{T^2}{r^3} = K \qquad \text{or} \qquad \frac{T_1^2}{r_1^3} = \frac{T_2^2}{r_2^3}$$

$$v = \sqrt{\frac{Gm_E}{r}}$$

$$T = \frac{2\pi r^{3/2}}{\sqrt{Gm_E}} \qquad \text{or} \qquad T = \sqrt{\frac{4\pi^2 r^3}{Gm_E}}$$

WORK AND POWER

The mathematical definition of work is
$$W = Fd$$

The definition of power is the rate of doing work or using energy.

$$P = \frac{W}{t} \qquad \text{or} \qquad P = \frac{\Delta E}{t}$$

ENERGY AND THE CONSERVATION OF MECHANICAL ENERGY

Kinetic energy is energy of motion.

$$E_k = \frac{1}{2}mv^2$$

Potential energy is stored energy or energy due to position.
- Gravitational potential energy

$$E_p = mgh$$

- Mechanical energy $= E_k + E_p$

- Work-energy theorem for net force

$$W = \Delta E_k$$

or

$$Fd = \frac{1}{2}m\left(v_f^2 - v_i^2\right)$$

- Work is defined as the transfer of energy.
- Work-energy theorem provides a framework to solve motion problems.
- Law of Conservation of Mechanical Energy.
  - In an isolated system (frictionless system) mechanical energy is conserved.
  - Provides a framework in which to solve motion problems.
  - $\Delta E_k + \Delta E_p = 0$

REVIEW EXERCISE

1. A car travels with a constant speed of 26.0 m/s around a curved path that has a radius of 225 m. What is the centripetal acceleration of the car?

2. How fast can a 1.6×10^3 kg car round an unbanked curve of radius 55 m if the coefficient of friction between the car and the road is 0.60?

3. A 0.150 kg mass is twirled from the end of a string in a horizontal circle (radius = 0.750 m) at a rate of 2.50 revolutions per second. Assuming the string is also horizontal, what is the tension in the string?

4. A 0.10 kg mass is twirled from the end of a string in a horizontal circle of radius 0.620 m at a rate of 1.66 revolutions per second (or Hz). Assuming the string is also horizontal, what is the speed of the mass?

5. You are riding your bike (total mass = 95.0 kg) over a rise with a radius of curvature of 10.0 m. How fast must you be travelling on this bike path for your bike to lose contact with the ground?

6. A student (mass = 50.0 kg) is riding through a dip on a roller coaster with a radius of curvature of 15.0 m. If her speed is 10.0 m/s, calculate the student's apparent weight in Newtons at the bottom of the dip.

7. A 1.75 kg mass is swung in a vertical circle (radius = 1.10 m) using a cord that will break if it is subjected to a force greater than 262 N. What is the maximum speed that this mass can travel as it passes through the bottom of the circular trajectory without breaking the string?

8. Calculate Kepler's constant for objects rotating around the sun given that the Earth has a period of revolution about the sun of 3.16×10^7 s and an orbital radius of 1.49×10^{11} m.

9. If a planet is orbiting our sun with a period of revolution of 7.82×10^9 s, how far is it from the sun? (Use information in Problem 8 to answer this question.)

10. An artificial satellite is put into a circular orbit around the sun. If the radius of this orbit is 1.52×10^{12} m, how long would it take the satellite to make one revolution around the sun? (Use information in Problem 8.)

11. What is the speed of an artificial satellite with a mass of 625 kg and which is placed in an orbit 1.00×10^6 m above the surface of a planet? $\left(m_p = 3.18 \times 10^{23} \text{ kg}, r_p = 2.43 \times 10^6 \text{ m} \right)$

12. An artificial satellite $\left(m_s = 572 \text{ kg} \right)$ is put into a circular orbit about the Earth $\left(m_E = 5.98 \times 10^{24} \text{ kg} \right)$. If the radius of this orbit is 1.2×10^7 m, how long will it take the satellite to make one revolution?

13. Mars orbits the sun (radius of Mars' orbit $= 2.28 \times 10^{11}$ m, $m_M = 6.42 \times 10^{23}$ kg, $m_s = 1.98 \times 10^{30}$ kg).

    a) Calculate the orbital speed of Mars.

    b) Calculate the period of the motion.

14. An artificial satellite $m_s = 611$ kg is put into a circular orbit around Jupiter ($m_J = 1.90 \times 10^{27}$ kg, $r_J = 6.99 \times 10^7$ m). If this satellite has an orbital velocity of 3.12×10^4 m/s, how far above Jupiter's surface is the satellite?

15. How much work is done in accelerating an 11.0 kg object from 15.0 m/s to 20.0 m/s in 4.30 s?

16. A 7.6 kg object is pulled 6.0 m at a constant velocity of 5.0 m/s along a horizontal surface. If a force of 2.0 N is used, what is the work done to overcome friction?

17. What is the gravitational potential energy with respect to the ground of a 20.0 N object that is 2.0 m above the ground?

18. Calculate the kinetic energy of a 1 250 kg car travelling at a speed of 40.0 km/h.

19. What is the average power of a 50.0 kg sprinter accelerating from rest to 1.50 m/s in 4.0 s?

20. What work is done on a 50.0 kg object to accelerate it from rest to 5.00 m/s along a 3.00 m horizontal frictionless surface? (Can be done using work-energy theorem.)

21. An electric motor is used to lift an elevator and occupants $\left(m = 1.50 \times 10^3 \text{ kg} \right)$ to a height of 15.0 m in 30.0 s at a constant velocity. What is the power output of the motor?

22. A 1.00×10^3 kg object is raised vertically at a constant velocity of 4.00 m/s by a crane. What is the power output of the crane?

23. A 10.0 kg box is accelerated from rest along a horizontal frictionless surface by a horizontal force of 20.0 N. What is the speed of the box after travelling 6.00 m? (NOTE: use the work-energy theorem to find net force.)

24. What is the gravitational potential energy with respect to the ground of a 91.2 N object that is 25.0 m above the ground?

25. A 3.0 kg object travels vertically at a constant speed of 2.0 m/s. What is the increase in gravitational potential energy after 4.0 s?

26. A roller coaster is travelling without friction as shown in the diagram. If the speed of the roller coaster at A is 3.0 m/s, what is the speed at B?

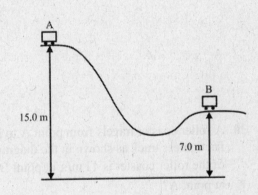

27. At what speed would a heavy object hit the ground if it was lifted vertically from the ground at a constant speed of 1.2 m/s for 2.5 s and then dropped?

28. A 2.0 kg object is thrown vertically downward at a speed of 5.0 m/s from a height of 12.0 m above the ground. Calculate the speed of the object as it hits the ground.

29. A heavy object was dropped from some distance above the ground. When it reached the ground, it had a speed of 10.0 m/s. From what height was the object dropped?

30. A roller coaster travels from point A to point B along a frictionless track as shown in the diagram. If the speed of the roller coaster is 11 m/s at point B, what is its speed at point A?

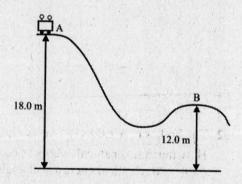

18.0 m

12.0 m

A

B

31. A ball player hits a ball $(m = 0.145 \text{ kg})$ that goes straight up. Given that the ball leaves the bat at a speed of 15.0 m/s, and ignoring air friction, find:

a) the mechanical energy of the ball when it is halfway to its maximum height.

b) the gravitational potential energy when the ball reaches its maximum height.

c) the speed of the ball when it is halfway to its maximum height.

32. The brakes of a 1.00×10^3 kg car are applied. The car skids 67.2 m while coming to a stop in 4.00 s. How much mechanical energy is converted to thermal energy while the car is skidding to a stop? (Note: Mechanical energy is changed to thermal energy when there is friction.)

33. A toy car (mass = 2.0 kg) starts from rest at point A and slides along the track described in the diagram. Assume that the track is frictionless.

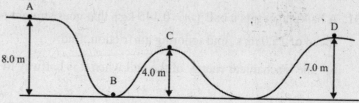

a) What is the speed of the car at point D?

b) What is the total mechanical energy of the car at point B? (Assume the gravitational potential energy of the car is zero at point B.)

34. An 8.00 kg object is dropped from a height above the ground. When it is 2.00 m from the ground, it has 627 J of mechanical energy. Ignoring air friction, find:

a) its speed when it is 2.00 m above the ground.

b) the height from which it was dropped.

35. A heavy box slides down a frictionless incline as shown in the diagram. If the box starts from rest at the top of the incline, what is its speed at the bottom?

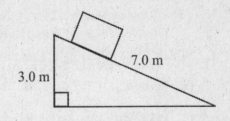

36. The diagram shows a simple pendulum bob swinging back and forth in simple harmonic motion. If the speed of the pendulum bob at the equilibrium position is 1.370 m/s , to what height (h) will the pendulum reach?

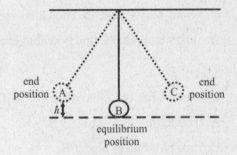

37. A 12.0 N object is lifted at a constant velocity from the floor to a height of 2.30 m. How much work is done in moving the object against gravity?

PRACTICE TEST

1. Which of the following is a unit of power?

   A. kg•m/s

   B. kg•m/s^2

   C. kg•m^2/s^2

   D. kg•m^2/s^3

2. As a heavy object falls, it

   A. loses potential energy and gains kinetic energy

   B. loses kinetic energy and gains potential energy

   C. gains both kinetic and potential energy

   D. loses both kinetic and potential energy

3. If object A has twice the mass and half the speed of object B, then the kinetic energy of object A is

   A. one eighth that of object B

   B. one quarter that of object B

   C. one half that of object B

   D. the same as object B

4. If you are travelling along a straight level highway at 5.0 m/s and you apply the brakes and slide to a stop in distance d, how far would you slide if you have been travelling 10.0 m/s?

   A. d

   B. $\sqrt{2.0}d$

   C. 2.0d

   D. 4.0d

5. An object with a mass m travels a distance d along a horizontal surface. What is the work done by gravity on this object?

   A. mgd

   B. md

   C. zero

   D. $\dfrac{mg}{d}$

6. An object (mass = m) accelerates uniformly (acceleration = a) from rest for t seconds through a distance d along a horizontal frictionless surface. The work done on this object is

   A. mad

   B. mgh

   C. $\dfrac{1}{2}mv^2$

   D. $\dfrac{Fd}{t}$

7. When an object is travelling east at a velocity $\bar{v}$, it has kinetic energy E. What is the kinetic energy of this object if its velocity is $3\bar{v}$ east?

A. $\sqrt{3}E$

B. $3E$

C. $6E$

D. $9E$

8. Units of kinetic energy are

A. kg•m/s

B. $kg•m/s^2$

C. $kg•m^2/s^2$ ²

D. $kg^2•m^2/s^2$

9. What is the work required to accelerate an object from rest to 10.0 m/s along a horizontal frictionless surface if the mass of the object is 2.50 kg?

A. 0

B. 31.3 J

C. 125 J

D. 245 J

10. A projectile (mass 10.0 g) is travelling horizontally at a velocity of 335 m/s when it hits a fixed block of wood. If the projectile penetrates the wood 3.15 cm, what is the work done on the projectile by the wood?

A. -1.68×10^2 J

B. -5.61×10^2 J

C. -2.81×10^3 J

D. -6.30×10^7 J

11. When a student runs up a flight of stairs with a velocity $\bar{v}$, her potential energy at the top of the stairs is E_p. What is the student's potential energy at the top of the stairs if she runs up at velocity of $2\bar{v}$?

A. E_p

B. $\sqrt{2}E_p$

C. $2E_p$

D. $4E_p$

12. This is a position-time graph for an object that is thrown vertically into the air. Which of the following statements is true concerning the mechanical energy of the object?

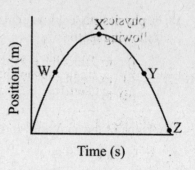

Position (m) / Time (s)

A. The mechanical energy is greatest at point **X**.

B. The mechanical energy is greatest at point **Z**.

C. The sum of the mechanical energies at points **X** and **Z** is greater than the sum of the mechanical energies at points **W** and **Y**.

D. The sum of the mechanical energies at points **X** and **Y** equal the sum of the mechanical energies at points **W** and **Y**.

13. A ball starts from rest at point A on the diagram and rolls along the frictionless track to point B. What is the velocity at point B?

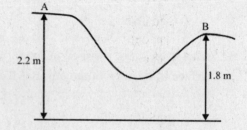

A. 2.8 m/s   B. 3.9 m/s

C. 4.8 m/s   D. 6.4 m/s

14. A student pushes against a wall with a force of 25 N for 15 s. The work done by the student on the wall is

A. 0 J   B. 1.7 J

C. 25 J   D. 3.8×10^2 J

15. A physics student claimed that when work is done on an object, the following can happen:

   i)   the gravitational potential energy of the object is changed
   ii) the kinetic energy of the object is changed
   iii) mechanical energy is changed to thermal energy

Which of the above are correct?

A. i) and ii) only   B. ii) and iii) only

C. i) and iii) only   D. i), ii), and iii) are all correct

16. A physics student was explaining to his friend that work is done on an object for the following reasons:

    i)   to overcome gravity
    ii) to accelerate the object
    iii) to overcome friction

Which of the above are correct?

A. i) and ii) only   **B.** ii) and iii) only

C. i) and iii) only   **D.** i), ii), and iii) are all correct

17. In which of the following cases is there no work done on the object?

    i)   an object is held 1.5 m above the ground
    ii) an object moves at a constant velocity of 0.50 m/s across a horizontal frictionless surface
    iii) an object falls freely from a height of 1.5 m above the floor

A. i) and ii) only   **B.** ii) and iii) only

C. i) and iii) only   **D.** There is no work done in any of the above.

18. A heavy box is pushed across a horizontal surface at a constant velocity. Which of the following represents the force-displacement graph for this motion? (Assume constant friction between the box and the surface.)

A.
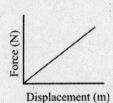

B.
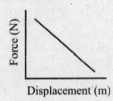

C.
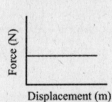

D.
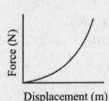

19. A physics student was explaining to her friend that when work is done on an object in lifting it to a height of 1.5 m at a constant velocity, the work done on the object is stored in the object as

    i)   gravitational potential energy
    ii) kinetic energy
    iii) thermal energy

Which of the above is/are correct?

A. i) only   **B.** ii) only

C. iii) only   **D.** All are correct: i), ii) and iii)

20. A heavy box is pushed up an incline at a constant velocity as shown in the diagram.

Assuming that the friction is constant along the incline, which of the following force-displacement graphs best represents this situation?

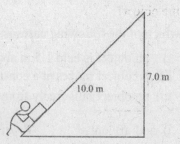

A.

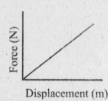

B.

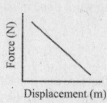

C.

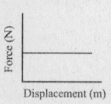

D.

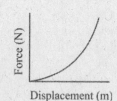

21. A physics student told his friend that the work done on a heavy object in dragging it over a horizontal surface at a constant velocity resulted in:

    i)   potential energy converted to kinetic energy
    ii) mechanical energy converted to thermal energy

Which of the above is/are correct if any? (Note: there is friction.)

A. i) only.   **B.** ii) only.

C. Both i) and ii) are correct.   **D.** Neither i) nor ii) are correct.

22. When a feather is freely falling in a vacuum, which of the following is correct?

    A. Kinetic energy is converted to potential energy.

    B. Potential energy is converted to kinetic energy.

    C. Mechanical energy is converted to kinetic energy.

    D. Potential energy is converted to mechanical energy.

23. An object is dropped from a certain height above the ground. Assuming negligible air resistance, which of the following graphs represent the relationship between the kinetic energy and the velocity of the object?

A.
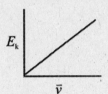

B.
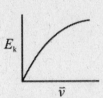

C.
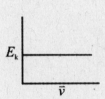

D.
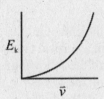

24. A child is swinging on a playground swing reaching the same height on each swing. Which of the following graphs shows the kinetic energy as a function of time for this motion?

A.
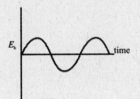

B.
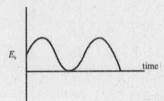

C.
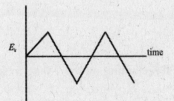

D.
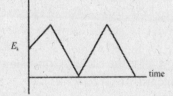

25. When an object is travelling in a circular path, the direction of the velocity of the object at any given time is:

   A. toward the centre of the circular path

   B. away from the centre of the circular path

   C. tangent to the circular path

   D. along the circular path followed by the object

26. When an object is travelling in a circular path, the direction of the acceleration of the object at any given time is:

   A. toward the centre of the circular path

   B. away from the centre of the circular path

   C. tangent to the circular path

   D. along the circular path followed by the object

27. Consider the motion of a 1.0 kg mass tied to the end of a 0.70 m cord. This mass is swung clockwise in a vertical circle as shown in the diagram to the right. Which of the following is a correctly labelled free-body diagram showing the forces acting on the 1.0 kg mass when it is at the top of the circle (T = tension in cord)?

   A.

   B.

   C.

   D.

28. In question 27, what is the correct expression for the centripetal force acting on the 1.0 kg mass? ($\vec{T}$ = tension in cord)

   A. $\vec{F}_c = \vec{F}_g - \vec{T}$

   B. $\vec{F}_c = \vec{F}_g + \vec{T}$

   C. $\vec{F}_c = \sqrt{\vec{F}_g^{\,2} + \vec{T}^2}$

   D. $\vec{F}_c = \vec{T}$

29. When an object is twirled in a horizontal circle at the end of a cord at a constant speed, which of the following graphs best represents the relationship between the tension $(\vec{T})$ in the cord and the time (t)?

A.

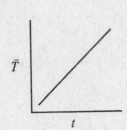

B.

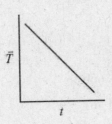

C.

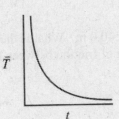

D.

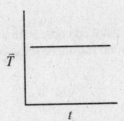

30. What is the definition of centripetal force?

   A. Applied force causing an object to travel in a circle.

   B. Product of the mass and the velocity of an object travelling in a circle.

   C. Net force causing an object to travel in a circle.

   D. Sum of the applied force and the net force causing an object to travel in a circle.

31. A student predicts that the speed of a satellite in its orbit depends on

   i)   gravitational field in the orbit

   ii) radius of the orbit

   iii) mass of the satellite

   Which of the above are correct?

   A. i) and ii) only

   B. i) and iii) only

   C. ii) and iii) only

   D. i), ii), and iii)

32. A student predicts that the speed of a satellite in an orbit around the Earth depends on

    i)   mass of the satellite

    i)   mass of the earth

    iii) radius of the orbit

Which of the above are correct?

  A. i) and ii) only   **B.** i) and iii) only

  C. ii) and iii) only   **D.** i), ii), and iii)

33. A car is travelling on a road that has an unbanked curve with a radius of 40.0 m. What is the maximum speed that the car can safely round the curve if the coefficient of friction between the tires and the road is 0.50?

  A. 4.5 m/s   **B.** 9.0 m/s

  C. 14 m/s   **D.** 20 m/s

34. When an astronaut is orbiting the Earth at a distance of 600 km above the Earth, she is weightless. The reason for this is that

  A. the gravitational field strength is zero at that distance from the Earth

  B. the astronaut is in freefall

  C. there are no forces acting on the astronaut at that distance from the Earth

  D. the net force acting on the astronaut is zero at that distance from the Earth

35. A satellite orbits Planet A. If we know the period and the radius of this motion, which of the following can also be calculated, if any?

    i)   speed of the satellite

    ii) mass of planet A

  A. i) only   **B.** ii) only

  C. both i) and ii)   **D.** neither i) nor ii)

36. Two geosynchronous satellites are placed in an orbit 400 km above the Earth. Satellite 1 has a mass of 1.2×10^4 kg and Satellite 2 has a mass of 2.4×10^4 kg. Which of these satellites, if any, has the greatest orbital velocity?

A. Satellite 1

B. Satellite 2

C. Both satellites have the same speed

37. The adjective "centripetal" in centripetal force is best described as meaning

A. parallel   B. perpendicular

C. toward the centre   D. away from the centre

38. Kepler's laws are important because they describe

     i) how the planets move

     ii) why the planets move

Which of the following is the best answer?

A. i) only   B. ii) only

C. both i) and ii)

39. When the speed of an object is doubled, its kinetic energy is

A. quartered   B. halved

C. doubled   D. quadrupled

OSCILLATORY MOTION AND MECHANICAL WAVES

When you are finished this unit, you will be able to...

- describe mechanical waves as particles of a medium that are moving in simple harmonic motion
- compare and contrast energy transmission by matter that moves and by waves
- define longitudinal and transverse waves in terms of the direction of motion of the medium particles in relation to the direction of propagation of the wave
- define the terms wavelength, wave velocity, period, frequency, amplitude, wave front and ray as they apply to describing transverse and longitudinal waves
- describe how the speed of a wave depends on the characteristics of the medium
- predict, quantitatively, and verify the effects of changing one or a combination of the variables in the universal wave equation $(v = f\lambda)$
- explain, qualitatively, the phenomenon of reflection as exhibited by mechanical waves
- explain, qualitatively, the conditions for constructive and destructive interference of waves and for acoustical resonance
- explain, qualitatively and quantitatively, the Doppler effect on a stationary observer with a moving source and on a moving observer with a stationary source
- describe oscillatory motion in terms of period and frequency
- define simple harmonic motion as a motion due to a restoring force that is directly proportional and opposite to the displacement from an equilibrium position
- explain, quantitatively, the relationships among displacement, acceleration, velocity and time for simple harmonic motion, as illustrated by a frictionless horizontal mass-spring system or a pendulum, using the small-angle approximation
- determine, quantitatively, the relationships among kinetic gravitational potential and total mechanical energies of a mass executing simple harmonic motion
- define mechanical resonance
- explain that the goal of science is knowledge about the natural world
- explain that the goal of technology is to provide solutions to practical problems

NOTES

Lesson 1   Oscillatory Motion

In the last unit we studied uniform circular motion. Uniform circular motion repeats itself in equal time intervals and at a constant frequency. The following diagram shows an object moving at a constant speed (uniform circular motion).

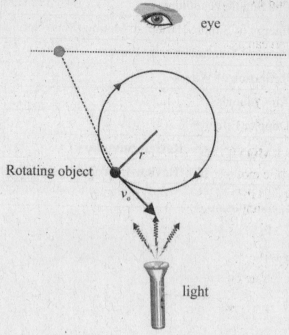

We observe that when an object is rotating in a circle at a constant speed, the shadow of this object oscillates back and forth just like a pendulum will swing back and forth along a path, or just like a mass in a mass-spring system.

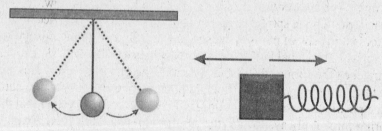

The motion of the swinging pendulum and the mass in the mass-spring system is called oscillatory motion.

Both uniform circular motion and oscillatory motion are examples of periodic motion. Any motion that repeats itself over and over again is called periodic motion.

Periodic motion:

• uniform circular motion
• oscillatory motion

Periodic motion gets its name from the fact that this motion repeats itself over and over again in equal time intervals (each repetition takes the same time as the previous motion).

The time for each complete oscillation (also called vibration or cycle) is called the period (T) of the motion.

Periodic motion can also be described in terms of frequency (f).

Remember: $f = \dfrac{1}{T}$

SIMPLE HARMONIC MOTION

Simple harmonic motion (SHM) is the simplest form of oscillatory motion. The motion of the pendulum and the mass-spring system described earlier are examples of simple harmonic motion.

HOOKE'S LAW

We will concentrate on a mass-spring system now.

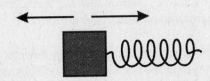

If we displace the mass slightly to the right and release it, the mass will vibrate back and forth. This motion is simple harmonic motion. Why does it do this? The answer to this question is given by Hooke's Law.
When we stretch the spring by applying a force on the spring, according to Newton's third law of motion, the spring exerts an equal but opposite force back on us. This equal but opposite force varies directly with how much we stretched the spring (the displacement). The displacement is measured from the equilibrium position (the mid position of the motion or we can say the position in which the motion will come to rest). We note that the restoring force is always toward the equilibrium position. The maximum displacement is called the amplitude.

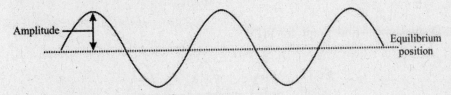

Hooke's Law
    $\vec{F}_s \propto -kx$ or $\vec{F}_s = -kx$
    where k is the proportionality constant, and
    x is the displacement from the equilibrium

Hooke's Law: the restoring force is directly proportional to the displacement

Equilibrium position is the position in which the motion will come to rest

Maximum displacement is called the amplitude

Hooke's Law
$\vec{F}_s = -kx$

Physics 20 SNAP

NOTES

When we are discussing springs, k is called the spring constant. The stiffer the spring, the greater the value of k.

Usually this equation is written with a negative sign. This is to indicate that the restoring force (elastic force) is in the opposite direction to the displacement.

$$\vec{F}_s = -kx$$

Any vibrating system for which the restoring force is directly proportional to the displacement is said to illustrate simple harmonic motion.

From Newton's second law of motion $\left(\vec{F}_{net} = m\vec{a} \right)$, the acceleration is directly proportional to the force. Therefore, simple harmonic motion can also be defined as motion where the acceleration is directly proportional to the restoring force.

$$\vec{a} \propto \vec{F}_s$$

$$\vec{a} \propto \vec{F}_s$$
$$\vec{F}_s = -kx$$
$$m\vec{a} = kx$$
$$\vec{a} = \frac{-kx}{m}$$

You will note from the above equation that the acceleration of the object undergoing simple harmonic motion is not uniform.

Simple harmonic motion can be referred to as sinusoidal motion. This is because if we were to graph the displacement, velocity and acceleration versus time for simple harmonic motion, we would obtain sine graphs.

SINE GRAPH

If we plot a graph of the sine of the angles from $0°$ to $720°$ as a function of the angle, we obtain the following graph.

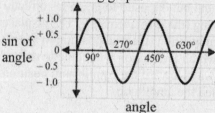

Displacement-time graph for SHM

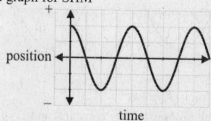

Velocity-time graph for SHM

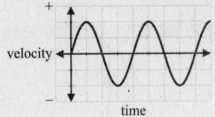

Acceleration-time graph for SHM

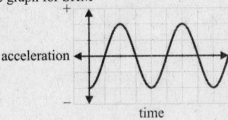

We note when we study these graphs that when the displacement is a maximum, the velocity is zero and the acceleration is a maximum. When the displacement is zero, the velocity is a maximum and the acceleration is zero.

Study the following diagram.

A Spring in Motion

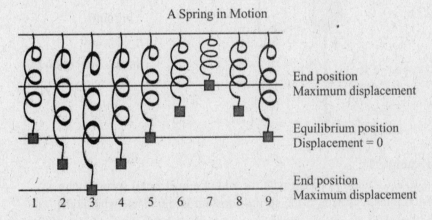

At positions 1, 5, and 9, the mass is at the equilibrium position. At this position, the mass's

displacement = 0

velocity = maximum

acceleration = maximum

To this point, we have used a mass-spring system to explain simple harmonic motion, but as we said earlier, a simple pendulum swinging back and forth at a small angle is also simple harmonic motion.

In the mass-spring system, the restoring force is the elastic force of the spring. In a simple pendulum, the restoring force is a component of the weight of the pendulum bob. It is the component of the weight that is tangent to the direction that the bob is moving.

For a pendulum: $\vec{F}_s = -mg\sin\theta$

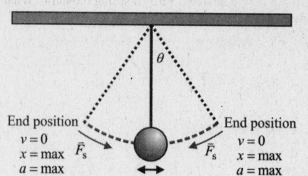

End position
$v = 0$
$x = \text{max}$
$a = \text{max}$

$\vec{F}_s$

$\vec{F}_s$

End position
$v = 0$
$x = \text{max}$
$a = \text{max}$

$\vec{F}_s$

Equilibrium position
$v = \text{max}$
$x = 0$
$a = 0$

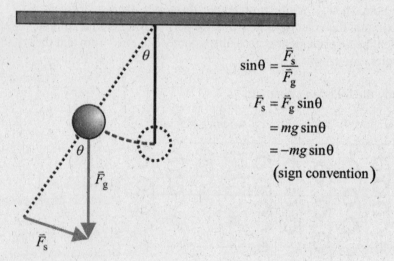

$\sin\theta = \dfrac{\vec{F}_s}{\vec{F}_g}$

$\vec{F}_s = \vec{F}_g \sin\theta$

$\quad = mg\sin\theta$

$\quad = -mg\sin\theta$

$\quad$ (sign convention)

Example 1

A 0.40 kg mass is vibrating at the end of a horizontal spring along a frictionless surface. If the spring constant is 6.0 N/m, what is the restoring force acting on the mass when it is 0.070 m from its equilibrium position?

Solution

$\vec{F} = -kx$

$\quad = -(6.0\ \text{N/m})(0.070\ \text{m})$

$\quad = -0.42\ \text{N}$

The negative sign indicates that the force is in the opposite direction to the displacement.

Example 2

A weight of 4.6 N will stretch a vertical spring 0.048 m. What is the spring constant?

Solution

$$\vec{F}_s = -kx$$

$$k = \frac{\vec{F}_s}{x}$$

$$= \frac{4.0 \text{ N}}{0.048 \text{ m}}$$

$$= 96 \text{ N/m}$$

Remember that the negative sign is included in the formula to remind us that the restoring force has a direction opposite to the displacement vector.

PRACTICE EXERCISE

Formulae: $\vec{F}_s = -kx$ $\vec{F}_s = -mg\sin\theta$

1. A 1.00 kg mass on a spring is 0.100 m from its equilibrium position. If the spring constant is 20.0 N/m, what is the restoring force acting on the mass?

2. The restoring force acting on a 0.50 kg object on a spring is 2.0 N. If the spring constant is 15 N/m, what is the displacement of the object?

3. The restoring force acting on a 0.60 kg object on a spring is 1.2 N. If the displacement of the object is 0.025 m, what is the spring constant?

4. A weight of 1.65 N will stretch a vertical spring 0.110 m. What is the spring constant?

5. A mass of 5.0 kg will stretch a vertical spring 3.25 cm. What is the spring constant?

6. A weight of 9.3 N is hung on a vertical spring that has a spring constant of 25 N/m. How far will the spring stretch?

7. A 0.25 kg mass is vibrating at the end of a horizontal spring along a frictionless surface. If the spring constant is 4.2 N/m, what is the acceleration of the mass when the displacement of the mass is 0.050 m?

8. A 0.11 kg mass is vibrating at the end of a horizontal spring along a frictionless surface. If the spring constant is 0.52 N/m, what is the displacement of the mass when its acceleration is 0.25 m/s^2?

9. What is the maximum acceleration of a 0.042 kg mass vibrating at the end of a horizontal spring if the maximum displacement of the mass is 0.012 m? Assume the mass is vibrating along a frictionless horizontal surface and the spring constant is 0.37 N/m .

10. A 0.18 kg pendulum bob is swinging back and forth from the end of a 0.75 m string.

   a) What is the acceleration of the pendulum bob when the bob is at the equilibrium position?

   b) What is the acceleration of the pendulum bob when the bob is at the end position if the string is making an angle of 9.0° with the vertical as shown in the diagram?

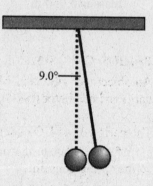

9.0°

Lesson 2   ENERGY OF SIMPLE HARMONIC MOTION

In the last unit we studied the energy changes in a swinging pendulum. As a pendulum swings back and forth (SHM), the energy changes back and forth from kinetic to potential energy.

In the same way, when a mass-spring system is vibrating, the energy in the system is also changing back and forth from kinetic to potential energy.

In a pendulum the potential energy is gravitational potential energy, but in a horizontal mass-spring system the potential energy is elastic potential energy.

$$E_p = mgh \quad \text{(gravitational)}$$

$$E_{p.} = \frac{1}{2}kx^2 \quad \text{(elastic)}$$

DERIVATION

When work is done to compress or stretch a spring, energy is stored in the system.

$$\text{Work} = \text{Force} \times \text{Displacement}$$

When work is done on a spring, this force is elastic force (restoring force or spring force). Remember from Hooke's Law that the elastic force is defined mathematically as:

$$\vec{F}_s = kx$$

where k = spring constant

x = displacement of the spring

PERIOD OF A SIMPLE HARMONIC OSCILLATOR

An object that vibrates with simple harmonic motion is called a simple harmonic oscillator (SHO).

The period of a SHO depends on the:
- stiffness of the spring (or other vibrating object). That is, it depends on k (the spring constant).
- mass that is oscillating (m).

$$T = 2\pi\sqrt{\frac{m}{k}}$$

where T = period
m = mass oscillating
k = spring constant

DERIVATION

To derive this equation, we make use of a reference circle.

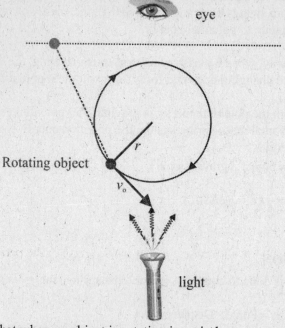

eye

Rotating object

r

v_o

light

We assume that when an object is rotating in a circle at a constant speed (v_o), the motion of a shadow of this object along a horizontal axis is analogous to SHM.

The speed of the object travelling in a circle is the circumference $(2\pi r)$ divided by the time it takes to complete the circle.

$$v_o = \frac{2\pi r}{T} \qquad A = r$$

where $r =$ radius $(\text{analagous to } A)$

Amplitude (A) is defined as maximum displacement.

Now, $\dfrac{1}{2}kA^2 = \dfrac{1}{2}mv_o^2$

or $\dfrac{A^2}{v_o^2} = \dfrac{m}{k}$

or $\dfrac{A}{v_o} = \sqrt{\dfrac{m}{k}}$

Return to

$$v_o = \frac{2\pi r}{T}$$

or $\quad v_o = \dfrac{2\pi A}{T}$

Therefore

$$T = \dfrac{2\pi A}{v_o}$$

but $\quad \dfrac{A}{v_o} = \sqrt{\dfrac{m}{k}}$

Therefore $\quad T = 2\pi\sqrt{\dfrac{m}{k}}$

$$T = 2\pi\sqrt{\dfrac{m}{k}}$$

THE FREQUENCY OF SHM

The frequency of simple harmonic motion is the inverse of the period (time) of vibration.

$$f = \dfrac{1}{T}$$

$$f = \dfrac{1}{T}$$

Activity 12

- Design an experiment to determine the spring constant of a spring.

  Suggestion: Make use of $T = 2\pi\sqrt{\dfrac{m}{k}}$

- Determine the spring constant using your design.

- Determine the effect of mass on the period.

Example 1

A 0.23 kg object vibrates at the end of a horizontal spring $(k = 32\ \text{N/m})$ along a frictionless surface. What is the period of the vibration?

Solution

$$T = 2\pi\sqrt{\dfrac{m}{k}}$$

$$= 2\pi\sqrt{\dfrac{0.23\ \text{kg}}{32\ \text{N/m}}}$$

$$= 0.53\ \text{s}$$

Example 2

A 2.7 N object vibrates at the end of a vertical spring. If the frequency of the vibration is 1.1 Hz, what is the spring constant?

Solution

$$\vec{F}_g = mg$$

$$m = \frac{\vec{F}_g}{g}$$

$$= \frac{2.7 \, \text{N}}{9.81 \, \text{m/s}^2}$$

$$= 0.28 \, \text{kg}$$

$$T = \frac{1}{f}$$

$$= \frac{1}{1.1 \, \text{Hz}}$$

$$= 0.91 \, \text{s}$$

$$T = 2\pi \sqrt{\frac{m}{k}}$$

$$0.91 \, \text{s} = 2\pi \sqrt{\frac{0.28 \, \text{kg}}{k}}$$

$$k = 13 \, \text{N/m}$$

PRACTICE EXERCISE

Formulae: $T = 2\pi\sqrt{\dfrac{m}{k}}$ $f = \dfrac{1}{T}$

1. A 0.50 kg object vibrates at the end of a vertical spring $(k = 82 \text{ N/m})$. What is the period of its vibration?

2. A 0.70 kg object vibrates at the end of a horizontal spring $(k = 75 \text{ N/m})$ along a frictionless surface. What is the frequency of the vibration?

3. An 8.8 N object vibrates at the end of a horizontal spring along a frictionless surface. If the period of vibration is 1.1 s, what is the spring constant?

4. A 1.00 kg object vibrates at the end of a vertical spring. If the frequency of the vibration is 1.25 Hz, what is the spring constant?

5. An object vibrates at the end of a horizontal spring $(k = 115 \text{ N/m})$ along a frictionless surface. If the frequency of the vibration is 1.50 Hz, what is the mass of the object?

6. A 0.40 kg mass vibrates with a frequency of 1.0 Hz at the end of a spring. If the 0.40 kg mass is replaced by a 0.80 kg mass, what is the frequency of the vibration?

7. After a bungee jump, a 75 kg student bobs up and down at the end of the bungee cord at a frequency of 0.23 Hz. What is the spring constant of the bungee cord?

8. A 0.025 kg object vibrates in SHM at the end of a spring. If the maximum displacement of the object is 0.030 cm, and its period is 0.50 s, what is the maximum acceleration of the object?

Lesson 3   THE SIMPLE PENDULUM

The motion of a pendulum is simple harmonic motion when the amplitude of the motion is small. That is, the restoring force is directly proportional to the displacement only for small displacements.

The period of vibration for a pendulum depends on
- the length of pendulum (L)
- the gravitational field strength (g)

$$T = 2\pi\sqrt{\frac{L}{g}}$$

To derive this equation, we determine the sum of forces acting on the pendulum bob. These forces are the weight of the bob (mg), and the tension in the string $(\bar{T})$.

$$T = 2\pi\sqrt{\frac{L}{g}}$$

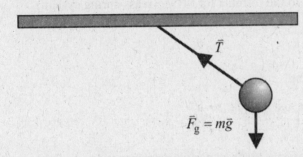

If we add these forces using a vector diagram, we get:

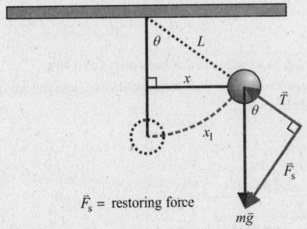

$\bar{F}_s$ = restoring force

For a small angle $x \approx x_1$. (x_1 = displacement of the pendulum bob.)

$$\sin\theta = \frac{\bar{F}_s}{mg} \qquad \text{OR} \qquad \bar{F}_s = mg\sin\theta \ \text{ for a pendulum}$$

From the triangle formed by the length of the string (L), we can conclude the following:

$$\sin\theta = \frac{x}{L}$$

Remember, $x \approx x_1$ (the pendulum bob displacement)

Therefore

$$\vec{F}_s = \frac{mgx}{L} \qquad \text{OR} \qquad \vec{F}_s = \left(\frac{mg}{L}\right)x$$

But for SHM,

$$\vec{F}s = kx \quad \text{(in a mass-spring system)}$$

Therefore

$$k = \frac{mg}{L}$$

Now if we return to the formula for SHM, (mass-spring system)

$$T = 2\pi\sqrt{\frac{m}{k}}$$

And by substituting

$\dfrac{mg}{L}$ for k, we get $T = 2\pi\sqrt{\dfrac{L}{g}}$

One approximation was made in deriving this equation. In the previously mentioned triangle, $x \approx x_1$ when θ is small; if θ is greater than 15°, this becomes less true. The motion of a pendulum is SHM only for angles less than 15°.

Example 1

Find the length of a pendulum that has a period of 0.90 s.

NOTE: Use $9.81\,\text{m/s}^2$ for g in these problems unless you are told otherwise.

Solution

$$T = 2\pi\sqrt{\frac{L}{\bar{g}}}$$

$$0.90\,\text{s} = 2\pi\sqrt{\frac{L}{9.81\,\text{m/s}^2}}$$

$$L = \left(\frac{0.90\,\text{s}}{2\pi}\right)^2\left(9.81\,\text{m/s}^2\right)$$

$$= 0.20\,\text{m}$$

Activity 13

- Design an experiment to determine the acceleration due to gravity using a pendulum. Suggestion: make use of $T = 2\pi\sqrt{\dfrac{L}{g}}$

- Determine the acceleration due to gravity using your design.

- Determine the effect of mass on the period.

- Determine the effect of the length of the pendulum on the period.

PRACTICE EXERCISE

Formulae: $T = 2\pi\sqrt{\dfrac{L}{g}}$

1. A pendulum has a period of 3.6 s. What is its frequency?

2. A spring vibrates 32 times in 56 s. Find its:
    a) period.

    b) frequency (in Hertz).

3. Find the length of a pendulum that has a period of 2.0 s.

4. Find the length of a pendulum that has a frequency of 0.80 Hz.

5. Determine the acceleration due to gravity at a location where a pendulum 0.75 m long has a frequency of 0.57 Hz.

6. The acceleration due to gravity on the moon is 1.6 m/s^2. If a pendulum on the moon has a period of 1.0 s, how long must it be?

7. The bob of a pendulum has a mass of 0.25 kg. If this pendulum is 1.0 m long, what is its frequency?

8. In the pendulum of Problem 7, the bob is replaced with a 0.50 kg bob. If the length of the pendulum remains at 1.0 m, what is its frequency?

9. Elwin, the bungee clown, swings back and forth like a simple pendulum at the end of a bungee cord. If a student determines the time of one complete swing is 6.9 s, how long is the bungee cord when Elwin is swinging from it?

Lesson 4 ENERGY OF SIMPLE HARMONIC MOTION (MASS-SPRING SYSTEM)

In stretching or compressing a spring, the force depends on the displacement. That is, the force will increase from zero (at equilibrium position) to a maximum value at maximum stretch or compression (maximum displacement). Therefore, the work done on the spring is:

$$W = \frac{1}{2}Fx$$

or, potential energy stored in a spring is

$$E_p = \frac{1}{2}Fx$$

but $F = kx$

Therefore

$$E_p = \frac{1}{2}kx^2$$

Now, as the spring vibrates back and forth, this potential energy is changing back and forth from potential energy to kinetic energy.

$$E_k = \frac{1}{2}mv^2$$

In an ideal spring, the total mechanical energy remains constant.

$$E_T = E_p + E_k \quad (E_T = \text{total mechanical energy})$$

At equilibrium position the kinetic energy (E_k) is a maximum and potential energy (E_p) is zero.

At maximum displacement the kinetic energy (E_k) is zero and the potential energy (E_p) is a maximum.

$$E_T = E_p = \frac{1}{2}kA^2 \quad (\text{where } A = \text{maximum displacement})$$

We use A as the symbol for maximum displacement because maximum displacement is called amplitude.

We see $\frac{1}{2}kA^2 = \frac{1}{2}mv_i^2$

As an object vibrates back and forth, the potential energy is changing back and forth from potential energy to kinetic energy

Ideal spring: no mechanical energy is lost

Example 1

A 0.30 kg mass vibrates at the end of a horizontal spring along a frictionless surface. If the spring constant is $45 \, \text{N/m}$, and the maximum displacement of the mass is 0.080 m, what is the maximum speed of the mass?

Solution

$$E_T = \frac{1}{2}kA^2$$

$$= \frac{1}{2}(45 \, \text{N/m})(0.080 \, \text{m})^2$$

$$= 0.14 \, \text{J}$$

$$E_T = \frac{1}{2}mv_i^2$$

$$v_i = \sqrt{\frac{2E_T}{m}}$$

$$= \sqrt{\frac{2(0.14 \, \text{J})}{0.30 \, \text{kg}}}$$

$$= 0.98 \, \text{m/s}$$

Example 2

An object vibrates at the end of a vertical spring $(k = 121 \, \text{N/m})$. If the potential energy of the object is 2.20 J, what is its displacement?

Solution

$$E_p = \frac{1}{2}kx^2$$

$$x = \sqrt{\frac{2E_p}{k}}$$

$$= \sqrt{\frac{2(2.20 \, \text{J})}{121 \, \text{N/m}}}$$

$$= 0.191 \, \text{m}$$

Example 3

An object vibrates at the end of a horizontal spring $(k = 2.0 \, \text{N/m})$ along a frictionless surface. If the maximum speed of the object is $0.50 \, \text{m/s}$, and its maximum displacement is 0.25 m, what is the speed of the object when its displacement is 0.20 m?

Solution

$$E_p = \frac{1}{2}kx^2$$

$$= \frac{1}{2}(2.0 \, \text{N/m})(0.20 \, \text{m})^2$$

$$= 4.0 \times 10^{-2} \, \text{J}$$

$$E_T = \frac{1}{2}kA^2$$

$$= \frac{1}{2}(2.0\ \text{N/m})(0.25\ \text{m})^2$$

$$= 6.25 \times 10^{-2}\ \text{J}$$

$$E_k = 6.25 \times 10^{-2}\ \text{J} - 4.0 \times 10^{-2}\ \text{J}$$

$$= 2.25 \times 10^{-2}\ \text{J}$$

Find mass

$$E_T = \frac{1}{2}mv_i^2$$

$$m = \frac{2E_T}{v_i^2}$$

$$= \frac{2\left(6.25 \times 10^{-2}\ \text{J}\right)}{(0.50\ \text{m/s})^2}$$

$$= 0.50\ \text{kg}$$

$$E_k = \frac{1}{2}mv^2$$

$$v = \sqrt{\frac{2E_k}{m}}$$

$$= \sqrt{\frac{2\left(2.25 \times 10^{-2}\ \text{J}\right)}{0.50\ \text{kg}}}$$

$$= 0.30\ \text{m/s}$$

PRACTICE EXERCISE

Formulae: $\quad E_p = \dfrac{1}{2}kx^2 \qquad E_T = \dfrac{1}{2}kA^2 \qquad E_k = \dfrac{1}{2}mv^2 \qquad E_T = \dfrac{1}{2}mv_o{}^2$

1. A 0.60 kg mass is vibrating at the end of a spring. If the spring constant is 26 N/m , and the maximum displacement of the mass is 0.15 m, what is the speed of the object at its equilibrium position?

2. A 0.40 kg mass vibrates at the end of a horizontal spring along a frictionless surface reaching a maximum speed of 0.50 m/s . If the maximum displacement of the mass is 0.11 m, what is the spring constant?

3. A 0.20 kg mass vibrates at the end of a horizontal spring $(k = 15 \text{ N/m})$ along a frictionless surface. What is the maximum displacement if it reaches a maximum speed of 0.12 m/s ?

4. An object vibrates at the end of a vertical spring $(k = 25 \text{ N/m})$. If the maximum speed of the object is 0.15 m/s , and its maximum displacement is 0.11 m, what is the mass of the object?

5. An object vibrates at the end of a horizontal spring $(k = 32 \text{ N/m})$ along a frictionless surface. If the object's potential energy is 4.5 J, what is its displacement?

6. An object vibrates at the end of a vertical spring $(k = 28 \text{ N/m})$. If the object's displacement is 0.18 m, what is its potential energy?

7. A 0.46 kg object vibrates at the end of a horizontal spring $(k = 12 \text{ N/m})$. If the object's kinetic energy is 7.32 J, what is its speed?

8. An object vibrates at the end of a horizontal spring $(k = 18 \text{ N/m})$ along a frictionless surface. If the maximum speed of the object is 0.35 m/s, what is the speed of the object when its displacement is

   a) 0.29 m?

   b) 0.10 m?

9. An object vibrates at the end of a vertical spring $(k = 23 \text{ N/m})$. The speed of the object is 0.12 m/s when the displacement is 0.15 m. If the maximum displacement is 0.20 m, what is the maximum speed?

10. A 75 g object vibrates in SHM at the end of a spring $(k = 5.0 \text{ N/m})$. If the maximum displacement of the object is 0.80 m, what is the maximum displacement?

11. How much work was done on a spring $(k = 76.0 \text{ N/m})$ in stretching it 3.50 cm?

Lesson 5 ENERGY: TRANSMISSION BY WAVES

Energy travels by either waves or particles. If you get hit with a ball at a ball game, the energy was transferred from the bat to you by means of a particle (ball). When you hear the crack of the bat against the ball (sound), that energy travelled from the bat to you as a wave.

The rest of this unit deals with energy transmitted as a mechanical wave. It deals with some mechanical wave characteristics and uses sound waves and water waves as examples of energy transmitted by waves.

DEFINITION OF A WAVE

A wave is a disturbance (vibration) that carries energy from one point to another without the transmission of matter (particles).

TYPES OF WAVES

Until the 1860s it was believed that all waves were mechanical waves. With mechanical waves, it is the medium (air, water, string, etc.) that is vibrating as the disturbance travels through it. During the 1860s, James Clerk Maxwell developed a theory in which he proposed that waves can travel by vibrating electric and magnetic fields. These waves are called electromagnetic waves. Mechanical and electromagnetic waves have common properties; however, there is one important difference. Mechanical waves require a medium (air, water, string, etc.), but electromagnetic waves can travel in a vacuum.

Waves are also classified as longitudinal or transverse. In mechanical waves, the medium is vibrating in simple harmonic motion. This vibration can be parallel to the direction of energy flow, or it can be perpendicular to the direction of energy flow.

Vibration of medium (parallel)

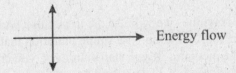

Energy flow

Vibration of medium (perpendicular)

Energy flow

NOTES

Whenever we talk about a wave or vibration travelling through a medium, we are talking about the transmission of energy through the medium

Mechanical waves require a medium through which to travel

Electromagnetic waves can travel in a vacuum

Types of waves:
• longitudinal
• transverse

355

NOTES

If the vibration is parallel, we call the wave a longitudinal wave. Sound is an example of energy that travels by longitudinal waves. If the vibration is perpendicular, we call the wave a transverse wave. Water waves are largely transverse, but they have a small longitudinal component.

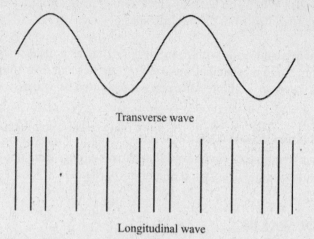

Transverse wave

Longitudinal wave

The motion of every point on a wave is SHM

The motion of the vibration in both longitudinal and transverse waves is simple harmonic motion like the swinging of a pendulum.

TERMS USED TO DESCRIBE WAVES

Compression: Used with a longitudinal wave to describe where the medium is most dense due to the disturbance (vibrations) in the medium.

Rarefaction: Used with a longitudinal wave to describe where the medium is least dense due to the disturbance (vibrations) in the medium.

Crest: Used with a transverse wave to describe the maximum displacement of the medium due to the disturbance (vibrations) in the medium.

Trough: Used with a transverse wave to describe the maximum displacement of the medium due to the disturbance (vibration) in the opposite direction from a crest.

Pulse: Sometimes we will use the term pulse. A pulse is a wave of short duration, or a single vibration that travels through the medium. If you slap your desk, you create a single compression. This would be a pulse.

Wavelength: The length of a wave is the distance between two adjacent points on a wave that are in phase. We often say it is the distance from one crest to the next. The Greek letter lambda (λ) is the symbol for wavelength.

The symbol for wavelength is λ

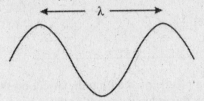

In Phase: Two points in a medium that are vibrating together are said to be in phase. Soldiers march in phase. That is, they all move their left foot together. They all move their right foot together. A and C are in phase.

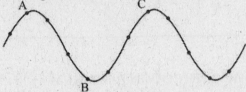

Out of Phase: Two points in a medium that are not vibrating together are out of phase. Students walk the halls out of phase. That is, when one student is moving her left foot, the other student is moving his right foot—they are not moving together. B and C are out of phase.

Period: Period is the time it takes a wave to travel one wavelength, or the time of one vibration of the medium. The symbol for period is T.

Frequency: Frequency is, as the name suggests, the number of waves that pass a point in a given time (usually 1 second), or the number of vibrations of a point in the medium in a given time. The symbol for frequency is f, and the unit is the hertz (Hz). A hertz is a defined unit meaning vibrations per second.

Remember, there is an inverse relationship between the period and frequency of a wave.

$$T = \frac{1}{f} \qquad f = \frac{1}{T}$$

The direction of motion is always perpendicular to the wave front

Amplitude: The amplitude is the maximum displacement of the medium from the equilibrium position.

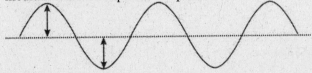

NOTES

The direction of motion is always perpendicular to the wave front

Wave front: We sometimes use this term in diagrams as a representation of the wave. (This diagram is called a wave front diagram.)

incoming wave front   reflected wave front

Ray: A ray is a means of showing the direction that the energy carried by the wave is travelling from source to receiver. (This diagram is called a ray diagram.)

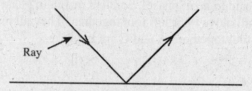

Ray

The speed of a wave depends on the nature of the medium through which it is travelling

SPEED OF A WAVE THROUGH A MEDIUM

Just as the speed of a horse in a horse race depends on the nature of the track (track conditions), the speed of a wave depends on the nature of the medium through which it is travelling.

In general terms, the speed of a wave through a medium depends on the elasticity and the density of the medium. Elasticity is the ability of a substance to recover its original length or volume after the stress is removed.

$$v = \sqrt{\frac{\text{elasticity}}{\text{density}}}$$

The speed of sound through air (0°C) = 331 m/s

The speed of sound through air (15°C) = 343 m/s

The speed of sound through water (15°) = 1 500 m/s

UNIVERSAL WAVE EQUATION

The speed of a wave can also be determined from its wave characteristics (wave length and frequency).

$$v = \lambda f \quad \text{(universal wave equation)}$$

This equation is really a form of the definition of uniform motion

$$v = \frac{d}{t}$$

When we are talking about a wave, the distance from crest to crest is a wavelength. That is, wavelength is a distance. The time it takes a wave to travel one wavelength is the period (T) of the wave.

$$v = \frac{\lambda}{T}$$

but $\qquad T = \frac{1}{f}$

therefore
$$v = \lambda f$$

Activity 14

- Design an experiment to determine the speed of water waves.
- Determine the speed of the wave using your design.
- Suggestion: Use a ripple tank and create a wave pulse. Measure with a stopwatch the time it takes the pulse to travel a certain distance.

  Calculate the speed using $v = \dfrac{d}{t}$.

Example 1

A wave has a frequency of 2.10 Hz and a wavelength of 5.30 m. What is its speed?

Solution

$$v = \lambda f$$
$$= (5.30\text{ m})(2.10\text{ Hz})$$
$$= 11.1\text{ m/s}$$

Example 2

A wave has a speed of 5.0×10^{-1} m/s and a wavelength of 2.0 m. What is its period?

Solution

$$v = \lambda f$$

$$f = \frac{v}{\lambda}$$

$$= \frac{5.0 \times 10^{-1}\text{ m/s}}{2.0\text{ m}}$$

$$= 0.25\text{ Hz}$$

$$T = \frac{1}{f}$$

$$= \frac{1}{0.25}$$

$$= 4.0\text{ s}$$

PRACTICE EXERCISES

Formulae: $T = \dfrac{1}{f}$ $v = \lambda f$ $v = \dfrac{d}{t}$

1. A wave has a frequency of 5.0×10^{-1} Hz and a speed of 3.3×10^{-1} m/s. What is the wavelength of this wave?

2. A form of energy travels as a wave front that moves 4.60 m in 2.00 s. What is the speed of the wave?

3. A water wave has a wavelength of 5.0 m and a speed of 2.5 m/s. What is the period of this wave?

4. A student counts 9.5 waves breaking on the beach in 1.0 min. What is the frequency in hertz of these waves?

5. If sound waves travel at 335 m/s, what is the wavelength of sound that has a period of 1.00×10^{-2} s?

6. A radio station broadcasts at a frequency of 1.00×10^6 Hz. If the speed of this wave is 3.00×10^8 m/s, what is its wavelength?

7. While floating on your air mattress on a lake, you note that you bob up and down 4.0×10^1 times in 5.0 minutes, and you estimate that the distance between the crests is 4.0 m. What is the estimated speed of the water waves?

8. A light wave has a speed of 3.00×10^8 m/s. If the length of this wave is 5.00×10^{-7} m, what is its period?

9. How deep is a lake if a sonar signal reflected from its bottom is detected 0.62 s after the original signal was transmitted? $\left(v_w = 1.46 \times 10^3 \text{ m/s}\right)$

10. While fishing near a high cliff, a fisherman shouts. If he hears the echo 1.05 s after he shouts, how far is he from the cliff?

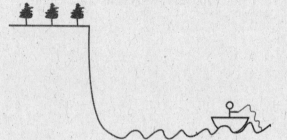

Lesson 6 REFLECTION OF WAVES

When a wave reaches a boundary between two media, some or all of the wave reflects. Waves obey the same law of reflection that particles do. The law of reflection states that the angle of reflection equals the angle of incidence. A billiard ball moving toward the cushion without any sideways spin will obey this law as it bounces off the cushion. Waves, both electromagnetic and mechanical, obey this law as well. The following is a ray diagram.

The angle of incidence and the angle of reflection are measured from the normal

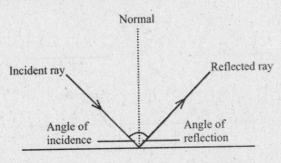

Incidence means incoming. Normal is a line perpendicular to the reflecting surface.

Note that the angle of incidence and the angle of reflection are measured with respect to the normal.

In the construction of a concert hall, the builder wants to eliminate echoes. Echoes are simply the reflection of sound. Sonar devices are used to detect the presence of objects (fish, submarines) in water. These devices emit a sound wave and detect the reflected wave. By knowing the time between the transmission and reflection, it is possible to determine the depth of the object in the water.

Mirrors and satellite dishes are other devices that make use of reflection.

Activity 15

• Draw a wave front diagram illustrating reflection.

• Draw a ray diagram illustrating reflection.

SUPERPOSITION PRINCIPLE

The superposition principle states that when there are two or more sources of waves in a medium, these waves will combine to give a resultant wave that is the algebraic sum of all the waves.

a)

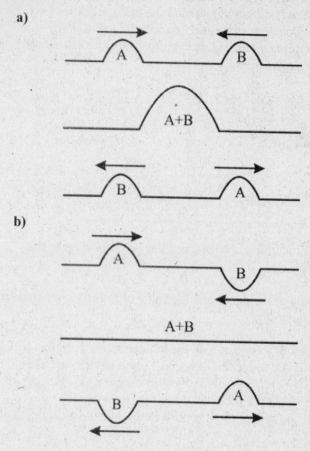

b)

This superposition principle explains constructive and destructive interference.

When a crest from one source meets a crest from another source, the energies combine to displace the medium (we add the energies together). When a trough meets a trough, the same thing happens. When a crest and trough meet, the energies combine to work against each other—they tend to cancel out. In each case, the energies (crest and trough) pass through each other, only having an effect where they meet. This is what we call constructive and destructive interference. In water two point sources will produce an interference pattern as shown below.

Note that we are observing both constructive interference (max) and destructive interference (min).

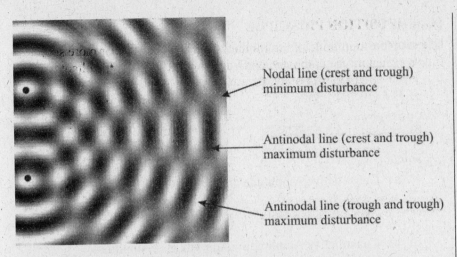

Nodal line (crest and trough)
minimum disturbance

Antinodal line (crest and trough)
maximum disturbance

Antinodal line (trough and trough)
maximum disturbance

Constructive interference:
a maximum

Destructive interference:
a minimum

If you were sunning yourself on an air mattress on the middle of a lake, and a giant started dipping his fingers into the corners of the lake, you would be in for a rough ride if you were on one of the maximums. However, you would not be aware the giant was around if you were on one of the minimums. On the water, these maximums define lines called antinodal lines that represent constructive interference (crest plus crest and trough plus trough).

Regions on the water where crests from one source meet troughs from another undergo destructive interference. Such regions, where the water surface is calm, are called nodal lines.

Constructive and destructive interference of sound waves result in beats. If the sound waves combine in phase, there is constructive interference. If the sound waves combine out of phase, there is destructive interference. Beats can be produced by using two tuning forks of slightly different frequencies. As the waves move together in and out of phase, the sound will reach a maximum (constructive interference) and then a minimum (destructive interference).

This is a wave front diagram illustrating interference.

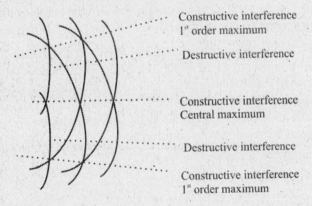

Constructive interference
1st order maximum

Destructive interference

Constructive interference
Central maximum

Destructive interference

Constructive interference
1st order maximum

Example 1

Calculate the amplitude of the combined wave when waves with the following amplitude combine in phase.

a) 2.3 cm and 1.9 cm

b) 5.2 cm and 2.5 cm

Solution

a) Constructive Amplitude $=$ Amplitude$_1 +$ Amplitude$_2$

$$= 2.3\ \text{cm} + 1.9\ \text{cm}$$

$$= 4.2\ \text{cm}$$

b) Constructive Amplitude $=$ Amplitude$_1 +$ Amplitude$_2$

$$= 5.2\ \text{cm} + 2.5\ \text{cm}$$

$$= 7.7\ \text{cm}$$

Example 2

Calculate the amplitude of the combined wave when waves with the following amplitudes combine out of phase.

a) 2.3 cm and 1.9 cm

b) 5.2 cm and 2.5 cm

Solution

a) Destructive Amplitude $= \left| \text{Amplitude}_1 - \text{Amplitude}_2 \right|$

$$= \left| 2.3\ \text{cm} - 1.9\ \text{cm} \right|$$

$$= 0.4\ \text{cm}$$

b) Destructive Amplitude $= \left| \text{Amplitude}_1 - \text{Amplitude}_2 \right|$

$$= \left| 5.2\ \text{cm} - 2.5\ \text{cm} \right|$$

$$= 2.7\ \text{cm}$$

INTERFERENCE OF WAVES

An important application of interference of waves occurs in musical instruments. When a stretched string of a string instrument or an air column in a wind instrument is set in motion by plucking the string or by putting the air in the column in motion by a vibrating object (like a reed or lips), standing waves are set up in the string and air column. Standing waves are produced by interference.

STANDING WAVES

A standing wave gets its name from the fact that the wave pattern does not move.

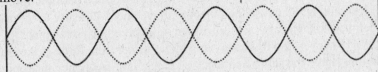

A standing wave results when two wave trains of equal wavelength and amplitudes travel in opposite directions through the same medium. This can happen when a wave train is reflected from a fixed object.

Standing waves have alternating nodes and antinodes. It should be noted that the distance between nodes is $\frac{1}{2}\lambda$.

Node: Region of medium where there is zero amplitude.

Antinode: Region of medium where there is maximum amplitude.

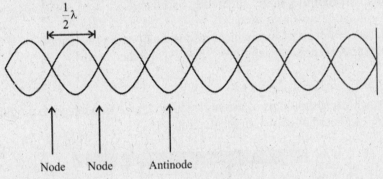

Node   Node   Antinode

Standing waves are produced by the reflecting wave interfering with the incident wave.

A pendulum or a mass vibrating at the end of a spring has one frequency at which it vibrates. A stretched string or air column of a musical instrument will vibrate at a number of frequencies. The lowest frequency that a stretched string will vibrate at is called the fundamental frequency or 1st harmonic. All the other frequencies at which the string will vibrate are whole number multiples of the fundamental frequency.

f = fundamental frequency (or first harmonic)

$2f$ = second harmonic

$3f$ = third harmonic

etc.

It should be noted that many standing wave patterns can form simultaneously on a stretched string or air column. The combined vibration is complex and results from the superposition of the fundamental standing wave with all of the harmonic standing waves. It is these different harmonic combinations that give different musical instruments their characteristic sounds.

The distance between alternating nodes of a standing wave is $\frac{1}{2}\lambda$

Standing waves are produced by the reflecting wave interfering with the incident wave

A node is formed by destructive interference

An antinode is formed by constructive interference

MECHANICAL RESONANCE

In mechanical waves, the energy is carried as a wave. When this wave strikes an object that is free to vibrate, the wave exerts a periodic force on the object which will cause the object to move and eventually to vibrate. In other words, the energy is transmitted as a wave from one object to another. However, the frequency at which this periodic force strikes the object must have the same frequency as the natural frequency that object can vibrate: its resonant frequency. That is, the force must be applied at the right time.

Let's use a playground swing to illustrate this. If you are pushing a child on a swing, there is a right time to push and a wrong time to push. If you push at the right time, the child will swing higher and higher. If you push at the wrong time, the child will not swing higher and higher. There is a right time and a wrong time to add the energy.

Mechanical resonance occurs when two objects have the same natural frequency and one of them is set to vibrate. In a short time, the second object will start to vibrate, apparently on its own.

You can demonstrate mechanical resonance by tying two simple pendulums of the same length to a tightly stretched cord.

Try this:
- Attach two pendulums of the same length (same frequency) to a tightly stretched cord as shown in the diagram.

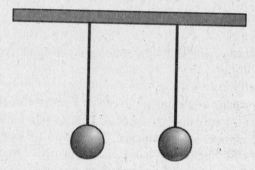

- Start one of the pendulums vibrating.
- Wait a short time (a few seconds), and the other pendulum will begin to vibrate with increasing amplitude.

Why does the second pendulum start to vibrate?

Go back to the example of a child on a playground swing. In order for the child to swing higher and higher, he must pump at the right time. From our study of pendulums, the swing has a natural frequency. That is, it swings so many times per second—the child cannot increase or decrease this. If the child pumps (supplies the force) at the proper times, the swing will go higher and higher.

Remember:

- $f = \dfrac{1}{T}$
- The natural frequency of a mass-spring system depends on the
  - mass
  - spring constant
- The natural frequency of a simple pendulum depends on the
  - length
  - gravitational field

This is what happens to the second pendulum. The energy of the vibration of the first pendulum is transferred through the cord supplying a force just at the right time to the second pendulum.

Now try this:

- Attach two pendulums of different lengths (different frequency) to a tightly stretched cord as shown in the diagram.

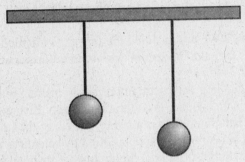

- Start one of the pendulums vibrating.

Question: What happens to the second pendulum?

Answer: It does not begin to vibrate with increasing amplitude.

The vibration of our car at a certain speed is an example of resonance that is annoying. Resonance caused by gusts of wind was responsible for the collapse of the Tacoma Narrows Suspension Bridge in 1940.

Soldiers, marching in step, have been known to set up resonance in bridges strong enough to cause the bridge to collapse. It is now the rule that when soldiers cross a bridge, they break step. Of course, there is the story of the opera singer shattering a glass goblet by hitting a high musical note, but this has never been accomplished without amplification of the volume.

Using the internet, research Tacoma Narrows Bridge

ACOUSTICAL RESONANCE

Acoustical resonance can be demonstrated by holding a vibrating tuning fork over a closed air column as shown in the diagram.

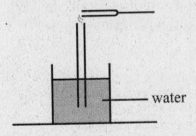
water

Try this:

Adjust the length of the air column and at certain points you will hear the resonance as standing waves are set up in the air column.

And try this:

- Place two tuning forks, mounted on resonating boxes, on opposite sides of a desk.
- Strike the tine of one tuning fork with a rubber mallet.
- Wait a few seconds, and eliminate the vibration of this tuning fork.
- Observe the second fork—it should be vibrating.

How can we explain what we have just observed?

The energy of the wave produced by the first fork supplied periodic force at the right times to make the second fork vibrate further and further.

Resonance and standing waves are important to music

Resonance and standing waves are important in making music. The source of the sound, as in any sound, is a vibrating object. In a musical instrument, the vibrating object is a string, a reed, or the lips of the musician. Musical instruments are classified by scientists as stringed instruments and wind instruments. In the case of stringed instruments, the source of the sound is the vibrating string; however, these strings are attached to a resonating box (guitar), or a resonating surface (piano). This box or surface serves to amplify the sound. Acoustical resonance is no different than mechanical resonance studied in the previous section.

STRETCHED STRINGS

One condition in a vibrating string is that the standing wave produced will always have nodes at the fixed ends.

The following are the simplest examples of this:

$$L = \frac{\lambda}{2}$$

Fundamental frequency (1st Harmonic)

$$L = \lambda$$

2nd Harmonic

$$L = \frac{3\lambda}{2}$$

3rd Harmonic

Recall that a stretched string can vibrate at all harmonics: 1st, 2nd, 3rd, 4th, etc.

Note that the λ of the 2nd harmonic is $\frac{1}{2}$ that of the 1st harmonic.

This is why the frequency is 2 times as large. $(v = \lambda f)$

Note that the λ of the 3rd harmonic is $\frac{1}{3}$ that of the 1st harmonic. This is why the frequency is 3 times as large.

The λ has to be a function of L (length of string) as shown above.

The frequency of a vibrating string depends on its tension and mass as well as its length. We have explained how the frequency depends on its length. We will now focus on the explanation of the relationship between frequency of vibration and the tension and mass.

The speed of vibration through a string depends on the tension and the mass (actually mass/length) according to

$$v = \sqrt{\frac{T}{m/L}}$$

where v = speed

T = tension

m = mass

L = length

This equation is really a form of

$$v = \sqrt{\frac{elasticity}{density}}$$

Knowing the speed of propagation of a wave through a string along with the wavelength (obtained from understanding the relationship of λ and L for a given harmonic) allows a determination of frequency (using the universal wave equation).

$$f = \frac{v}{\lambda}$$

The frequency of a vibrating string depends on its tension and mass as well as its length

m/L is called the linear density

Example 3

A 0.60 m string vibrates at a fundamental frequency of 125 Hz. What is the speed of the wave through the string?

Solution

$$\lambda = 2L$$
$$= 2(0.60 \text{ m})$$
$$= 1.2 \text{ m}$$
$$v = \lambda f$$
$$= (1.2 \text{ m})(125 \text{ Hz})$$
$$= 1.5 \times 10^2 \text{ m/s}$$

Example 4

A vibrating string has a frequency of 375 Hz. If this string is vibrating in four segments, what is its fundamental frequency?

Solution

$$\text{Fundamental } f = \frac{375 \text{ Hz}}{4}$$
$$= 93.8 \text{ Hz}$$

Example 5

A 1.2 m string has a mass of 1.9 g. This string is tightened to a tension of 18.9 N. What is the speed of the wave travelling on this string?

Solution

$$v = \sqrt{\frac{T}{m/L}}$$
$$= \sqrt{\frac{18.9 \text{ N}}{1.9 \times 10^{-3} \text{ kg}/1.2 \text{ m}}}$$
$$= 1.1 \times 10^2 \text{ m/s} \quad .$$

PRACTICE EXERCISE

Formulae: $v = \lambda f$ $v = \sqrt{\dfrac{T}{m/L}}$

1. A 1.2 m string vibrates at a fundamental frequency of 65 Hz. What is the speed of the wave through the string?

2. A vibrating string has a frequency of 144 Hz. If this string is vibrating in three segments, what is its fundamental frequency?

3. If the fundamental frequency of a vibrating string is 354 Hz, what is the frequency of its 3rd harmonic?

4. If the frequency of the 4th harmonic of a vibrating string is 2.5×10^3 Hz, what is the fundamental frequency of this string?

5. If the frequency of the 3rd harmonic of a vibrating string is 1.2×10^3 Hz, what is the frequency of its 2nd harmonic?

6. A string on a musical instrument vibrates in three segments at a frequency of 335 Hz. If this same string vibrates in four segments, what is its frequency?

7. The fundamental frequency of a 27.0 cm string is 637 Hz. What would the fundamental frequency of this same string be if it was 22.0 cm long?

8. The fundamental frequency of a string that is 25 cm long is 441 Hz. In order to produce a fundamental frequency of 525 Hz using the same string, to what length must the string be shortened?

9. A 0.80 m string has a mass of 1.9 g. This string is tightened to a tension of 23 N. What is the speed of the wave travelling on this string?

10. What is the fundamental frequency of the sound produced by the vibrating string in Question 9?

11. A 5.0 m cord has a mass of 195 g. This cord is tightened to a tension of 80.0 N. What is the fundamental frequency of the vibrating cord?

12. A 2.6 m cord has a mass of 98 g. To what tension must this cord be tightened in order that its fundamental frequency of vibration is 133 Hz?

13. Musicians tune their stringed instruments by changing the tension on the strings. If a 0.600 m string under a tension of 1.00×10^2 N produces a fundamental frequency of 224 Hz, what tension would be required to produce a fundamental frequency of 231 Hz?

14. A string 0.50 m long is tightened to a tension of 12 N. If the speed of the wave travelling in the string is 65 m/s, what is the mass of the string?

Lesson 7 AIR COLUMNS

In the case of wind instruments, the reed or lips vibrate at various frequencies; however, the resonating air column (it is the air column that resonates—not a box) can only resonate at certain specific frequencies.

When studying air columns, we need to classify them as
- closed air columns
- opened air columns

Air columns:
- closed air columns
- open air columns

CLOSED AIR COLUMNS

For a standing wave in a closed air column, there is always a node at the closed end and an antinode at the open end.

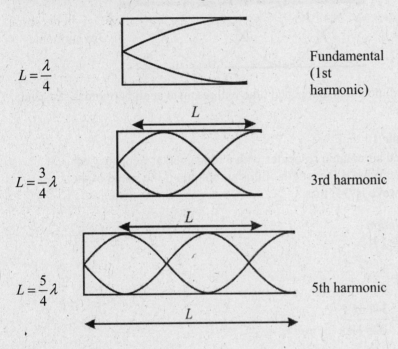

$L = \dfrac{\lambda}{4}$ Fundamental (1st harmonic)

$L = \dfrac{3}{4}\lambda$ 3rd harmonic

$L = \dfrac{5}{4}\lambda$ 5th harmonic

You will note that closed tubes will resonate (vibrate) at only odd numbered harmonics: 1st, 3rd, 5th, 7th, etc.

Note that the wavelength of the 3rd harmonic is $\dfrac{1}{3}$ that of the 1st harmonic.

Most brass and woodwind instruments can be classified as opened air columns

OPENED AIR COLUMNS

For a standing wave in an opened air column, there is always an antinode at both ends.

$$L = \frac{\lambda}{2}$$ Fundamental 1st harmonic

$$L = \lambda$$ 2nd harmonic

$$L = \frac{3\lambda}{2}$$ 3rd harmonic

Opened tubes resonate at all harmonics

You will note that an opened tube will resonate at all harmonics, 1st, 2nd, 3rd, etc.

Example 1

A closed air column resonates with a fundamental frequency of 225 Hz. What is the length of this air column if the speed of the sound wave is 341 m/s ?

Solution

$$v = \lambda f$$

$$\lambda = \frac{v}{f}$$

$$= \frac{341 \, \text{m/s}}{225 \, \text{Hz}}$$

$$= 1.52 \, \text{m}$$

$$\lambda = 4L$$

$$L = \frac{\lambda}{4}$$

$$= \frac{1.52 \, \text{m}}{4}$$

$$= 0.379 \, \text{m}$$

Example 2

An opened air column resonates with a fundamental frequency of 334 Hz. If the length of the air column is 51.0 cm, what is the speed of the sound wave?

Solution

$$\lambda = 2L$$
$$= 2(0.510\,\text{m})$$
$$= 1.02\,\text{m}$$
$$v = \lambda f$$
$$= (1.02\,\text{m})(334\,\text{Hz})$$
$$= 341\,\text{m/s}$$

Activity 16

- Design an experiment to determine the speed of sound.

- Determine the speed of sound using your design.

- Suggestion: Use a closed tube that you can vary the length of and a tuning fork of known frequency.

PRACTICE EXERCISE

Formulae: $v = \lambda f$ **For fundamental frequencies:**   −closed tubes $\lambda = 4L$
−opened tubes $\lambda = 2L$

1. A closed air column resonates with a fundamental frequency of 256 Hz. What is the length of this air column if the speed of the sound wave is 343 m/s ?

2. A closed air column resonates with a fundamental frequency of 4.40×10^2 Hz. If the length of the air column is 18.9 cm, what is the speed of the sound wave?

3. If a closed air column resonates with a fundamental frequency of 384 Hz, what is the frequency of its 3rd harmonic?

4. A 55 cm closed air column will resonate to many frequencies; however, the lowest frequency to which it resonates is 156 Hz. What is the speed of the sound wave?

5. What is the shortest closed air column that will resonate to a sound source (tuning fork) that has a frequency of 4.40×10^2 Hz, assuming that the speed of sound is 341 m/s ?

6. An opened air column resonates with a fundamental frequency of 256 Hz. What is the length of the air column if the speed of the sound wave is 341 m/s ?

7. An opened air column resonates with a fundamental frequency of 512 Hz. If the length of the air column is 33.0 cm, what is the speed of the sound wave?

8. If an opened air column resonates with a fundamental frequency of 384 Hz, what is the frequency of the next greatest harmonic to which this column will resonate?

9. If a closed air column resonates with a fundamental frequency of 384 Hz, what is the frequency of the next greatest harmonic to which this column will resonate?

Lesson 8   DOPPLER EFFECT

If there is a relative motion between the source of a wave and the receiver of the wave, the frequency received will be different from the frequency of the source. If the source is moving away from the receiver, the frequency received will be less than the frequency of the source.

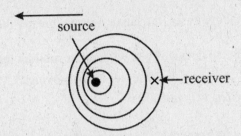

If the source is moving toward the receiver, the frequency received will be greater than the frequency of the source.

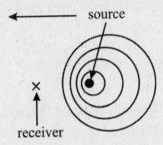

This is known as the Doppler effect. We are aware of this with sound waves. Have you ever been waiting at a railroad crossing for a train to go by? As the train approaches with its whistle blowing, you hear a high frequency sound (we call it pitch). When the train (source of whistle) has passed, the sound drops to a low frequency (low pitch)—this is an example of the Doppler effect in action.

MATHEMATICS OF DOPPLER EFFECT

$$f' = f_0 \left(\frac{v \pm v_o}{v \pm v_s} \right)$$

where f' = apparent frequency

f_0 = frequency of source

v = speed of wave

v_o = speed of observer

v_s = speed of wave source

You will note that this equation tells us that the apparent frequency equals the frequency of the source times some factor.

$$f' = f_0 \,(\text{factor})$$

NOTES

You know that the apparent frequency is greater than frequency of the source when:

- the observer is moving toward the source
- the source is moving toward the observer
- or both of the above

Therefore, in the above cases, the factor must be greater than 1.

Use this knowledge to decide if you will add or subtract the value of v_o and v_s. Now, of course, if the observer is not moving, $v_o = \text{zero}$. If the source is not moving, $v_s = \text{zero}$.

In the same way, you know that the apparent frequency is less than the frequency of the source when:

- the observer is moving away from the source
- the source is moving away from the observer
- or both

In the above cases, the factor must be less than 1.

Example 1

A car travelling 29 m/s toward a stationary sound (whistle) that has a frequency of 625 Hz. If the speed of sound is 337 m/s, what is the apparent frequency of the sound as heard by the driver of the car?

Solution

$$f' = f_o \left(\frac{v \pm v_o}{v \pm v_s} \right)$$

$$= (625 \text{ Hz}) \left(\frac{337 \text{ m/s} + 29 \text{ m/s}}{337 \text{ m/s} - 0} \right)$$

$$= 679 \text{ Hz}$$

Example 2

If the car in the Example 1 was travelling away from the stationary sound, what would the apparent frequency of the sound be as heard by the driver of the car?

Solution

$$f' = f_o \left(\frac{v \pm v_o}{v \pm v_s} \right)$$

$$= (625 \text{ Hz}) \left(\frac{337 \text{ m/s} - 29 \text{ m/s}}{337 \text{ m/s} - 0} \right)$$

$$= 571 \text{ Hz}$$

Example 3

A whistle with a frequency of 965 Hz is moving at a speed of 23 m/s toward a stationary observer. If the speed of sound is 342 m/s, what is the apparent frequency of the sound as heard by the observer?

Solution

$$f' = f_o \left(\frac{v \pm v_o}{v \pm v_s} \right)$$

$$= (965 \text{ Hz}) \left(\frac{342 \text{ m/s} - 0}{342 \text{ m/s} - 23 \text{ m/s}} \right)$$

$$= 1.03 \times 10^3 \text{ Hz}$$

Example 4

If the whistle in Example 3 was moving away from the stationary observer, what would the apparent frequency of the sound be as heard by the observer?

Solution

$$f' = f_o \left(\frac{v \pm v_o}{v \pm v_s} \right)$$

$$= (965 \text{ Hz}) \left(\frac{342 \text{ m/s} - 0}{342 \text{ m/s} + 23 \text{ m/s}} \right)$$

$$= 904 \text{ Hz}$$

PRACTICE EXERCISE

Formula: $\quad f' = f_0 \left(\dfrac{v \pm v_0}{v \pm v_s} \right)$

1. A train is moving at a speed of 32 m/s toward a stationary observer with its whistle $\left(f_0 = 1.85 \times 10^3 \text{ Hz} \right)$ sounding. If the speed of sound is 341 m/s, what is the apparent frequency as heard by the stationary observer?

2. If the train in Problem 1 is moving away from the observer, what would the apparent frequency be as heard by the observer?

3. You are approaching a stationary whistle ($f_0 = 2.15 \times 10^3$ Hz) at a speed of 25 m/s. If the speed of sound is 339 m/s, what is the apparent frequency that you hear?

4. You are moving away from the whistle in Problem 3 at a speed of 25 m/s. If the speed of sound is still 339 m/s, what is the apparent frequency that you hear?

5. A whistle $\left(f_0 = 2.50 \times 10^3 \text{ Hz} \right)$ is travelling south at a velocity of 27 m/s. You are travelling north toward this whistle at a velocity of 15 m/s. If the speed of sound is 341 m/s, what is the apparent frequency of the whistle as heard by you?

6. A whistle $\left(f_0 = 2.50 \times 10^3 \text{ Hz} \right)$ is travelling south at a velocity of 27 m/s. You are travelling north away from the whistle at a velocity of 15 m/s. If the speed of sound is 341 m/s, what is the apparent frequency of the whistle as heard by you?

7. You are travelling toward a stationary whistle ($f_0 = 2.90 \times 10^3$ Hz), The apparent frequency of this whistle is 3.13×10^3 Hz. If the speed of sound is 343 m/s, how fast are you travelling?

8. A whistle $\left(f_0 = 2.20 \times 10^3 \text{ Hz} \right)$ is moving away from a stationary observer. The apparent frequency of the sound as heard by the observer is 2.08×10^3 Hz. If the speed of sound is 3.40×10^2 m/s, what is the speed of the whistle?

9. You are moving toward a stationary whistle at a speed of 3.00×10^1 m/s. The sound that you hear has an apparent frequency of 1.50×10^3 Hz. If the speed of sound is 3.40×10^2 m/s, what is the actual frequency of the whistle?

REVIEW SUMMARY

In this unit, we studied:
- oscillatory motion (simple harmonic motion)
- waves as a means of transmitting energy

Simple harmonic motion is motion in which the restoring force (elastic force) is directly proportional to the displacement.

Hooke's Law: the restoring force (elastic force) is directly proportional to the displacement.
$$\vec{F}_s = -kx$$

A mass at the end of a spring will vibrate back and forth, moving with simple harmonic motion.

A simple pendulum will also oscillate back and forth, moving with simple harmonic motion. The restoring force acting on the simple pendulum is found using:
$$\vec{F}_s = -mg\sin\theta$$

Simple harmonic motion can be described in terms of its frequency or period.
- For a mass-spring system:
$$T = 2\pi\sqrt{\frac{m}{k}}$$
- For a simple pendulum:
$$T = 2\pi\sqrt{\frac{L}{g}}$$

Remember: $f = \dfrac{1}{T}$

When a frictionless mass-spring system or a simple pendulum undergoes simple harmonic motion, kinetic energy is changed to potential energy and back into kinetic energy over and over. However, the mechanical energy remains constant.
$$\text{mechanical energy} = E_k + E_p$$

WAVES
- Waves are a means of transmitting energy.
- Every point in a wave vibrates in simple harmonic motion.
- The universal wave equation describes the relationship between speed, wavelength and frequency of a wave.
$$v = \lambda f$$

- The superposition principle states that when there are two or more sources of waves in a medium, these waves will combine to give a resultant wave that is the algebraic sum of all the waves.
  - This results in constructive and destructive interference.
  - Standing waves may also be the result of constructive and destructive interference when the wave reflects back along the incident wave.
  - The distance between adjacent nodes in a standing wave is a half a wavelength.
- Standing waves and resonance are important to music.
- Stretched strings produce all harmonics (1st, 2nd, 3rd, etc. harmonics).
- The speed of a wave through a string depends on the tension and the density of the string.

$$v = \sqrt{\frac{T}{m/L}}$$

- The length of the fundamental wavelength is described by
  $$\lambda = 2L \qquad (L = \text{length of string})$$

AIR COLUMNS

- Closed air columns produce only odd numbered harmonics (1st, 3rd, 5th, etc. harmonics).
- The length of the fundamental wavelength in a closed air column is described by:
  $$\lambda = 4L \qquad (L = \text{length of column})$$
- Open air columns produce all harmonics (1st, 2nd, 3rd, etc. harmonics).
- The length of the fundamental wavelength in an open air column is described by
  $$\lambda = 2L \qquad (L = \text{length of column})$$
- Doppler Effect
  - If there is relative motion between the source of a wave and the receiver of a wave, the frequency received will be different from the frequency of the source.

$$f' = f_0 \left(\frac{v \pm v_0}{v \pm v_s} \right)$$

where f' = apparent frequency

f_0 = frequency of source

v = speed of wave

v_0 = speed of observer

v_s = speed of wave source

REVIEW EXERCISE

Ignore air friction in all problems unless otherwise stated.

1. A 0.18 kg mass is vibrating at the end of a horizontal spring along a frictionless surface. If the spring constant is 0.21 N/m, what is the displacement of the mass when its acceleration is $0.13 \, \text{m/s}^2$?

2. A 0.250 kg mass vibrates at the end of a horizontal spring $(k = 94.5 \, \text{N/m})$ along a frictionless surface. When the displacement is 0.030 0 m, what is its acceleration?

3. A 1.20 kg mass vibrates at the end of a horizontal spring along a frictionless surface. What is the spring constant if the mass has an acceleration of $8.20 \, \text{m/s}^2$ when the displacement is 0.050 m?

4. A 0.22 kg pendulum bob is swinging back and forth from the end of a 0.62 m string. What is the acceleration of the pendulum bob when the bob is at the end position if the string is making an angle of 8.0° with the vertical?

5. A 0.300 kg mass is vibrating at the end of a horizontal spring $(k = 29.2 \text{ N/m})$ along a frictionless horizontal surface reaching a maximum speed of 0.620 m/s. What is the maximum displacement of this mass?

6. In Question 5, what is the speed of the mass when its displacement is 0.035 0 m?

7. A 0.750 kg mass is vibrating at the end of a horizontal spring $(k = 115 \text{ N/m})$ along a frictionless horizontal surface. The maximum displacement is 0.045 0 m. What is the kinetic energy of this mass when its displacement is 0.022 0 m?

8. If the period of vibration of a mass-spring system is 0.250 s when a 0.012 0 kg mass is attached to the spring, what is the spring constant?

9. A 7.20 N object vibrates up and down from the end of a vertical spring $(k = 21.3 \text{ N/m})$. What is the frequency of vibration?

10. An object vibrates at the end of a horizontal spring $(k = 112 \text{ N/m})$ along a horizontal frictionless surface. It reaches a maximum speed of 0.820 m/s and a maximum displacement of 0.041 0 m. What is the period of the vibration?

11. What is the acceleration due to gravity at a location where a 0.450 m pendulum has a frequency of 0.740 Hz?

12. A clock uses a pendulum to keep time. If the period of the oscillating pendulum is 1.00 s, how long is the pendulum? $(g = 9.81 \text{ m/s}^2)$

13. A 0.20 kg mass vibrates at the end of a horizontal spring $(k = 0.800 \text{ N/m})$ along a frictionless surface. The kinetic energy at the equilibrium position is 3.00×10^{-3} J.

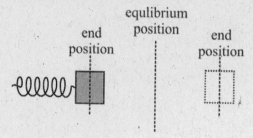

a) What is the speed of the object at the equilibrium position?

b) The formula for elastic potential energy is $E_p = \frac{1}{2}kx^2$ (k = spring constant, x = displacement). What is the maximum displacement?

c) Starting with Hooke's law and the mathematical definition of work, derive the equation in part **b)**.

d) What is the total mechanical energy when the mass is halfway between the end position and the equilibrium position?

14. A wave has a frequency of 5.00×10^{-1} Hz and a wavelength of 3.00×10^{-1} m. How long does it take a crest to travel 25.0 m?

15. If a laser beam takes 1.20 s to travel to a space craft and back, how far away is the craft?

16. An observer is moving at a speed of 22.0 m/s toward a stationary sound source $\left(f_o = 1.00 \times 10^3 \text{ Hz} \right)$.

    If the speed of sound is 341 m/s, what is the apparent frequency heard by the observer?

17. A sound source $\left(f_o = 1.00 \times 10^3 \text{ Hz} \right)$ is moving north at a speed of 30.0 m/s while you are also moving north along the same path at 25.0 m/s. If the speed of sound is 341 m/s, what is the apparent frequency of the sound that you hear? (Assume that you are in front of the source.)

18. The nodes of a standing wave on a stretched string are 15.0 cm apart. If the string vibrates at 375 Hz, what is the speed of the wave moving through the string?

19. A closed air column resonates with a fundamental frequency of 256 Hz. If the length of the air column is 0.330 m, what is the speed of the sound wave through air?

20. What is the fundamental frequency of a 20.0 cm opened air column? (Assume the speed of sound is 342 m/s)

21. A form of energy travels as a wave 25.5 m in 1.00 min. If the frequency of this wave is 10.0 Hz, what is the wavelength?

22. A form of energy travels as a wave 25.5 m in 1.00 min. If the frequency of this wave is 10.0 Hz, what is the wavelength?

PRACTICE TEST

1. Two physics students are discussing periodic motion. Student 1 says, "All periodic motion is simple harmonic motion." Student 2 says, "All simple harmonic motion is periodic motion."

   Which of these students, if any, is/are correct?

   A. Student 1

   B. Student 2

   C. Both students are correct.

   D. Neither student is correct.

2. If simple harmonic motion is defined as periodic motion in which the restoring force is directly proportional to the displacement, which of the following statements must also be correct?

   A. The acceleration is directly proportional to the displacement.

   B. The acceleration is inversely proportional to the displacement.

   C. The speed is directly proportional to the displacement.

   D. The speed is inversely proportional to the displacement.

3. In the diagram at right showing a vibrating simple pendulum, which of the vectors indicate best the direction of the acceleration of the pendulum bob when it is at position P?

   A. 1

   B. 2

   C. 3

   D. 4

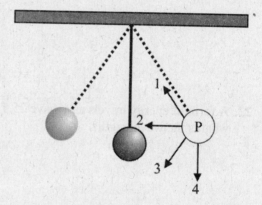

4. In the diagram at right showing a vibrating simple pendulum, which of the vectors indicate best the direction of the restoring force acting on the pendulum bob when it is at position P?

   A. 1

   B. 2

   C. 3

   D. 4

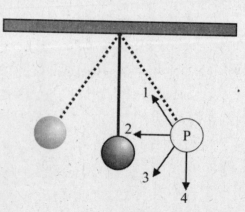

5. The diagrams at right show a mass vibrating at the end of a horizontal spring along a frictionless surface at three different positions. At what position, if any, is the speed of the mass the greatest?

   A. 1

   B. 2

   C. 3

   D. All have the same speed.

Position 1 (equilibrium position)

Position 2

Position 3 (end position)

6. Using the diagram in Question 5, at what position, if any, is the acceleration of the mass zero?

   A. 1   B. 2

   C. 3   D. All have the same acceleration

7. Using the diagram in Question 5, at what position, if any, is the mechanical energy the greatest?

   A. 1   B. 2

   C. 3   D. All have the same mechanical energy

8. Using the diagram in Question 5, at what position, if any, is the kinetic energy of the mass the greatest?

   A. 1   B. 2

   C. 3   D. All have the same mechanical energy

9. If an object vibrates back and forth 100 times per minute, what is the period of the motion?

   A. 0.600 s   B. 1.67 s

   C. 60.0 s

10. Which of the following graphs best shows the relationship of the restoring force as a function of time for a mass vibrating in simple harmonic motion at the end of a horizontal spring along a frictionless surface?

A.

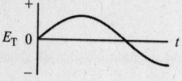

B.

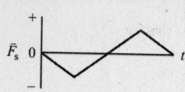

C.

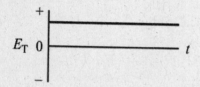

D.

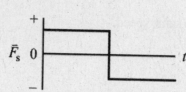

11. Which of the following graphs best shows the relationship of the mechanical energy as a function of time for a mass vibrating in simple harmonic motion at the end of a horizontal spring along a frictionless surface?

A.

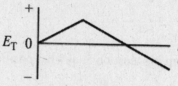

B.

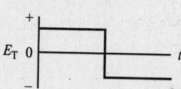

C.

D.

12. The frequency of a simple pendulum depends on

   i)   the mass of the pendulum bob

   ii) the length of the pendulum

The correct answer is:

A. i) only

B. ii) only

C. both i) and ii)

D. neither i) nor ii)

13. The frequency of a mass vibrating in simple harmonic motion at the end of a horizontal spring along a frictionless surface depends on

    i)   the mass

    ii) the spring constant

The correct answer is

A. i) only   **B.** ii) only

C. both i) and ii)   **D.** neither i) nor ii)

14. The spring constant of a 10.0 cm spring is 4.2 N/m . If this spring is cut in half, what is the spring constant of each half?

A. 2.1 N/m   **B.** 4.2 N/m

C. 8.2 N/m

15. The amplitude of a mass vibrating at the end of a horizontal spring along a frictionless surface depends on

    i)   the frequency of the vibration

    ii) the energy of the vibration

The correct answer is

A. i) only   **B.** ii) only

C. both i) and ii)   **D.** neither i) nor ii)

16. A physics student tells her friend that when a mass is vibrating at the end of a horizontal spring along a frictionless surface, the following quantities are zero at the equilibrium position:

    i)   restoring force

    ii) mechanical energy

    iii) elastic potential energy

Which of these quantities are correct?

A. i) and ii) only   **B.** i) and iii) only

C. ii) and iii) only   **D.** i), ii), and iii) are all correct

17. If you know the wavelength of a wave and its period, which of the following information about the wave can you calculate?

    i) .the speed of the wave

    ii) the frequency of the wave

    iii) the amplitude of the wave

A. All of the above: i), ii) and iii)

B. i) and ii) only

C. ii) and iii) only

D. i) and iii) only

18. When a train that is travelling at a speed of 80 km/h goes by you with its whistle blowing as you stand near the railroad track, the frequency of the whistle sound appears to fall (decrease). This phenomenon is most closely related to or referred to as

A. refraction

B. diffraction

C. the superposition principle

D. the Doppler effect

19. A transverse wave is travelling through a medium at a speed of 10.0 cm/s. If this wave has an amplitude of 5.0 cm and a wavelength of 2.0 cm/s, what is the frequency of the wave?

A. 2.0 Hz

B. 5.0 Hz

C. 20 Hz

D. 50 Hz

20. If a longitudinal wave is traveling through a medium, the particles in the medium are vibrating

A. parallel to the directions that the energy is transmitted through the medium

B. perpendicular to the direction that the energy is transmitted through the medium

C. in a circular path relative to the direction that the energy is transmitted through the medium

D. in an elliptical path relative to the direction that the energy is transmitted through the medium

21. In an interference pattern, there are maxima and minima. The maxima result when waves meet

A. out of phase

B. in phase

C. with the same frequencies

D. with the same amplitudes

22. A police car with its siren sounding is travelling at 100 km/h as it goes by you as you sit alongside the road as shown. At which position would the frequency of the siren appear to be the lowest?

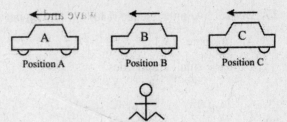

Position A   Position B   Position C

You

A. Position A

B. Position B

C. Position C

D. It would appear to be the same at all positions.

23. P represents a point on a transverse wave. Over a period of time, the motion of point P can best be described as

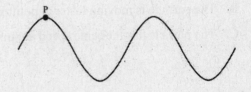

A. stopped

B. uniform motion

C. uniformly accelerated motion

D. simple harmonic motion

24. The diagram represents a transverse wave. A wavelength can best be described as the distance between

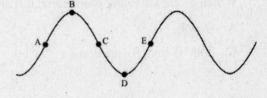

A. A and C   B. B and D

C. A and E   D. C and E

25. Constructive interference can best be explained using

A. the Doppler effect   B. resonance

C. the superposition principle   D. reflection

26. In order to explain the production of a standing wave, we need to make use of which of the following?

    i) The superposition principle

    ii) Reflection

    iii) Resonance

The best answer is

A. i) and ii) only   B. ii) and iii) only

C. i) and iii) only   D. i), ii) and iii)

27. Destructive interference results when waves

    A. resonate

    C. have small amplitudes

    B. meet out of phase

    D. reflect from a fixed end

28. A particle in a mechanical wave moves from point B to point A. Which of the following is correct concerning the speed of this particle?

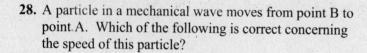

    A. The particle is moving faster at point A

    B. The particle is moving faster at point B

    C. The particle has the same speed at points A and B

29. A student is telling his friend that when the frequency of sound increases, the

    i)   the wavelength decreases, and

    ii) the speed of the wave increases

Which of the following is/are correct, if any?

    A. i) only

    C. both i) and ii) are correct

    B. ii) only

    D. neither i) nor ii) are correct

30. Which of the following points on a vibrating string are in phase with point A?

    A. All points: B, C, D and E

    B. B and C only

    C. C and E only

    D. B and D only

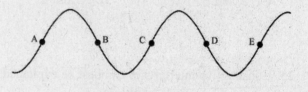

CONSTANTS

Acceleration due to gravity near Earth	$g = 9.81 \text{ m/s}^2$ (or N/kg)
Gravitation field near Earth	$g = 9.81 \text{ m/s}^2$ (or N/kg)
Gravitational Constant	$G = 6.67 \times 10^{-11} \ \dfrac{\text{N} \cdot \text{m}^2}{\text{kg}^2}$
Mass of Earth	$M_E = 5.98 \times 10^{24} \text{ kg}$
Radius of Earth	$r_E = 6.37 \times 10^6 \text{ m}$

EQUATIONS

KINEMATICS AND DYNAMICS

$$v = \frac{d}{t}$$

$$\vec{a} = \frac{\vec{v}_f - \vec{v}_i}{t}$$

$$\vec{d} = \vec{v}_i t + \frac{1}{2} \vec{a} t^2$$

$$\vec{d} = \left(\frac{\vec{v}_f + \vec{v}_i}{2} \right) t$$

$$\vec{v}_f^{\,2} = \vec{v}_i^{\,2} + 2 \vec{a} \vec{d}$$

$$\vec{F}_{net} = m \vec{a}$$

$$\vec{F}_g = mg$$

$$F_N = mg \cos \theta$$

$$\vec{F}_f = \mu \vec{F}_N \quad \text{or} \quad \vec{F}_f = \mu mg \cos \theta$$

$$\vec{F}_g = \frac{G m_1 m_2}{r^2}$$

$$g = \frac{Gm}{r^2}$$

ENERGY

$$W = Fd$$

$$P = Wt \quad \text{or} \quad P = \frac{\Delta E}{t} \quad \text{or} \quad P = Fv$$

$$E_k = \frac{1}{2} mv^2$$

$$E_p = mgh \quad \text{(gravitational)}$$

$$E_p = \frac{1}{2} kx^2 \quad \text{(elastic)}$$

SIMPLE HARMONIC MOTION

$\vec{F}_s = -kx$ (mass-spring) $T = 2\pi\sqrt{\dfrac{m}{k}}$

$\vec{F}_s = mg\sin\theta$ (pendulum) $T = 2\pi\sqrt{\dfrac{L}{g}}$

CIRCULAR MOTION

$v = 2\pi r f$ $\dfrac{T^2}{r^3} = K$ or $\dfrac{T_1^2}{r_1^3} = \dfrac{T_2^2}{r_2^3}$

$v = \dfrac{2\pi r}{T}$ $v = \sqrt{\dfrac{Gm_E}{r}}$

$a_c = \dfrac{v^2}{r}$ $T = \dfrac{2\pi r^{3/2}}{\sqrt{Gm_E}}$ or $T = \sqrt{\dfrac{4\pi^2 r^3}{Gm_E}}$

$\vec{F}_c = mv^2$

WAVES

$f = \dfrac{1}{T}$ $v = \sqrt{\dfrac{T}{m/L}}$

$v = \lambda f$ $f' = f_o\left(\dfrac{v \pm v_o}{v \pm v_s}\right)$

$\lambda = 2L$ (opened tubes) $\lambda = 4L$ (closed tubes)

TRIGONOMETRY AND VECTORS

$\sin\theta = \dfrac{\text{opposite}}{\text{hypotenuse}}$ $c^2 = a^2 + b^2$

$\cos\theta = \dfrac{\text{adjacent}}{\text{hypotenuse}}$ $R = \sqrt{R_x^2 + R_y^2}$

$\tan\theta = \dfrac{\text{opposite}}{\text{adjacent}}$ $R_x = R\cos\theta$
$R_y = R\sin\theta$

QUADRATIC FORMULA

$x = \dfrac{-b \pm \sqrt{b^2 - 4ac}}{2a}$

Student Notes and Problems

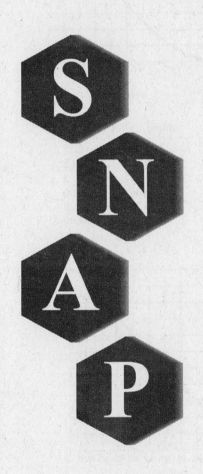

Answers
and
Solutions

INTRODUCTION TO PHYSICS

Lesson 2—Significant Digits and Scientific Notation

1. **a)** 3   **b)** 2

    c) 3   **d)** 1

    e) 3

3. **a)** 72.3 m   **b)** 559 m

    c) 490 m or 4.90×10^2 m

Lesson 3—Graphing

1. **a)** A vs. B

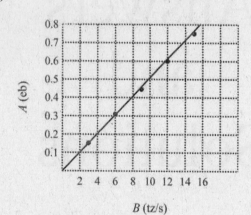

A (eb)

B (tz/s)

b) $\text{slope} = \dfrac{\text{rise}}{\text{run}} = \dfrac{y_2 - y_1}{x_2 - x_1}$

$= \dfrac{0.750 \text{ eb} - 0}{15.0 \text{ tz/s} - 0}$

$= 5.00 \times 10^{-2} \text{ eb} \cdot \text{s/tz}$

c) $A \propto B$ or $A = kB$

3. **a)**

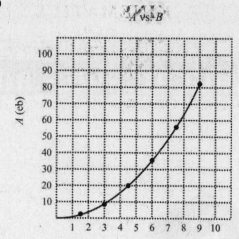

A (eb)

B (tz/s)

b)

B (tz/s)	A (eb)	$B2$ (tz²/s²)
1.5	2.25	2.25
3.0	9.00	9.00
4.5	20.25	20.25
6.0	36.00	36.00
7.5	56.25	56.25
9.0	81.00	81.00

A vs. B^2

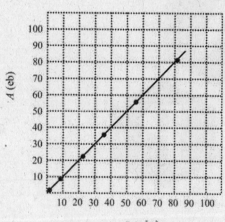

A (eb)

B (tz²/s²)

c) $\text{slope} = \dfrac{\text{rise}}{\text{run}} = \dfrac{y_2 - y_1}{x_2 - x_1}$

$= \dfrac{70 \text{ eb} - 0}{70 \text{ tz}^2/\text{s}^2 - 0}$

$= 1.00 \text{ eb} \cdot \text{s}^2/\text{tz}^2$

d) $A \propto B^2$ or $A = kB^2$

KINEMATICS

Lesson 1—Introduction to Kinematics

1. **a)** $275 + 425 = 700$ m

b) $425 - 275 = 150$ m

3. **a)** $\dfrac{36 \text{ m}}{52 \text{ s}} = \dfrac{9}{13} \text{ m/s}$

b) $\dfrac{14 \text{ m}}{52 \text{ s}} = \dfrac{7}{26} \text{ m/s}$

Lesson 2—Instantaneous Velocity and Speed

1. $v = \dfrac{d}{t}$

$= \dfrac{1.00 \times 10^2 \text{ m}}{11.2 \text{ s}}$

$= 8.93$ m/s west

3. $v = \dfrac{d}{t}$

$t = \dfrac{d}{v}$

$= \dfrac{2.5 \text{ m}}{9.8 \text{ m/s}}$

$= 0.26$ s

5. $v = \dfrac{d}{t}$

$= \dfrac{64.0 \text{ m}}{3.61 \text{ s}}$

$= 17.7$ m/s down

7. Both speed and velocity are equal to the slope of the graph.

$\text{slope} = \dfrac{\text{rise}}{\text{run}}$

$= \dfrac{(8.0 - 0) \text{ m}}{(8.0 - 0) \text{ s}}$

$= 1.0$ m/s

a) speed $= 1.0$ m/s

b) velocity $= 1.0$ m/s north

9. Both the displacement and distance are found by determining the area under the graph.

$\text{area} = l \times w$

$= (5.0 \text{ s})(2.5 \text{ m/s})$

$= 13$ m

a) displacement $= 13$ m west

b) distance $= 13$ m

11. 1st part of the motion

$v = \dfrac{d}{t}$

$d = vt$

$= (8.0 \text{ m/s})(25 \text{ min})(60 \text{ s/min})$

$= 1.2 \times 10^4$ m north

2nd part of the motion

$d = vt$

$= (5.0 \text{ m/s})(15 \text{ min})(60 \text{ s/min})$

$= 4.5 \times 10^3$ m south

Displacement is

$1.2 \times 10^4 \text{ m} - 4.5 \times 10^3 \text{ m} = 7.5 \times 10^3$ m north

Distance is $1.2 \times 10^4 \text{ m} + 4.5 \times 10^3 \text{ m} = 1.65 \times 10^4$ m

a) Average velocity $= \dfrac{\text{displacement}}{t}$

$= \dfrac{7.5 \times 10^3 \text{ m}}{40 \text{ min} \times 60 \text{ s/min}}$

$= 3.1$ m/s north

b) Average speed $= \dfrac{\text{distance}}{t}$

$= \dfrac{1.65 \times 10^4 \text{ m}}{40 \text{ min} \times 60 \text{ s/min}}$

$= 6.9$ m/s

13. **a)**

time (s)	displacement (m)	displacement during time interval (m)	average velocity during time interval (m/s)
0	0		
0.10	0.012	0.012	0.12
0.20	0.024	0.012	0.12
0.30	0.035	0.011	0.11
0.40	0.047	0.012	0.12
0.50	0.060	0.013	0.13
0.60	0.072	0.012	0.12
0.70	0.085	0.013	0.13
0.80	0.097	0.012	0.12
0.90	0.108	0.011	0.11
1.00	0.120	0.012	0.12

b) Position-time graph

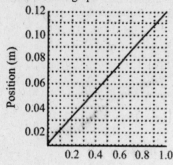

c) Velocity-Time Graph

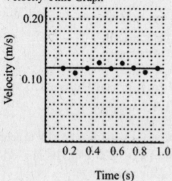

d) slope $= \dfrac{\text{rise}}{\text{run}}$

$$= \dfrac{(0.12 - 0) \text{ m}}{(1.0 - 0) \text{ s}}$$

$$= 0.12 \text{ m/s right}$$

e) displacement = area
area $= l \times w$

$$= (0.95 \text{ s})(0.12 \text{ m/s})$$

$$= 0.11 \text{ m right}$$

Lesson 3—Uniform Accelerated Motion

1. **a) b)** Answers will vary according to your data.

3. **a)** Acceleration is the slope of the velocity-time graph

$$\text{slope} = \dfrac{\text{rise}}{\text{run}}$$

$$= \dfrac{(15.0 - 0) \text{ m/s}}{(7.0 - 0) \text{ s}}$$

$$= 2.1 \text{ m/s}^2 \text{ north}$$

b) Displacement is the area under the velocity-time graph.

$$\text{area} = \dfrac{1}{2}(l \times w)$$

$$= \dfrac{1}{2}(7.0 \text{ s} \times 15.0 \text{ m/s})$$

$$= 53 \text{ m north}$$

5. **a)** Velocity of A = 9.0 m/s east.
Velocity of B = 4.5 m/s east.

$$\text{ratio} = \dfrac{\text{velocity of A}}{\text{velocity of B}}$$

$$= \dfrac{9.0 \text{ m/s}}{4.5 \text{ m/s}}$$

$$= 2.0 \text{ times}$$

A is travelling 2.0 times faster than B.

b) Distance = area

$$\text{area} = \dfrac{1}{2}(l \times w)$$

Distance A travels

$$= \dfrac{1}{2}(5.0 \text{ s} \times 9.0 \text{ m/s})$$

$$= 22.5 \text{ m}$$

Distance B travels

$$= \dfrac{1}{2}(5.0 \text{ s} \times 4.5 \text{ m/s})$$

$$= 11.3 \text{ m}$$

Difference

$$= 22.5 \text{ m} - 11.3 \text{ m}$$

$$= 11 \text{ m}$$

7. **a)** Acceleration = slope

$$\text{slope} = \dfrac{\text{rise}}{\text{run}}$$

$$= \dfrac{(10.0 - 4.0) \text{ m/s}}{(16.0 - 0) \text{ s}}$$

$$= 0.38 \text{ m/s}^2 \text{ west}$$

b) Displacement = area

$$area = (l \times w) + \frac{1}{2}(l \times w)$$

$$= (16.0 \text{ s} \times 4.0 \text{ m/s}) + \frac{1}{2}(16.0 \text{ s} \times 6.0 \text{ m/s})$$

$$= 1.1 \times 10^2 \text{ m west}$$

9. a) Velocity-Time Graph

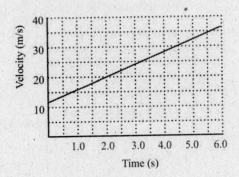

b) i) Acceleration = slope

$$slope = \frac{rise}{run}$$

$$= \frac{(31.8 - 12.0) \text{m/s}}{(6.0 - 0) \text{ s}}$$

$$= 3.3 \text{ m/s}^2 \text{ north}$$

ii) Displacement = area

$$area = (l \times w) + \frac{1}{2}(l \times w)$$

$$= (6.0 \text{ s} \times 12.0 \text{ m/s}) + \frac{1}{2}(6.0 \text{ s} \times 20.0 \text{ m/s})$$

$$= 1.3 \times 10^2 \text{ m north}$$

11. a)

time (s)	displacement from t = 0 (m)	displacement during time interval (m)	average velocity during time interval (m/s)
0	0.0		
0.10	0.02	0.02	0.20
0.20	0.09	0.07	0.70
0.30	0.20	0.11	1.10
0.40	0.36	0.16	1.60
0.50	0.56	0.20	2.00
0.60	0.80	0.24	2.40
0.70	1.09	0.29	2.90

b) Position-Time Graph

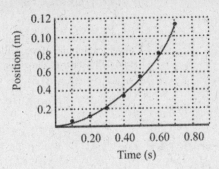

c) Velocity-Time Graph

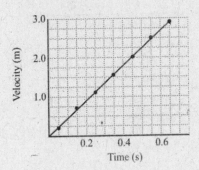

d) acceleration = slope of velocity-time graph

$$slope = \frac{rise}{run}$$

$$= \frac{(2.25 - 0) \text{m/s}}{(0.50 - 0) \text{s}}$$

$$= 4.5 \text{ m/s}^2 \text{ right}$$

Acceleration-Time Graph

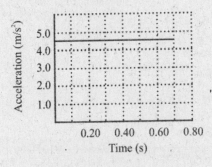

e) To find the velocity, read your velocity-time graph.
At 0.30 s, velocity = 1.3 m/s right.
At 0.60 s, velocity = 2.7 m/s right.

Lesson 4—Uniformly Accelerated Motion—Mathematical Analysis

1.

$\vec{v}_i$	$\vec{v}_f$	$\vec{a}$	$\vec{d}$	t
0	12.0 m/s	?	×	3.40 s

$$a = \frac{\vec{v}_f - \vec{v}_i}{t}$$
$$= \frac{12.0 \text{ m/s} - 0}{3.40 \text{ s}}$$
$$= 3.53 \text{ m/s}^2 \text{ west}$$

3.

$\vec{v}_i$	$\vec{v}_f$	$\vec{a}$	$\vec{d}$	t
0	?	1.9 m/s²	?	5.0 s

a) $\vec{d} = \vec{v}_i t + \frac{1}{2}\vec{a}t^2$

$$= \frac{1}{2}(1.9 \text{ m/s}^2)(5.0 \text{ s})^2$$
$$= 24 \text{ m right}$$

b) $\quad a = \frac{\vec{v}_f - \vec{v}_i}{t}$

$$1.9 \text{ m/s}^2 = \frac{\vec{v}_f - 0}{5.0 \text{ s}}$$
$$\vec{v}_f = 9.5 \text{ m/s right}$$

c) magnitude of displacement: 24 m

d) magnitude of velocity: 9.5 m/s

5.

$\vec{v}_i$	$\vec{v}_f$	$\vec{a}$	$\vec{d}$	t
5.0 m/s	?	3.0 m/s²	×	2.9 s

$$a = \frac{\vec{v}_f - \vec{v}_i}{t}$$
$$3.0 \text{ m/s} = \frac{\vec{v}_f - 5.0 \text{ m/s}}{2.9 \text{ s}}$$
$$\vec{v}_f = (3.0 \text{ m/s}^2)(2.9 \text{ s}) + 5.0 \text{ m/s}$$
$$= 14 \text{ m/s north}$$

7.

$\vec{v}_i$	$\vec{v}_f$	$\vec{a}$	$\vec{d}$	t
0	×	?	20.0 m	8.10 s

$$\vec{d} = \vec{v}_i t + \frac{1}{2}\vec{a}t^2$$
$$20.0 \text{ m} = \frac{1}{2}(\vec{a})(8.10 \text{ s})^2$$
$$\vec{a} = 0.610 \text{ m/s}^2 \text{ right}$$

9.

$\vec{v}_i$	$\vec{v}_f$	$\vec{a}$	$\vec{d}$	t
0	122.0 km/h			10.5 s

$$\vec{v}_{average} = \frac{\vec{v}_f + \vec{v}_i}{2}$$
$$= \frac{122.0 \text{ km/h} + 0}{2}$$
$$= 61.0 \text{ km/hr north}$$
$$= 61.0 \text{ km/hr} \times 1\,000 \text{ m/km} \times \frac{1 \text{ h}}{3\,600 \text{ s}}$$
$$= 16.9 \text{ m/s north}$$

or

$$\vec{v}_{average} = \frac{\vec{d}}{t}$$
$$\vec{v}_f = 122.0 \text{ km/hr} \times 1\,000 \text{ m/km} \times \frac{1 \text{ h}}{3\,600 \text{ s}}$$
$$= 33.9 \text{ m/s}$$
$$\vec{d} = \left(\frac{\vec{v}_f + \vec{v}_i}{2}\right)t$$
$$= \left(\frac{33.9 \text{ m/s} + 0}{2}\right)10.5 \text{ s}$$
$$= 178 \text{ m}$$
$$\vec{v}_{average} = \frac{178 \text{ m}}{10.5 \text{ s}}$$
$$= 16.9 \text{ m/s north}$$

11.

$\vec{v}_i$	$\vec{v}_f$	$\vec{a}$	$\vec{d}$	t
0	?	×	19.0 m	7.10 s

$$\vec{d} = \left(\frac{\vec{v}_f + \vec{v}_i}{2}\right)t$$
$$19.0 \text{ m} = \left(\frac{\vec{v}_f + 0}{2}\right)7.10 \text{ s}$$
$$\vec{v}_f = \frac{2(19.0 \text{ m})}{7.10 \text{ s}}$$
$$= 5.35 \text{ m/s north}$$

13.

$\vec{v}_i$	$\vec{v}_f$	$\vec{a}$	$\vec{d}$	t
15.0 m/s	35.0 m/s	?	43.0 m	×

$$\vec{v}_f^2 = \vec{v}_i^2 + 2\vec{a}\vec{d}$$
$$(35.0 \text{ m/s})^2 = (15.0 \text{ m/s})^2 + 2(\vec{a})(43.0 \text{ m})$$
$$\vec{a} = 11.6 \text{ m/s}^2 \text{ west}$$

15.

$\vec{v}_i$	$\vec{v}_f$	$\vec{a}$	$\vec{d}$	t
?	25.0 m/s	1.50 m/s²	×	10.0 s

$$\vec{a} = \frac{\vec{v}_f - \vec{v}_i}{t}$$

$$1.50 \text{ m/s}^2 = \frac{25.0 \text{ m/s} - \vec{v}_i}{10.0 \text{ s}}$$

$$\vec{v}_i = 25.0 \text{ m/s} - (10.0 \text{ s})(1.50 \text{ m/s}^2)$$

$$= 10.0 \text{ m/s east}$$

17.

$\vec{v}_i$	$\vec{v}_f$	$\vec{a}$	$\vec{d}$	t
0	?	×	31.0 m	5.6 s

$$\vec{d} = \left(\frac{\vec{v}_f + \vec{v}_i}{2}\right)t$$

$$31.0 \text{ m} = \left(\frac{\vec{v}_f + 0}{2}\right)(5.6 \text{ s})$$

$$\vec{v}_f = \frac{2(31.0 \text{ m})}{5.6 \text{ s}}$$

$$= 11 \text{ m/s west}$$

19.

$\vec{v}_i$	$\vec{v}_f$	$\vec{a}$	$\vec{d}$	t
0	?	1.4 m/s²	?	5.0 s

a) $d = v_i t + \frac{1}{2}at^2$

$$= \frac{1}{2}(1.4 \text{ m/s}^2)(5.0 \text{ s})^2$$

$$= 18 \text{ m}$$

b) $\vec{a} = \frac{\vec{v}_f - \vec{v}_i}{t}$

$$1.4 \text{ m/s}^2 = \frac{\vec{v}_f - 0}{5.0 \text{ s}}$$

$$\vec{v}_f = 7.0 \text{ m/s down}$$

21.

$\vec{v}_i$	$\vec{v}_f$	$\vec{a}$	$\vec{d}$	t
0	12.4 m/s	3.10 m/s²	?	4.00 s

You can use any formula except $\vec{a} = \frac{\vec{v}_f - \vec{v}_i}{t}$

$$\vec{d} = \vec{v}_i t + \frac{1}{2}\vec{a}t^2$$

$$= \frac{1}{2}(3.10 \text{ m/s}^2)(4.00 \text{ s})^2$$

$$= 24.8 \text{ m south}$$

23.

$\vec{v}_i$	$\vec{v}_f$	$\vec{a}$	$\vec{d}$	t
0	×	?	19.6 m	Find from $\vec{v}_{average}$

$$\vec{v}_{average} = \frac{\vec{d}}{t}$$

$$t = \frac{\vec{d}}{\vec{v}_{average}}$$

$$= \frac{19.6 \text{ m}}{5.00 \text{ m/s}}$$

$$= 3.92 \text{ s}$$

$$\vec{d} = \vec{v}_i t + \frac{1}{2}\vec{a}t^2$$

$$19.6 \text{ m} = \frac{1}{2}(\vec{a})(3.92 \text{ s})^2$$

$$\vec{a} = 2.55 \text{ m/s}^2 \text{ east}$$

Lesson 5—Freely Falling Objects

1.

$\vec{v}_i$	$\vec{v}_f$	$\vec{a}$	$\vec{d}$	t
0	?	9.81 m/s²	15.0 m	×

$$\vec{v}_f^{\,2} = \vec{v}_i^{\,2} + 2\vec{a}\vec{d}$$

$$= 2(9.81 \text{ m/s}^2)(15.0 \text{ m})$$

$$\vec{v}_f = 17.2 \text{ m}$$

3.

$\vec{v}_i$	$\vec{v}_f$	$\vec{a}$	$\vec{d}$	t
0	×	9.81 m/s²	1.75 m	?

$$\vec{d} = \vec{v}_i t + \frac{1}{2}\vec{a}t^2$$

$$1.75 \text{ m} = \frac{1}{2}(9.81 \text{ m/s}^2)t^2$$

$$t = \sqrt{\frac{2(1.75 \text{ m})}{9.81 \text{ m/s}^2}}$$

$$= 0.597 \text{ s}$$

5.

$\vec{v}_i$	$\vec{v}_f$	$\vec{a}$	$\vec{d}$	t
0	?	9.81 m/s²	×	2.5 s

$$\vec{a} = \frac{\vec{v}_f - \vec{v}_i}{t}$$

$$9.81 \text{ m/s}^2 = \frac{\vec{v}_f - 0}{2.5 \text{ s}}$$

$$\vec{v}_f = 25 \text{ m/s down}$$

7.

$\vec{v}_i$	$\vec{v}_f$	$\vec{a}$	$\vec{d}$	t
10.0 m/s	25.0 m/s	9.81 m/s²	×	?

$$\vec{a} = \frac{\vec{v}_f - \vec{v}_i}{t}$$

$$9.81 \text{ m/s}^2 = \frac{25.0 \text{ m/s} - 10.0 \text{ m/s}}{t}$$

$$t = \frac{25.0 \text{ m/s} - 10.0 \text{ m/s}}{9.81 \text{ m/s}^2}$$

$$= 1.53 \text{ s}$$

9.

$\vec{v}_i$	$\vec{v}_f$	$\vec{a}$	$\vec{d}$	t
?	10.0 m/s	9.81 m/s²	×	0.880 s

$$\vec{a} = \frac{\vec{v}_f - \vec{v}_i}{t}$$

$$9.81 \text{ m/s}^2 = \frac{10.0 \text{ m/s} - v_i}{0.880 \text{ s}}$$

$$\vec{v}_i = 1.37 \text{ m/s down}$$

11. a) $\vec{v}_{average} = \frac{\vec{v}_f + \vec{v}_i}{2}$

$$= \frac{50.0 \text{ m/s} + 0}{2}$$

$$= 25.0 \text{ m/s left}$$

b) Reading the graph: 4.0 s

13. $\vec{v}_{average} = \frac{\vec{d}}{t}$

$$t = \frac{\vec{d}}{\vec{v}_{average}}$$

$$= \frac{7.0 \text{ m}}{5.9 \text{ m/s}}$$

$$= 1.2 \text{ s}$$

15. $\vec{v}_{average} = \frac{\vec{v}_f + \vec{v}_i}{2}$

$$12.0 \text{ m/s} = \frac{\vec{v}_f - 0}{2}$$

$$\vec{v}_f = 24.0 \text{ m/s}$$

$\vec{v}_i$	$\vec{v}_f$	$\vec{a}$	$\vec{d}$	t
0	24.0 m/s	9.81 m/s²	×	?

$$\vec{a} = \frac{\vec{v}_f - \vec{v}_i}{t}$$

$$t = \frac{24.0 \text{ m/s} - 0}{9.81 \text{ m/s}^2}$$

$$= 2.45 \text{ s}$$

17.

$\vec{v}_i$	$\vec{v}_f$	$\vec{a}$	$\vec{d}$	t
0	19.6 m/s	?	24.0 m	×

$$\vec{v}_f^2 = \vec{v}_i^2 + 2\vec{a}\vec{d}$$

$$(19.6 \text{ m/s})^2 = 2(\vec{a})(24.0 \text{ m})$$

$$\vec{a} = \frac{(19.6 \text{ m/s})^2}{2(24.0 \text{ m})}$$

$$= 8.00 \text{ m/s}^2$$

19.

$\vec{v}_i$	$\vec{v}_f$	$\vec{a}$	$\vec{d}$	t
×	15.0 m/s	9.81 m/s²	10.0 m	?

Note: All equations require $\vec{v}_i$, therefore, we must find $\vec{v}_i$ first.

$$\vec{v}_f^2 = \vec{v}_i^2 + 2\vec{a}\vec{d}$$

$$(15 \text{ m/s})^2 = \vec{v}_i^2 + 2(9.81 \text{ m/s}^2)(10.0 \text{ m})$$

$$\vec{v}_i = 5.37 \text{ m/s}$$

Now use any equation that you like to find t.

$$\vec{a} = \frac{\vec{v}_f - \vec{v}_i}{t}$$

$$9.81 \text{ m/s}^2 = \frac{15.0 \text{ m/s} - 5.37 \text{ m/s}}{t}$$

$$t = 0.982 \text{ s}$$

21.

$\vec{v}_i$	$\vec{v}_f$	$\vec{a}$	$\vec{d}$	t
0	60.0 m/s	?	40.0 m	×

$$\vec{v}_f^2 = \vec{v}_i^2 + 2\vec{a}\vec{d}$$

$$(60.0 \text{ m/s})^2 = 2(\vec{a})(40.0 \text{ m})$$

$$\vec{a} = 45.0 \text{ m/s}^2$$

Lesson 6—Kinematics in One Dimension

1. Velocity = slope of position-time graph—we must draw a tangent line and find slope.

$$slope = \frac{rise}{run} = \frac{y_2 - y_1}{x_2 - x_1}$$

a) $slope = \dfrac{(12.0 - 5.0)\,m}{(4.0 - 0)\,s}$

$= 1.75\ m/s$

$= 1.4\ m/s\ up$

b) $slope = \dfrac{(6.0 - 12.0)\,m}{(10.0 - 6.0)\,s}$

$= -1.5\ m/s$

$= 1.5\ m/s\ down$

3. a) Displacement is read from graph.
   = 14.0 m north

b) Velocity = slope of position-time graph.

$$slope = \frac{rise}{run} = \frac{y_2 - y_1}{x_2 - x_1}$$

$$= \frac{(7.0 - 0)\ m}{(7.0 - 0)\ s}$$

$= 1.0\ m/s\ north$

c) Velocity = slope of position-time graph.
   slope = 0

d) Velocity = slope of position-time graph.

$$slope = \frac{rise}{run} = \frac{y_2 - y_1}{x_2 - x_1}$$

$$= \frac{(14.0 - 7.0)\ m}{(16.0 - 13.2)\ s}$$

$= 2.5\ m/s\ north$

e) $\bar{v}_{average} = \dfrac{\bar{d}}{t}$

$= \dfrac{14.0\ m}{16.0\ s}$

$= 0.875\ m/s\ north$

f) Since slope does not change, the velocity does not change.
   acceleration = 0

5. a) Velocity = slope of position-time graph.

$$slope = \frac{rise}{run} = \frac{y_2 - y_1}{x_2 - x_1}$$

$$= \frac{(-16.0 - 16.0)\ m}{(8.0 - 0)\ s}$$

$= -4.0\ m/s\ \ or\ \ 4.0\ m/s\ south$

b) same slope as a)
   $= -4.0\ m/s\ \ or\ \ 4.0\ m/s\ south$

c) Acceleration = 0 because velocity does not change.

7. a) Displacement = area of velocity-time graph.
   Greatest area = A

b) B

9. a) D   b) A

   c) C   d) B

11. a) Read velocity from velocity-time graph.
    Greatest velocity = A at 25.0 m/s.

b) Acceleration = slope of a velocity-time graph.
   slope = zero during A.

c) Greatest slope = D

Lesson 7—Uniformly Accelerated Motion—Mathematical Analysis (continued)

1.

$\bar{v}_i$	$\bar{v}_f$	$\bar{a}$	$\bar{d}$	t
14.0 m/s	×	−9.81 m/s²	?	1.80 s

$$\bar{d} = \bar{v}_i t + \frac{1}{2}\bar{a}t^2$$

$$= (14.0\ m/s)(1.80\ s) + \frac{1}{2}\left(-9.81\ m/s^2\right)(1.80\ s)^2$$

$$= 9.31\ m$$

3.

$\bar{v}_i$	$\bar{v}_f$	$\bar{a}$	$\bar{d}$	t
11.0 m/s	−7.3 m/s	?	×	9.3 s

$$\bar{a} = \frac{\bar{v}_f - \bar{v}_i}{t}$$

$$= \frac{-7.3\ m/s - 11.0\ m/s}{9.3\ s}$$

$$= -2.0\ m/s^2$$

5.

$\vec{v}_i$	$\vec{v}_f$	$\vec{a}$	$\vec{d}$	t
15.0 m/s	−8.0 m/s	−9.81 m/s²	?	×

$$\vec{v}_f^{\,2} = \vec{v}_i^{\,2} + 2\vec{a}\vec{d}$$

$$\left(-8.0\ \text{m/s}^2\right) = \left(15.0\ \text{m/s}\right)^2 + 2\left(-9.81\ \text{m/s}^2\right)\vec{d}$$

$$\vec{d} = \frac{\left(-8.0\ \text{m/s}\right)^2 - \left(15.0\ \text{m/s}\right)^2}{2\left(-9.81\ \text{m/s}^2\right)}$$

$$= 8.2\ \text{m}$$

7.

$\vec{v}_i$	$\vec{v}_f$	$\vec{a}$	$\vec{d}$	t
?	0	×	2.6 m	3.6 s

$$\vec{d} = \left(\frac{\vec{v}_f + \vec{v}_i}{2}\right)t$$

$$2.6\ \text{m} = \left(\frac{0 + \vec{v}_i}{2}\right)\left(3.6\ \text{s}\right)$$

$$\vec{v}_i = \frac{\left(2.6\ \text{m}\right)^2}{3.6\ \text{s}}$$

$$= 1.4\ \text{m/s}$$

9.

$\vec{v}_i$	$\vec{v}_f$	$\vec{a}$	$\vec{d}$	t
25.0 m/s	?	−9.81 m/s²	×	3.0 s

$$\vec{a} = \frac{\vec{v}_f - \vec{v}_i}{t}$$

$$-9.81\ \text{m/s}^2 = \frac{\vec{v}_f - 25.0\ \text{m/s}}{3.0\ \text{s}}$$

$$\vec{v}_f = \left(3.0\ \text{s}\right)\left(-9.81\ \text{m/s}^2\right) + 25.0\ \text{m/s}$$

$$= -4.4\ \text{m/s}$$

11.

$\vec{v}_i$	$\vec{v}_f$	$\vec{a}$	$\vec{d}$	t
?	×	−9.81 m/s²	5.0 m	3.0 s

$$\vec{d} = \vec{v}_i t + \frac{1}{2}\vec{a}t^2$$

$$5.0\ \text{m} = \vec{v}_i\left(3.0\ \text{s}\right) + \frac{1}{2}\left(-9.81\ \text{m/s}^2\right)\left(3.0\ \text{s}\right)^2$$

$$\vec{v}_i = \frac{5.0\ \text{m} - \frac{1}{2}\left(-9.81\ \text{m/s}^2\right)\left(3.0\ \text{s}\right)^2}{3.0\ \text{s}}$$

$$= 16\ \text{m/s}$$

13.

$\vec{v}_i$	$\vec{v}_f$	$\vec{a}$	$\vec{d}$	t
2.5 m/s	−1.6 m/s	?	1.0 m	×

$$\vec{v}_f^{\,2} = \vec{v}_i^{\,2} + 2\vec{a}\vec{d}$$

$$\left(-1.6\ \text{m/s}\right)^2 = \left(2.5\ \text{m/s}\right)^2 + 2\left(\vec{a}\right)\left(1.0\ \text{m}\right)$$

$$\vec{a} = \frac{\left(-1.6\ \text{m/s}\right)^2 - \left(2.5\ \text{m/s}\right)^2}{2\left(1.0\ \text{m}\right)}$$

$$= -1.8\ \text{m/s}^2$$

15.

$\vec{v}_i$	$\vec{v}_f$	$\vec{a}$	$\vec{d}$	t
5.0 m/s	−5.0 m/s	?	0	3.0 s

$$\vec{a} = \frac{\vec{v}_f - \vec{v}_i}{t}$$

$$= \frac{-5.0\ \text{m/s} - 5.0\ \text{m/s}}{3.0\ \text{s}}$$

$$= -3.3\ \text{m/s}^2$$

17.

$\vec{v}_i$	$\vec{v}_f$	$\vec{a}$	$\vec{d}$	t
11.0 m/s	×	−9.81 m/s²	−5.0 m	?

Find $\vec{v}_f$ first.

$$\vec{v}_f^{\,2} = \vec{v}_i^{\,2} + 2\vec{a}\vec{d}$$

$$= \left(11.0\ \text{m/s}\right)^2 + 2\left(-9.81\ \text{m/s}^2\right)\left(-5.0\ \text{m}\right)$$

$$\vec{v}_f = -14.8\ \text{m/s}$$

Now find t.

$$\vec{a} = \frac{\vec{v}_f - \vec{v}_i}{t}$$

$$-9.81\ \text{m/s}^2 = \frac{-14.8\ \text{m/s} - 11.0\ \text{m/s}}{t}$$

$$= 2.6\ \text{s}$$

19.

$\vec{v}_i$	$\vec{v}_f$	$\vec{a}$	$\vec{d}$	t
0		−9.81 m/s²	−25.0 m	

Either find $\vec{v}_f$ or t.

$$\vec{v}_f^{\,2} = \vec{v}_i^{\,2} + 2\vec{a}\vec{d}$$

$$= 2\left(-9.81\ \text{m/s}^2\right)\left(-25.0\ \text{m}\right)$$

$$\vec{v}_f = 22.1\ \text{m/s}$$

$$\vec{v}_{\text{average}} = \frac{\vec{v}_f + \vec{v}_i}{2}$$

$$= \frac{-22.1\ \text{m/s} - 0}{2}$$

$$= -11.1\ \text{m/s}$$

21.

$\bar{v}_i$		$\bar{v}_f$	$\bar{a}$	$\bar{d}$	t
×		−1.90 m/s	?	2.75 m	4.50 s

Find $\bar{v}_i$ first

$$\bar{d} = \left(\frac{\bar{v}_f + \bar{v}_i}{2}\right)t$$

$$2.75 \text{ m} = \left(\frac{-1.90 \text{ m/s} - \bar{v}_i}{2}\right)(4.50 \text{ s})$$

$$\bar{v}_i = \frac{2(2.75 \text{ m})}{4.50 \text{ s}} + 1.90 \text{ m/s}$$

$$= 3.12 \text{ m/s}$$

Now find $\bar{a}$.

$$\bar{a} = \frac{\bar{v}_f - \bar{v}_i}{t}$$

$$= \frac{-1.90 \text{ m/s} - 3.12 \text{ m/s}}{4.50 \text{ s}}$$

$$= -1.12 \text{ m/s}^2$$

Lesson 8—Kinematics in Two Dimensions

1. **a)** 3.0 m + 4.0 m
= 7.0 m south (7.0 m 270°)

b) −3.0 m + 4.0 m
1.0 m north (1.0 m 90°)

c)

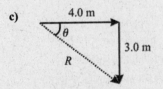

$$\bar{R} = \sqrt{(\bar{v}_1)^2 + (\bar{v}_2)^2}$$

$$= \sqrt{(4.0 \text{ m})^2 + (3.0 \text{ m})^2}$$

$$= 5.0 \text{ m}$$

$$\tan\theta = \frac{\text{opposite}}{\text{adjacent}}$$

$$= 0.75$$

$$\theta = 37°$$

$\bar{R} = 5.0$ m 37° S of E or 5.0 m 53° E of S

(5.0 m 323°)

d)

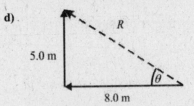

$$\bar{R} = \sqrt{(\bar{v}_1)^2 + (\bar{v}_2)^2}$$

$$= \sqrt{(8.0 \text{ m})^2 + (5.0 \text{ m})^2}$$

$$= 9.4 \text{ m}$$

$$\tan\theta = \frac{\text{opposite}}{\text{adjacent}}$$

$$= \frac{5.0 \text{ m}}{8.0 \text{ m}}$$

$$\theta = 32°$$

$\bar{R} = 9.4$ m 32° N of W or 9.4 m W of N

(9.4 m 148°)

e)

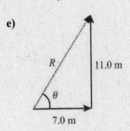

$$\bar{R} = \sqrt{(v_1)^2 + (v_2)^2}$$

$$= \sqrt{(7.0 \text{ m})^2 + (11.0 \text{ m})^2}$$

$$= 13.0 \text{ m}$$

$$\tan\theta = \frac{\text{opposite}}{\text{adjacent}}$$

$$\theta = 58°$$

$\bar{R} = 13.0$ m 58° N of E

or

13.0 m 32° E of N

(13.0 m 58°)

f)

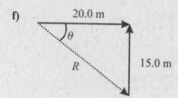

$$\vec{R} = \sqrt{(v_1)^2 + (v_2)^2}$$
$$= \sqrt{(20.0 \text{ m})^2 + (15.0 \text{ m})^2}$$
$$= 25.0 \text{ m}$$

$$\tan\theta = \frac{\text{opposite}}{\text{adjacent}}$$
$$= \frac{15.0 \text{ m}}{20.0 \text{ m}}$$
$$\theta = 36.9°$$

$\vec{R} = 25.0$ m 36.9° S of E

or 25.0 m 53.1° E of S

$(25.0$ m 232.1°$)$

g)

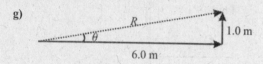

$$\vec{R} = \sqrt{(v_1)^2 + (v_2)^2}$$
$$= \sqrt{(6.0 \text{ m})^2 + (1.0 \text{ m})^2}$$

$$\tan\theta = \frac{\text{opposite}}{\text{adjacent}}$$
$$= \frac{1.0 \text{ m}}{6.0 \text{ m}}$$
$$\theta = 9.5°$$

$\vec{R} = 6.1$ m 9.5° N of E or 6.1 m E of N

$(6.1$ m 9.5°$)$

h)

$$\vec{R} = \sqrt{(v_1)^2 + (v_2)^2}$$
$$= \sqrt{(5.0 \text{ m})^2 + (12.0 \text{ m})^2}$$
$$= 13 \text{ m}$$

$$\tan\theta = \frac{\text{opposite}}{\text{adjacent}}$$
$$= \frac{12.0 \text{ m}}{5.0 \text{ m}}$$
$$\theta = 67°$$

$\vec{R} = 13$ m 67° N of E

or 13 m 23° E of N

$(13$ m 67°$)$

Lesson 9—Vector Components

1. a) x component $= 0$

y component $= 16.0$ m

b)

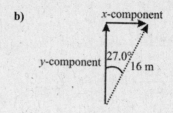

$$\sin\theta = \frac{\text{opposite}}{\text{hypotenuse}}$$
x component $= (16.0 \text{ m})(\sin 27.0°)$
$$= 7.3 \text{ m east } (7.3 \text{ m } 0°)$$

$$\cos\theta = \frac{\text{adjacent}}{\text{hypotenuse}}$$
y component $= (16.0 \text{ m})(\sin 27.0°)$
$$= 14.3 \text{ m north } (14.3 \text{ m } 90°)$$

c)

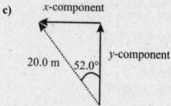

$$\sin\theta = \frac{\text{opposite}}{\text{hypotenuse}}$$
x component $= (20.0 \text{ m})(\sin 52.0°)$
$$= 15.8 \text{ m west } (15.8 \text{ m } 180°)$$

$$\cos\theta = \frac{\text{adjacent}}{\text{hypotenuse}}$$
y component $= (10.0 \text{ m})(\sin 33.0°)$
$$= 5.44 \text{ m south } (5.44 \text{ m } 270°)$$

d)

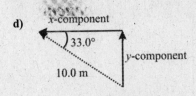

$$\cos\theta = \frac{adjacent}{hypotenuse}$$

x component $= (10.0\ m)(\cos 33.0°)$

$\qquad = 8.39\ m\ east\ (8.39\ m\ 0°)$

$$\sin\theta = \frac{opposite}{hypotenuse}$$

y component $= (10.0\ m)(\sin 33.0°)$

$\qquad = 5.44\ m\ south\ (5.44\ m\ 270°)$

Lesson 10—Velocity Vectors and Navigation

1.

15.0 m/s

θ

11.0 m/s

$\bar{R}$

$$\bar{R} = \sqrt{(\bar{v}_x)^2 + (\bar{v}_y)^2}$$

$$= \sqrt{(15.0\ m/s)^2 + (11.0\ m/s)^2}$$

$$= 18.6\ m/s$$

$$\tan\theta = \frac{opposite}{adjacent}$$

$$= \frac{11.0\ m/s}{15.0\ m/s}$$

$$\theta = 36.3°$$

$\bar{R} = 18.6\ m/s\ 36.3°\ S\ of\ E$

$\quad$ or $18.6\ m/s\ 53.7\ E\ of\ S$

$\quad (18.6\ m/s\ 324°)$

3.

$\bar{R}$

255 km/h

θ

112 km/n

$$\bar{R} = \sqrt{(\bar{v}_1)^2 + (\bar{v}_2)^2}$$

$$= \sqrt{(112\ km/h)^2 + (255\ km/h)^2}$$

$$= 279\ km/h$$

$$\tan\theta = \frac{opposite}{adjacent}$$

$$\theta = 66.3°$$

$\bar{R} = 279\ km/h\ 66.3°\ N\ of\ E$

$\quad$ or $279\ km/h\ 23.7\ E\ of\ N$

$\quad (279\ km/h\ 66.3°)$

5.

$\bar{R}$

32 m/s

θ

12 m/s

$$\bar{R} = \sqrt{(\bar{v}_1)^2 + (\bar{v}_2)^2}$$

$$= \sqrt{(12\ m/s)^2 + (32\ m/s)^2}$$

$$= 34\ m/s$$

$$\tan\theta = \frac{opposite}{adjacent}$$

$$= \frac{32\ m/s}{12\ m/s}$$

$$\theta = 69°$$

$\bar{R} = 34\ m/s\ 69°\ N\ of\ E$

$\quad$ or $34\ m/s\ 21°\ E\ of\ N$

$\quad (34\ m/s\ 69°)$

7.

125 m/s

θ

25 m/s

$\bar{R}$

$$\bar{R} = \sqrt{(\bar{v}_1)^2 + (\bar{v}_2)^2}$$

$$= \sqrt{(125\ m/s)^2 + (25.0\ m/s)^2}$$

$$= 127\ m/s$$

$$\tan\theta = \frac{opposite}{adjacent}$$

$$= \frac{25.0\ m/s}{125\ m/s}$$

$$\theta = 11°$$

$\bar{R} = 127\ m/s\ 11°\ S\ of\ E$

$\quad$ or $127\ m/s\ 79°\ E\ of\ S$

$\quad (127\ m/s\ 349°)$

9.

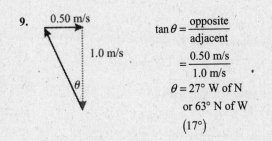

0.50 m/s

1.0 m/s

θ

$$\tan\theta = \frac{opposite}{adjacent}$$

$$= \frac{0.50\ m/s}{1.0\ m/s}$$

$$\theta = 27°\ W\ of\ N$$

$\quad$ or $63°\ N\ of\ W$

$\quad (17°)$

11.

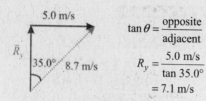

$\tan \theta = \dfrac{\text{opposite}}{\text{adjacent}}$

$R_y = \dfrac{5.0 \text{ m/s}}{\tan 35.0°}$

$= 7.1 \text{ m/s}$

13. a) 2.5 m/s east + 2.0 m/s east = 4.5 m/s east

$(4.5 \text{ m/s } 0°)$

b) 2.5 m/s west + 2.0 m/s east = 0.5 m/s west

$(-0.5 \text{ m/s } 180°)$

c)

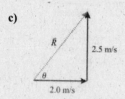

$\vec{R} = \sqrt{(\vec{v}_1)^2 + (\vec{v}_2)^2}$

$= \sqrt{(2.0 \text{ m/s})^2 + (2.5 \text{ m/s})^2}$

$= 3.2 \text{ m/s}$

$\tan \theta = \dfrac{\text{opposite}}{\text{adjacent}}$

$= \dfrac{2.5 \text{ m/s}}{2.0 \text{ m/s}}$

$\theta = 51°$

$\vec{R} = 3.2 \text{ m/s } 51° \text{ N of E}$

or 3.2 m/s 39° E of N

$(3.2 \text{ m/s } 51°)$

d) Find x and y components of 2.5 m/s 135°.

$\vec{R}_x = \vec{v} \cos \theta$

$= (2.5 \text{ m/s})(\cos 135°)$

$= -1.77 \text{ m/s}$

$\vec{R}_y = \vec{v} \sin \theta$

$= (2.5 \text{ m/s})(\sin 135°)$

$= 1.77 \text{ m/s}$

Add x components.

$\vec{R}_x = \vec{R}_{1x} + \vec{R}_{2x}$

$= 2.0 \text{ m/s} + (-1.77 \text{ m/s})$

$= 0.2 \text{ m/s}$

Add y components.

$\vec{R}_y = \vec{R}_{1y} + \vec{R}_{2y}$

$= 0 + 1.77 \text{ m/s}$

$= 1.77 \text{ m/s}$

Add Rx and Ry.

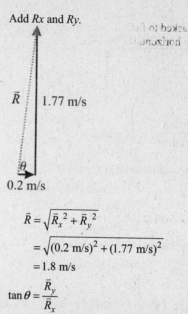

$\vec{R} = \sqrt{\vec{R}_x^{\,2} + \vec{R}_y^{\,2}}$

$= \sqrt{(0.2 \text{ m/s})^2 + (1.77 \text{ m/s})^2}$

$= 1.8 \text{ m/s}$

$\tan \theta = \dfrac{\vec{R}_y}{\vec{R}_x}$

$= \dfrac{1.77 \text{ m/s}}{0.2 \text{ m/s}}$

$\theta = 84°$

$\vec{R} = 1.8 \text{ m/s } 84° \text{ N of E}$

or 1.8 m/s 6.3 E of N

$(1.8 \text{ m/s } 84°)$

Lesson 11—Horizontal Projectile Motion

1. We are asked to find the horizontal component. Use $v = \dfrac{d}{t}$. Find t from vertical component.

$\vec{v}_i$	$\vec{v}_f$	$\vec{a}$	$\vec{d}$	t
0	×	9.81 m/s²	90.0 m	?

$\vec{d} = \vec{v}_i t + \dfrac{1}{2} \vec{a} t^2$

$90.0 \text{ m} = \dfrac{1}{2}\left(9.81 \text{ m/s}^2\right) t^2$

$t = \sqrt{\dfrac{2(90.0 \text{ m})}{9.81 \text{ m/s}^2}}$

$= 4.28 \text{ s}$

$\vec{v} = \dfrac{\vec{d}}{t}$

$\vec{d} = \vec{v} t$

$= (10.0 \text{ m/s})(4.28 \text{ s})$

$= 42.8 \text{ m}$

3. We are asked to find the vertical component. Find t from the horizontal component.

$$\bar{v} = \frac{\bar{d}}{t}$$

$$t = \frac{\bar{d}}{\bar{v}}$$

$$= \frac{100.0 \text{ m}}{18.0 \text{ m/s}}$$

$$= 5.56 \text{ s}$$

Vertical component

$\bar{v}_i$	$\bar{v}_f$	$\bar{a}$	$\bar{d}$	t
0	×	9.81 m/s^2	?	5.56 s

$$\bar{d} = \bar{v}_i t + \frac{1}{2}\bar{a}t^2$$

$$= \frac{1}{2}\left(9.81 \text{ m/s}^2\right)\left(5.56 \text{ s}\right)^2$$

$$= 151 \text{ m}$$

5. We are asked to find the vertical component.

$\bar{v}_i$	$\bar{v}_f$	$\bar{a}$	$\bar{d}$	t
0	×	9.81 m/s^2	?	5.50 s

$$\bar{d} = \bar{v}_i t + \frac{1}{2}\bar{a}t^2$$

$$= \frac{1}{2}\left(9.81 \text{ m/s}^2\right)\left(5.50 \text{ s}\right)^2$$

$$= 148 \text{ m}$$

7. We are asked to find the horizontal component. Find t from the vertical component.

$\bar{v}_i$	$\bar{v}_f$	$\bar{a}$	$\bar{d}$	t
0	×	9.81 m/s^2	85.0 m	?

$$\bar{d} = \bar{v}_i t + \frac{1}{2}\bar{a}t^2$$

$$85.0 \text{ m} = \frac{1}{2}\left(9.81 \text{ m/s}^2\right)t^2$$

$$t = 4.16 \text{ s}$$

Horizontal:

$$\bar{v} = \frac{\bar{d}}{t}$$

$$= \frac{67.8 \text{ m}}{4.16 \text{ s}}$$

$$= 16.3 \text{ m/s}$$

Lesson 12—Projectile Motion at an Angle

1. Find t from the vertical component.

$$\sin\theta = \frac{\text{vertical}}{\text{hypotenuse}}$$

$$\text{vertical} = \sin\theta\left(\text{hypotenuse}\right)$$

$$= \sin 40.0°\left(18.0 \text{ m/s}\right)$$

$$= 11.6 \text{ m/s}$$

$$\bar{a} = \frac{\bar{v}_f - \bar{v}_i}{t}$$

$$t = \frac{\bar{v}_f - \bar{v}_i}{\bar{a}}$$

$$= \frac{-11.6 \text{ m/s} - 11.57 \text{ m/s}}{-9.81 \text{ m/s}^2}$$

$$t = 2.4 \text{ s}$$

Find $\bar{d}$ from the horizontal component.

$$\cos\theta = \frac{\text{horizontal}}{\text{hypotenuse}}$$

$$\text{horizontal} = \cos\theta\left(\text{hypotenuse}\right)$$

$$= \left(\cos 40°\right)\left(18.0 \text{ m/s}\right)$$

$$= 13.8 \text{ m/s}$$

$$\bar{d} = \bar{v}t$$

$$= \left(13.8 \text{ m/s}\right)\left(2.4 \text{ s}\right)$$

$$= 32.5 \text{ m}$$

3. Find t from the vertical component.

$$\sin\theta = \frac{\text{vertical}}{\text{hypotenuse}}$$

$$\text{vertical} = \sin\theta\left(\text{hypotenuse}\right)$$

$$= \sin 32.0°\left(25.0 \text{ m/s}\right)$$

$$= 13.3 \text{ m/s}$$

$$\bar{a} = \frac{\bar{v}_f - \bar{v}_i}{t}$$

$$t = \frac{\bar{v}_f - \bar{v}_i}{\bar{a}}$$

$$= \frac{-13.3 \text{ m/s} - 13.3 \text{ m/s}}{-9.81 \text{ m/s}^2}$$

$$t = 2.7 \text{ s}$$

Find $\bar{d}$ from the the horizontal component.

$$\cos\theta = \frac{\text{horizontal}}{\text{hypotenuse}}$$

$$\text{horizontal} = \cos\theta\left(\text{hypotenuse}\right)$$

$$= \left(\cos 32°\right)\left(25.0 \text{ m/s}\right)$$

$$= 21.2 \text{ m/s}$$

$$\bar{d} = \bar{v}t$$

$$= \left(21.2 \text{ m/s}\right)\left(2.7 \text{ s}\right)$$

$$= 57.2 \text{ m}$$

5. Find the time it takes to reach maximum displacement.

$$\vec{a} = \frac{\vec{v}_f - \vec{v}_i}{t}$$

$$t = \frac{\vec{v}_f - \vec{v}_i}{\vec{a}}$$

$$t = \frac{0 - \vec{v}_i}{\vec{a}}$$

$$\vec{v}_i = -\vec{a}t$$

$$\vec{v} = \frac{\vec{d}}{t}$$

$$\vec{v}_i = \frac{\vec{d}}{t} \text{ and } \vec{v}_i = -\vec{a}t$$

$$\frac{\vec{d}}{t} = -\vec{a}t$$

$$t^2 = \frac{\vec{d}}{-\vec{a}}$$

$$t = \sqrt{\frac{5.75 \text{ m}}{9.81 \text{ m/s}^2}}$$

$$= 0.77 \text{ s}$$

$$\vec{v} = \frac{\vec{d}}{t}$$

$$= \frac{5.75 \text{ m}}{0.77 \text{ s}}$$

$$= 7.5 \text{ m/s}$$

$$\sin\theta = \frac{\text{vert}}{\text{hyp}}$$

$$\text{velocity} = \frac{\text{vert}}{\sin\theta}$$

$$= \frac{7.5 \text{ m/s}}{\sin 30.0°}$$

$$= 15 \text{ m/s}$$

7. Find horizontal velocity first.

$$\vec{v} = \frac{\vec{d}}{t}$$

$$= \frac{25.0 \text{ m}}{2.15 \text{ s}}$$

$$= 11.7 \text{ m/s}$$

$$\cos\theta = \frac{\text{horizontal}}{\text{hypotenuse}}$$

$$= \frac{11.7 \text{ m/s}}{15.7 \text{ m/s}}$$

$$\theta = 42.8°$$

9. Find t from the vertical component. First, find the vertical component of the velocity.

$$\sin\theta = \frac{\text{vertical}}{\text{hypotenuse}}$$

$$\text{vertical} = \sin\theta(\text{hypotenuse})$$

$$= \sin 32.0°(22.0 \text{ m/s})$$

$$= 11.7 \text{ m/s down}$$

Since the ball does not go up into the air first, $\vec{v}_f$ will be different from $\vec{v}_i$. Find $\vec{v}_f$, then time.

$$\vec{v}_f^2 = \vec{v}_i^2 + 2\vec{a}\vec{d}$$

$$= (11.7 \text{ m/s}) + 2(9.81 \text{ m/s}^2)(9.0 \text{ m})$$

$$v_f = 17.7 \text{ m/s}$$

$$\vec{a} = \frac{\vec{v}_f - \vec{v}_i}{t}$$

$$t = \frac{\vec{v}_f - \vec{v}_i}{\vec{a}}$$

$$= \frac{-17.7\text{m/s} - (-11.7 \text{ m/s})}{-9.81 \text{ m/s}^2}$$

$$t = 0.62 \text{ s}$$

Find the horizontal displacement.

$$\cos\theta = \frac{\text{horizontal}}{\text{hypotenuse}}$$

$$\text{horizontal} = (\cos\theta)(\text{hypotenuse})$$

$$= (\cos 32°)(22 \text{ m/s})$$

$$= 18.7 \text{ m/s down}$$

$$\vec{v} = \frac{\vec{d}}{t}$$

$$\vec{d} = \vec{v}t$$

$$= (18.7 \text{ m/s})(0.62 \text{ s})$$

$$= 11.6 \text{ m}$$

Review Exercises—Kinematics

1. **a)** $\vec{v} = \frac{\vec{d}}{t}$

$$\vec{d} = \vec{v}t$$

$$= (1.7 \text{ m/s})(6.0 \text{ min} \times 60 \text{ s/min})$$

$$= 6.1 \times 10^2 \text{ m}$$

b) 0

3.

$\vec{v}_i$	$\vec{v}_f$	$\vec{a}$	$\vec{d}$	t
0	?	-9.81 m/s^2	-11.0 m	×

$$\vec{v}_f^2 = \vec{v}_i^2 + 2\vec{a}\vec{d}$$

$$= 2(-9.81 \text{ m/s}^2)(-11.0 \text{ m})$$

$$= -14.7 \text{ m/s}$$

5.

$\vec{v}_i$	$\vec{v}_f$	$\vec{a}$	$\vec{d}$	t
?	0	-9.81 m/s^2	?	1.6 s

a) Find $\vec{v}_i$ first (Do **b)** first).

$$\vec{d} = \left(\frac{\vec{v}_f + \vec{v}_i}{2}\right)t$$

$$= \left(\frac{0 + 16 \text{ m/s}}{2}\right)(1.6 \text{ s})$$

$$= 13 \text{ m}$$

b)

$$\vec{a} = \frac{\vec{v}_f - \vec{v}_i}{t}$$

$$-9.81 \text{ m/s}^2 = \frac{0 - \vec{v}_i}{1.6 \text{ s}}$$

$$\vec{v}_i = 16 \text{ m/s}$$

7.

$\vec{v}_i$	$\vec{v}_f$	$\vec{a}$	$\vec{d}$	t
8.0 m/s	?	-9.81 m/s^2	-25 m	?

a) Find $\vec{v}_f$ first (Do **b)** first).

$$\vec{a} = \frac{\vec{v}_f - \vec{v}_i}{t}$$

$$-9.81 \text{ m/s}^2 = \frac{-8.0 \text{ m/s} - (-23.5 \text{ m/s})}{t}$$

$$t = 1.6 \text{ s}$$

b) $\vec{v}_f^{\,2} = \vec{v}_i^{\,2} + 2\vec{a}\vec{d}$

$$= (-8.0 \text{ m/s})^2 + 2(-9.81 \text{ m/s}^2)(-25 \text{ m})$$

$$\vec{v}_f = -24 \text{ m/s}$$

9.

$\vec{v}_i$	$\vec{v}_f$	$\vec{a}$	$\vec{d}$	t
0	101 km/h	?	×	8.0 s

Change 101 km/h to m/s.

$$101 \text{ km/h} \times 1\,000 \text{ m/km} \times \frac{1 \text{ h}}{3\,600 \text{ s}} = 28 \text{ m/s}$$

11.

$\vec{v}_i$	$\vec{v}_f$	$\vec{a}$	$\vec{d}$	t
20.0 m/s	-20.0 m/s	-9.81 m/s^2	×	?

13. Convert 65 km/h to m/s

$$65 \text{ km/h} \times 1\,000 \text{ m/km} \times \frac{1 \text{ h}}{3\,600 \text{ s}} = 18 \text{ m/s}$$

$$\vec{v} = \frac{\vec{d}}{t}$$

$$\vec{d} = \vec{v}t$$

$$= (18 \text{ m/s})(0.35 \text{ s})$$

$$= 6.3 \text{ m}$$

15.

$\vec{v}_i$	$\vec{v}_f$	$\vec{a}$	$\vec{d}$	t
5.0 m/s	×	-9.81 m/s^2	?	4 s

Find the displacement during the 1st four seconds

$$\vec{d} = \vec{v}_i t + \frac{1}{2}\vec{a}t^2$$

$$= (-5.0 \text{ m/s})(4.0 \text{ s}) + \frac{1}{2}(-9.81 \text{ m/s}^2)(4.0 \text{ s})^2$$

$$= -59 \text{ m}$$

Find the displacement during the first three seconds.

$$\vec{d} = \vec{v}_i t + \frac{1}{2}\vec{a}t^2$$

$$= (-5.0 \text{ m/s})(3.0 \text{ s}) + \frac{1}{2}(-9.81 \text{ m/s}^2)(3.0 \text{ s})^2$$

$$= -59 \text{ m}$$

Stone falls $98 \text{ m} - 59 \text{ m} = 39 \text{ m}$

17. a) slope $= \dfrac{\text{rise}}{\text{run}}$

$$= \frac{(45 - 0) \text{ m}}{(32.5 - 0) \text{ s}}$$

$$= 1.4 \text{ m/s north}$$

b) slope $= \dfrac{(35 - 10) \text{ m}}{(37.5 - 0) \text{ s}}$

$$= 0.67 \text{ m/s north}$$

19. a) $\vec{v}_{average} = \dfrac{\vec{d}}{t}$

Displacement during A = area

$$= \frac{1}{2}(l \times w)$$

$$= \frac{1}{2}(10 \text{ s} \times 20 \text{ m/s})$$

$$= 1.0 \times 10^2 \text{ m}$$

Displacement during B = area

$$= l \times w$$

$$= 10 \text{ s} \times 20 \text{ m/s}$$

$$= 2.0 \times 10^2 \text{ m}$$

Total displacement $= 3.0 \times 10^2 \text{ m}$

$$\vec{v}_{average} = \frac{3.0 \times 10^2 \text{ m}}{20 \text{ s}}$$

$$= 15 \text{ m/s east}$$

b) Displacement = area under velocity-time graph
area = area above axis − area below axis

$$= \frac{1}{2}(3.5 \text{ s} \times 20 \text{ m/s}) - (1.5 \text{ s} \times 10 \text{ m/s})$$

$$= 55 \pm 5 \text{ m/s}$$

c) Acceleration = slope of velocity-time graph

$$slope = \frac{rise}{run}$$

i) $slope = \dfrac{20 \text{ m/s}}{10 \text{ s}}$

$= 2.0 \text{ m/s}^2$ east

ii) no slope

iii) $slope = \dfrac{-30 \text{ m/s}}{5.0 \text{ s}}$

$= -6.0 \text{ m/s}^2$ or 6.0 m/s^2 west

21. Find the x and y components.

a) $\vec{R}_x = \vec{v}\cos\theta$

$= (18 \text{ m/s})(\cos 55°)$

$= 1.0 \times 10^1 \text{ m/s}$

b) $\vec{R}_y = \vec{v}\sin\theta$

$= (18 \text{ m/s})(\sin 55°)$

$= 15 \text{ m/s}$

23. Find the x component.

$\vec{R}_x = 25 \text{ m} + (-15 \text{ m})$

$= 10 \text{ m}$

Find the y component.

$\vec{R}_y = -35 \text{ m}$

Add the x and y components.

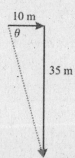

$\vec{R} = \sqrt{(\vec{R}_x)^2 + (\vec{R}_y)^2}$

$= \sqrt{(10 \text{ m})^2 + (-35 \text{ m})^2}$

$= 36 \text{ m}$

$\tan\theta = \dfrac{\vec{R}_y}{\vec{R}_x}$

$= \dfrac{35 \text{ m}}{10 \text{ m}}$

$\theta = 74°$

$\vec{R} = 36 \text{ m } 74°$ S of E

or $36 \text{ m } 16°$ E of S

$(36 \text{ m } 286°)$

25.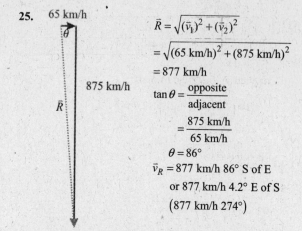

$\vec{R} = \sqrt{(\vec{v}_1)^2 + (\vec{v}_2)^2}$

$= \sqrt{(65 \text{ km/h})^2 + (875 \text{ km/h})^2}$

$= 877 \text{ km/h}$

$\tan\theta = \dfrac{opposite}{adjacent}$

$= \dfrac{875 \text{ km/h}}{65 \text{ km/h}}$

$\theta = 86°$

$\vec{v}_R = 877 \text{ km/h } 86°$ S of E

or $877 \text{ km/h } 4.2°$ E of S

$(877 \text{ km/h } 274°)$

Practice Test

1. The motion of a falling object is uniformly accelerated motion. This means that the acceleration of a falling object remains constant. Remember, the slope of a velocity-time graph is the acceleration. All of A, B, and D, represent a constant slope, but A shows no change in velocity; D shows that the velocity is decreasing.

B is the answer.

3. The acceleration of a falling object is constant. Therefore we are looking for a graph that shows a constant acceleration.

A is the answer.

5. Velocity is slope of a position-time graph.

$$slope = \frac{rise}{run}$$

$$= \frac{50 \text{ m} - 20 \text{ m}}{6 \text{ s}}$$

$$= 5.0 \text{ m/s}$$

C is the answer.

7. Velocity is a vector quantity; therefore it has direction. Once the object is released, it is at the mercy of gravity. The acceleration due to gravity is constant at -9.81 m/s^2. Therefore we are looking for a constant slope that starts at a high value and ends with a low value.

A is the answer.

9. The slope of a position-time graph is the velocity. In this graph, the slope is decreasing.

C is the answer.

11.

$\vec{v}_i$	$(t) + \vec{v}_f$	$\vec{a}$	$\vec{d}$	t
2.0 m/s	0	?	2.7 m	

$$v_f^2 = v_i^2 + 2\vec{a}\vec{d}$$
$$0 = (2.0\ \text{m/s})^2 + 2(\vec{a})(2.7\ \text{m})$$
$$\vec{a} = -0.74\ \text{m/s}^2$$

B is the answer.

13.

$\vec{v}_i$	$\vec{v}_f$	$\vec{a}$	$\vec{d}$	t
15 m/s		$-9.81\ \text{m/s}^2$	?	8.00 s

$$\vec{d} = \vec{v}_i t + \frac{1}{2}\vec{a}t^2$$
$$= (15\ \text{m/s})(8.00\ \text{s}) + \frac{1}{2}(-9.81\ \text{m/s}^2)(8.00\ \text{s})^2$$
$$= 1.9 \times 10^2\ \text{m}$$

B is the answer.

15. Convert 105 km/h to m/s

$$(105\ \text{km/h})\left(\frac{1\,000\ \text{m/km}}{3\,600\ \text{s/h}}\right) = 29.2\ \text{m/s}$$

$\vec{v}_i$	$\vec{v}_f$	$\vec{a}$	$\vec{d}$	t
0	29.2 m/s			9.0 s

$$\vec{v}_{average} = \frac{\vec{v}_f - \vec{v}_i}{t}$$
$$= \frac{29.2\ \text{m/s} + 0}{2}$$
$$= 14.6\ \text{m/s}$$

B is the answer.

17. All objects fall at the same rate if we ignore air friction. Also, the vertical component of the motion is independent of the horizontal component.

C is the answer.

19. All objects fall at the same rate. Also the vertical component of the motion is independent of the horizontal component. Therefore, the lower the cliff, the sooner the object will hit the ground.

C is the answer.

21. Slope of a position-time graph represents the velocity. All these graphs have a constant slope; therefore they have a constant velocity. If the velocity is constant, here is no acceleration.

D is the answer.

23. Sections A, B, C have a constant slope, which means that in these sections they have a constant velocity.

D is the answer.

25. When it reaches its highest point, its velocity is zero at that instant; however, the acceleration is due to gravity, which is constant.

B is the answer.

27. $\vec{R}_y = \vec{R}\sin\theta$
Convert 33° W of S to 57° S of W.
$$\vec{R}_y = (12\ \text{m})(\sin 57°)$$
$$= -10\ \text{m}$$

D is the answer.

29. From #3,

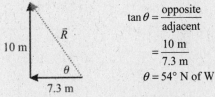

$$\tan\theta = \frac{\text{opposite}}{\text{adjacent}}$$
$$= \frac{10\ \text{m}}{7.3\ \text{m}}$$
$$\theta = 54°\ \text{N of W}$$

D is the answer.

31. From #30,

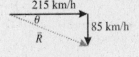

$$\tan\theta = \frac{\text{opposite}}{\text{adjacent}}$$
$$= \frac{85\ \text{km/h}}{215\ \text{km/h}}$$
$$\theta = 22°\ \text{S of E}$$

B is the answer.

33. Ignoring air friction, if the speed of a ball that is thrown horizontally from the roof of a building is increased, the vertical velocity with which the ball hits the ground will remain the same. The only force pulling the ball down is gravity, which is constant, independent of the horizontal speed.

C is the answer.

35. At maximum vertical displacement, the object passes through 0 velocity before beginning its downward velocity. The acceleration is constant at $-9.81\ \text{m/s}^2$.

B is the answer.

37. The vertical motion of projectile that is thrown horizontally starts at zero, then continues downward at an accelerated rate (g).

C is the answer.

39. Acceleration is constant (g).

A is the answer.

DYNAMICS

Lesson 1—Introduction to Dynamics

1. $\vec{F}_{net} = m\vec{a}$

$$\vec{a} = \frac{\vec{F}_{net}}{m}$$

$$= \frac{9.0 \text{ N}}{20.0 \text{ kg}}$$

$$= 0.45 \text{ m/s}^2 \text{ east}$$

3. $\vec{F}_{net} = m\vec{a}$

$$= (16.0 \text{ kg})(2.0 \text{ m/s}^2)$$

$$= 32 \text{ N}$$

5. $\vec{F}_{net} = m\vec{a}$

$$= (5.2 \text{ kg})(6.0 \text{ m/s}^2)$$

$$= 31 \text{ N}$$

7. $\vec{a} = \frac{\vec{v}_f - \vec{v}_i}{t}$

$$= \frac{25.0 \text{ m/s} - 0}{10.0 \text{ s}}$$

$$= 2.50 \text{ m/s}^2$$

$\vec{F}_{net} = m\vec{a}$

$$= (925 \text{ kg})(2.5 \text{ m/s}^2)$$

$$= 2.31 \times 10^3 \text{ N south}$$

9. $\vec{v}_f^2 = \vec{v}_i^2 + 2\vec{a}\vec{d}$

$$(12 \text{ m/s})^2 = (5.0 \text{ m/s})^2 + 2(\vec{a})(94 \text{ m})$$

$$\vec{a} = 0.633 \text{ m/s}^2$$

$\vec{F}_{net} = m\vec{a}$

$$= (1.20 \times 10^3 \text{ kg})(0.633 \text{ m/s}^2)$$

$$= 7.6 \times 10^2 \text{ N east}$$

11. **a)** $\vec{F}_{net} = m\vec{a}$

$$\vec{a} = \frac{\vec{F}_{net}}{m}$$

$$= \frac{6.6 \text{ N}}{9.0 \text{ kg}}$$

$$= 0.73 \text{ m/s}^2$$

$$\vec{v}_f^2 = \vec{v}_i^2 + 2\vec{a}\vec{d}$$

$$\vec{d} = \frac{\vec{v}_f^2 - \vec{v}_i^2}{2\vec{a}}$$

$$= \frac{(3.0 \text{ m/s}) - 0}{2(0.73 \text{ m/s}^2)}$$

$$= 2.1 \text{ m east}$$

b) $\vec{a} = \frac{\vec{v}_f - \vec{v}_i}{t}$

$$t = \frac{\vec{v}_f - \vec{v}_i}{\vec{a}}$$

$$= \frac{(3.0 \text{ m/s}) - 0 \text{ m/s}}{0.73 \text{ m/s}^2}$$

$$= 4.1 \text{ s}$$

Lesson 2—Forces in Nature

1. $\vec{F}_N = \vec{F}_g$

$$= mg$$

$$= (14.0 \text{ kg})(9.81 \text{ m/s}^2)$$

$$= 137 \text{ N}$$

3. $\vec{F}_f = \mu\vec{F}_N$

$$\mu = \frac{\vec{F}_f}{\vec{F}_N}$$

$$= \frac{3.0 \text{ N}}{20.0 \text{ N}}$$

$$= 0.15$$

5. $\vec{F}_f = \mu\vec{F}_N$

$$\vec{F}_N = -(mg\cos\theta)$$

$$\vec{F}_f = -(\mu)(mg\cos\theta)$$

$$= -(0.300)(15.0 \text{ N})(-9.81 \text{ m/s}^2)(\cos 35.0°)$$

$$= 36.0 \text{ N}$$

7. Weight $= \vec{F}_g$

$$= mg$$

$$= (25.0 \text{ kg})(9.81 \text{ m/s}^2)$$

$$= 245 \text{ N}$$

9. $\vec{F}_g = mg$

$$g = \frac{\vec{F}_g}{m}$$

$$= \frac{36.0 \text{ N}}{22.0 \text{ kg}}$$

$$= 1.64 \text{ m/s}^2$$

11. Weight $= \vec{F}_g$

$$\vec{F}_g = mg$$

$$m = \frac{\vec{F}_g}{g}$$

$$= \frac{127 \text{ N}}{9.81 \text{ m/s}^2}$$

$$= 13.0 \text{ kg}$$

Lesson 3—Applied Force or Tension

Draw a free-body diagram to solve the following problems.

1. $\vec{F}_{net} = \vec{T} + \vec{F}_g$

$$= 145 \text{ N} + (11.0 \text{ kg})(-9.81 \text{ m/s}^2)$$

$$= 37.1 \text{ N}$$

$$\vec{F}_{net} = m\vec{a}$$

$$\vec{a} = \frac{\vec{F}_{net}}{m}$$

$$= \frac{37.1 \text{ N}}{11.0 \text{ kg}}$$

$$= 3.37 \text{ m/s}^2$$

3. $\vec{F}_{net} = m\vec{a}$

$$= (15.0 \text{ kg})(8.80 \text{ m/s}^2)$$

$$= 132 \text{ N}$$

$$\vec{F}_{net} = \vec{T} + \vec{F}_g$$

$$\vec{T} = \vec{F}_{net} - \vec{F}_g$$

$$= 132 \text{ N} - (15.0 \text{ kg})(-9.81 \text{ m/s}^2)$$

$$= 279 \text{ N}$$

5. Solve for acceleration first.

$$\vec{v}_f^{\,2} = \vec{v}_i^{\,2} + 2\vec{a}\vec{d}$$

$$\vec{a} = \frac{\vec{v}_f^{\,2} - \vec{v}_i^{\,2}}{2\vec{d}}$$

$$= \frac{(4.0 \text{ m/s})^2 - 0}{2(5.0 \text{ m})}$$

$$= 1.6 \text{ m/s}^2$$

$$\vec{F}_{net} = m\vec{a}$$

$$m = \frac{\vec{F}_{net}}{\vec{a}}$$

$$= \frac{12.0 \text{ N}}{1.6 \text{ m/s}^2}$$

$$= 7.5 \text{ kg}$$

7. **a)** $\vec{F}_{net} = m\vec{a}$

$$= (1.20 \times 10^3 \text{ kg})(-1.05 \text{ m/s}^2)$$

$$= -1.26 \times 10^3 \text{ N}$$

$$\vec{F}_{net} = \vec{T} + \vec{F}_g$$

$$\vec{T} = \vec{F}_{net} - \vec{F}_g$$

$$= (-1.26 \times 10^3 \text{ N}) - (-1.18 \times 10^4 \text{ N})$$

$$= 1.06 \times 10^4 \text{ N}$$

b) Use $\vec{F}_g$ from part **a)** to reduce calculations.

$$\vec{F}_{net} = m\vec{a}$$

$$= (1.20 \times 10^3 \text{ kg})(1.05 \text{ m/s}^2)$$

$$= 1.26 \times 10^3 \text{ N}$$

$$\vec{T} = \vec{F}_{net} - \vec{F}_g$$

$$= (1.26 \times 10^3 \text{ N}) - (-1.18 \times 10^4 \text{ N})$$

$$= 1.3 \times 10^4 \text{ N}$$

c) Use $\vec{F}_g$ from part **a)** to reduce calculations.

$$\vec{F}_{net} = m\vec{a}$$

$$= (1.20 \times 10^3 \text{ kg})(0)$$

$$= 0$$

$$\vec{F}_{net} = \vec{T} + \vec{F}_g$$

$$\vec{T} = \vec{F}_{net} - \vec{F}_g$$

$$= 0 - (-1.18 \times 10^4 \text{ N})$$

$$= 1.18 \times 10^4 \text{ N}$$

9. $\vec{F}_{net} = m\vec{a}$

$$= (75.0 \text{ kg})(0)$$

$$= 0$$

$$\vec{F}_{net} = \vec{T} + \vec{F}_f$$

$$\vec{F}_f = \vec{F}_{net} - \vec{T}$$

$$= 0 - 90.0 \text{ N}$$

$$= 90.0 \text{ N (magnitude only)}$$

11. $\vec{F}_{net} = \vec{T} + \vec{F}_f$

$$= (2.5 \times 10^2 \text{ N}) + (-1.4 \times 10^2 \text{ N})$$

$$= 110 \text{ N}$$

$$m = \frac{\vec{F}_g}{g}$$

$$= \frac{1.0 \times 10^2 \text{ N}}{-9.81 \text{ m/s}^2}$$

$$= 10.2 \text{ kg}$$

$$\vec{F}_{net} = m\vec{a}$$

$$\vec{a} = \frac{\vec{F}_{net}}{m}$$

$$= \frac{11.0 \text{ N}}{10.2 \text{ kg}}$$

$$= 1.1 \times 10^1 \text{ m/s}^2 \text{ north}$$

13. $\vec{F}_{net} = \vec{F}_f$

$$\vec{F}_{net} = m\vec{a}$$

$$\vec{a} = \frac{\vec{F}_f}{m}$$

$$= \frac{-1.80 \times 10^4 \text{ N}}{1.50 \times 10^3 \text{ kg}}$$

$$= -12.0 \text{ m/s}^2$$

$$\vec{v}_f^{\,2} = \vec{v}_i^{\,2} + 2\vec{a}\vec{d}$$

$$\vec{d} = \frac{\vec{v}_f^{\,2} - \vec{v}_i^{\,2}}{2\vec{a}}$$

$$= \frac{0 - (24.0 \text{ m/s})^2}{2(-12.0 \text{ m/s}^2)}$$

$$= 24.0 \text{ m}$$

15. $\vec{F}_{net} = \text{weight of 1.5 kg mass}$

$$\vec{F}_{net} = \vec{F}_g$$

$$m_{net}\vec{a} = mg$$

$$\vec{a} = \frac{mg}{m_{net}}$$

$$= \frac{(1.5 \text{ kg})(-9.81 \text{ m/s}^2)}{(1.0 \text{ kg} + 1.5 \text{ kg})}$$

$$= 5.9 \text{ m/s}^2$$

17. $\vec{F}_{net} = \vec{T} + \vec{F}_f$

$\vec{T} = (60.0 \text{ N})(\cos 42.0°)$

$\phantom{\vec{T}} = 44.6 \text{ N}$

$\vec{F}_{net} = 44.6 \text{ N} + (-15 \text{ N})$

$\phantom{\vec{F}_{net}} = 29.6 \text{ N}$

$m = \dfrac{\vec{F}_g}{g}$

$ = \dfrac{125 \text{ N}}{9.81 \text{ m/s}^2}$

$ = 12.7 \text{ kg}$

$\vec{F}_{net} = m\vec{a}$

$\vec{a} = \dfrac{\vec{F}_{net}}{m}$

$\phantom{\vec{a}} = \dfrac{29.6 \text{ N}}{12.7 \text{ kg}}$

$\phantom{\vec{a}} = 2.33 \text{ m/s}^2$

19. $\vec{v}_f^2 = v_i^2 + 2\vec{a}\vec{d}$

$\vec{a} = \dfrac{v_f^2 - v_i^2}{2d}$

$\phantom{\vec{a}} = \dfrac{0 - (3.0 \text{ m/s})^2}{(2)(8.0 \text{ m})}$

$\phantom{\vec{a}} = -0.56 \text{ m/s}^2$

$\vec{F}_{net} = \vec{F}_f$

$\vec{F}_f = m\vec{a}$

$\phantom{\vec{F}_f} = (-0.56 \text{ m/s}^2)(0.48 \text{ kg})$

$\phantom{\vec{F}_f} = -0.27 \text{ N or } 0.27 \text{ N south}$

21. a) $\vec{F}_{net} = m\vec{a}$

$\vec{a} = \dfrac{\vec{F}_{net}}{m}$

$\phantom{\vec{a}} = \dfrac{20.0 \text{ N}}{5.0 \text{ kg}}$

$\phantom{\vec{a}} = 4.0 \text{ m/s}^2$

b) $\vec{F}_{net} = m\vec{a}$

$\phantom{\vec{F}_{net}} = (3.0 \text{ kg})(4.0 \text{ m/s}^2)$

$\phantom{\vec{F}_{net}} = 12 \text{ N}$

23. Find x components.

$x_1 = \vec{T}_1 \cos\theta$

$ = (40.0 \text{ N})(\cos 20.0°)$

$ = 37.6 \text{ N}$

$x_2 = \vec{T}_2 \cos\theta$

$ = (25.0 \text{ N})(\cos 30.0°)$

$ = 21.7 \text{ N}$

$x_{total} = 59.2 \text{ N}$

Find y components.

$y_1 = \vec{T}_1 \sin\theta$

$ = (40.0 \text{ N})(\sin 20.0°)$

$ = 13.7 \text{ N}$

$y_2 = \vec{T}_2 \sin\theta$

$ = (25.0 \text{ N})(\sin 30.0°)$

$ = 12.5 \text{ N}$

$y_{total} = 1.18 \text{ N}$

Add x_{total} and y_{total} $(\vec{T})$.

$\vec{T} = \sqrt{x^2 + y^2}$

$\phantom{\vec{T}} = \sqrt{(59.2 \text{ N})^2 + (1.18 \text{ N})^2}$

$\phantom{\vec{T}} = 59.25 \text{ N}$

$\tan\theta = \dfrac{\text{opp}}{\text{adj}}$

$ = \dfrac{1.18 \text{ N}}{59.2 \text{ N}}$

$\theta = 1.2°$ north of horizontal

$\vec{F}_{net} = \vec{T} - \vec{F}_f$

$\phantom{\vec{F}_{net}} = 59.25 \text{ N} - 5.0 \text{ N}$

$\phantom{\vec{F}_{net}} = 54.25 \text{ N}$

$\vec{F}_{net} = m\vec{a}$

$\vec{a} = \dfrac{\vec{F}_{net}}{m}$

$\phantom{\vec{a}} = \dfrac{54.25 \text{ N}}{25.0 \text{ kg}}$

$\phantom{\vec{a}} = 2.2 \text{ m/s}^2 \ 1.2°$ N of horizontal

Lesson 4—Physics of an Inclined Plane

1.

$\sin\theta = \dfrac{\text{opposite}}{\text{hypotenuse}}$

$\sin 25.0° = \dfrac{(\vec{F}_g)_x}{445 \text{ N}}$

$(\vec{F}_g)_x = (445 \text{ N})(\sin 25.0°)$

$\phantom{(\vec{F}_g)_x} = 188 \text{ N}$

3.

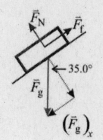

$$\sin\theta = \frac{\text{opposite}}{\text{hypotenuse}}$$

$$\sin 35° = \frac{(F_g)_x}{275\ N}$$

$$(F_g)_x = (275\ N)(\sin 35.0°)$$

$$= 158\ N$$

$$\vec{F}_g = mg$$

$$m = \frac{\vec{F}_g}{g}$$

$$= \frac{275\ N}{9.81\ m/s^2}$$

$$= 28.0\ kg$$

$$\vec{F}_{net} = m\vec{a}$$

$$\vec{a} = \frac{\vec{F}_{net}}{m}$$

$$= \frac{62\ N}{28.0\ kg}$$

$$= 28.0\ kg$$

5.

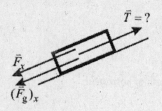

$$\vec{F}_f = \mu \vec{F}_g \cos\theta$$

$$= (0.180)(125\ N)(\cos 23.0°)$$

$$= 20.7\ N$$

$$(\vec{F}_g)_x = \vec{F}_g \sin\theta$$

$$= (125\ N)(\sin 23.0°)$$

$$= 48.8\ N$$

$$\vec{T} = \vec{F}_f + (\vec{F}_g)_x$$

$$= 20.7\ N + 48.8\ N$$

$$= 69.6\ N$$

7. **a)** $\vec{F}_f = \mu \vec{F}_N$

$$= \mu mg \cos\theta$$

$$= (0.25)(1.0\ kg)(9.81\ m/s^2)(\cos 30.0°)$$

$$= 2.12\ N$$

$$\vec{F}_{net} = \vec{F}_g - \vec{F}_x - \vec{F}_x$$

$$= 19.6\ N - 4.9\ N - 2.1\ N$$

$$= 12.6\ N$$

$$\vec{F}_{net} = m\vec{a}$$

$$\vec{a} = \frac{\vec{F}_{net}}{m}$$

$$= \frac{12.6\ N}{3.0\ kg}$$

$$= 4.2\ m/s^2$$

b)

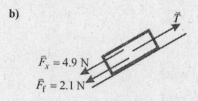

$$\vec{F}_x = 4.9\ N$$

$$\vec{F}_f = 2.1\ N$$

$$\vec{F}_{net} = m\vec{a}$$

$$= (1.0\ kg)(4.2\ m/s^2)$$

$$= 4.2\ N$$

$$\vec{F}_{net} = \vec{T} - \vec{F}_x - \vec{F}_f$$

$$\vec{T} = \vec{F}_{net} + \vec{F}_x + \vec{F}_f$$

$$= 4.2\ N + 4.9\ N + 2.1\ N$$

$$= 1.2\ N\ \text{or}\ 11\ N$$

Lesson 5—Newton's Third Law of Motion

1. $\vec{F}_1 = -\vec{F}_2$

$$m_A \vec{a}_A = -m_B \vec{a}_B$$

$$(38\ kg)(0.60\ m/s^2) = -m_B(-0.75\ m/s^2)$$

$$m_B = 3.0 \times 10^1\ kg$$

3. $\vec{a} = \dfrac{\vec{v}_f - \vec{v}_i}{t}$

$$= \frac{22\ m/s - 11\ m/s}{0.75\ s}$$

$$= 14.6\ m/s^2$$

$$\vec{F}_{net} = m\vec{a}$$

$$= (9.8 \times 10^3\ kg)(14.6\ m/s^2)$$

$$= 1.4 \times 10^5\ N\ \text{east}$$

5. **a)** $\vec{F}_f = \mu mg$

$$= (0.35)(4.0 \text{ kg})(9.81 \text{ m/s}^2)$$

$$= 13.7 \text{ N}$$

$\vec{F}_{net} = \vec{T} - \vec{F}_f$

$$= 14.0 \text{ N} - 13.7 \text{ N}$$

$$= 0.3 \text{ N}$$

$\vec{F}_{net} = m\vec{a}$

$$\vec{a} = \frac{\vec{F}_{net}}{m}$$

$$= \frac{0.3 \text{ N}}{4.0 \text{ kg}}$$

$$= 0.067 \text{ m/s}^2$$

b) $\vec{F}_{net} = m\vec{a}$

$$= (1.0 \text{ kg})(0.067 \text{ m/s}^2)$$

$$= 0.067 \text{ N}$$

$\vec{F}_{net} = \vec{T} + \vec{F}_f$

$\vec{T} = \vec{F}_{net} - \vec{F}_f$

$$= 0.067 \text{ N} + 3.43 \text{ N}$$

$$= 3.5 \text{ N}$$

$\vec{F}_f = \mu \vec{F}_N$ or $\vec{F}_f = \mu mg$

$$= (0.35)(1.0 \text{ kg})(9.81 \text{ m/s}^2)$$

$$= 3.43 \text{ N}$$

Lesson 6—Newton's Law of Universal Gravitation

1. $\vec{F}_g = \dfrac{Gm_1m_2}{r^2}$

$$= \frac{\left(6.67 \times 10^{-11} \frac{\text{N} \cdot \text{m}^2}{\text{kg}^2}\right)(70.0 \text{ kg})(52.0 \text{ kg})}{(1.50 \text{ m})^2}$$

$$= 1.08 \times 10^{-7} \text{ N}$$

3. $\vec{F}_g = \dfrac{Gm_1m_2}{r^2}$

$$m_2 = \frac{F_g r^2}{G}$$

$$= \frac{\left(2.30 \times 10^{-8} \text{ N}\right)(10.0 \text{ m})^2}{6.67 \times 10^{-11} \frac{\text{N} \cdot \text{m}^2}{\text{kg}^2}}$$

$$= 3.45 \times 10^4 \text{ kg}^2$$

$$m = 1.86 \times 10^2 \text{ kg}$$

5. $\vec{F}_g = \dfrac{Gm_1m_2}{r^2}$

$$m_2 = \frac{\vec{F}_g r^2}{Gm_1}$$

$$= \frac{\left(3.2 \times 10^{-6} \text{ N}\right)\left(2.1 \times 10^{-1} \text{ m}\right)^2}{\left(6.67 \times 10^{-11} \frac{\text{N} \cdot \text{m}^2}{\text{kg}^2}\right)\left(5.5 \times 10^1 \text{ kg}\right)}$$

$$= 3.8 \times 10^1 \text{ N}$$

7. $\vec{F}_g = \dfrac{Gm_1m_2}{r^2}$

$$= \frac{\left(6.67 \times 10^{-11} \frac{\text{N} \cdot \text{m}^2}{\text{kg}^2}\right)\left(5.98 \times 10^{24} \text{ kg}\right)(70.0 \text{ kg})}{\left(6.37 \times 10^6 \text{ m}\right)^2}$$

$$= 6.88 \times 10^2 \text{ N}$$

9. $\vec{F}_g = \dfrac{Gm_1m_2}{r^2}$

$$\vec{F}_g \propto \frac{1}{r^2}$$

Distance changes by a factor of:

$$\frac{\text{To}}{\text{From}} = \frac{1.27 \times 10^7 \text{ m}}{6.37 \times 10^6 \text{ m}} = 2.00$$

Distance changes by a factor of 2.00.
Therefore, $\vec{F}_g$ changes by a factor of 0.250 or

$$\frac{1}{(2.00)^2}$$

$$\vec{F}_g = 6.88 \times 10^2 \text{ N} \times 0.250$$

$$= 1.72 \times 10^2 \text{ N}$$

11.

Because $\vec{F}_1 = \vec{F}_2$, and because these forces are in opposite directions, the force will be zero.

13. $\vec{F}_g = \dfrac{Gm_1m_2}{r^2}$

$$\vec{F}_g \propto \frac{m_1 m_2}{r^2}$$

$$\propto \frac{(2)(2)}{(3)^2}$$

$$\propto 0.444$$

$$\vec{F}_g = \left(3.24 \times 10^{-7} \text{ N}\right)(0.444)$$

$$= 1.44 \times 10^{-7} \text{ N}$$

Lesson 7—Field Explanation

1. $\vec{F}_g = mg$

$= (25.0 \text{ kg})(9.81 \text{ m/s}^2)$

$= 245 \text{ N}$

3. $\vec{F}_g = mg$

$g = \dfrac{\vec{F}_g}{m}$

$= \dfrac{36.0 \text{ N}}{22.0 \text{ kg}}$

$= 1.64 \text{ m/s}^2$

5. $\vec{F}_g = mg$

$m = \dfrac{\vec{F}_g}{g}$

$= \dfrac{127 \text{ N}}{9.81 \text{ m/s}^2}$

$= 12.9 \text{ kg}$

Review Exercises—Dynamics

1.

$\vec{v}_i$	$\vec{v}_f$	$\vec{a}$	$\vec{d}$	t
0	3.50 m/s	?		2.00×10^{-1} s

$\vec{a} = \dfrac{\vec{v}_f - \vec{v}_i}{t}$

$= \dfrac{3.50 \text{ m/s}}{2.00 \times 10^{-1} \text{ s}}$

$= 17.5 \text{ m/s}$

$\vec{F}_{net} = m\vec{a}$

$m = \dfrac{\vec{F}_{net}}{\vec{a}}$

$= \dfrac{16.0 \text{ N}}{17.5 \text{ m/s}^2}$

$= 0.914 \text{ kg}$

3. **a)**

$\vec{F}_g = mg$

$= (1.20 \times 10^3 \text{ kg})(9.81 \text{ m/s}^2)$

$= -1.18 \times 10^4 \text{ N}$

$\vec{F}_{net} = m\vec{a}$

$= (1.20 \times 10^3 \text{ kg})(-1.05 \text{ m/s}^2)$

$= -1.26 \times 10^3 \text{ N}$

$\vec{F}_{net} = \vec{T} + \vec{F}_g$

$\vec{T} = \vec{F}_{net} - \vec{F}_g$

$= -1.26 \times 10^3 \text{ N} - (-1.18 \times 10^4 \text{ N})$

$= 1.05 \times 10^4 \text{ N}$

b)

$\vec{F}_{net} = m\vec{a}$

$= (1.20 \times 10^3 \text{ kg})(1.05 \text{ m/s}^2)$

$= 1.26 \times 10^3 \text{ N}$

$\vec{F}_{net} = \vec{T} + \vec{F}_g$

$\vec{T} = \vec{F}_{net} - \vec{F}_g$

$= 1.26 \times 10^3 \text{ N} - (-1.18 \times 10^4 \text{ N})$

$= 1.31 \times 10^4 \text{ N}$

c)

$\vec{F}_{net} = 0$

$\therefore \vec{T} = \vec{F}_g$

$= -1.18 \times 10^4 \text{ N}$

5. $\vec{F}_g = \dfrac{Gm_1 m_2}{r^2}$

$1.95 \times 10^3 \text{ N} =$

$\dfrac{\left(6.67 \times 10^{-11} \dfrac{\text{N} \bullet \text{m}^2}{\text{kg}^2}\right)(25)(5.98 \times 10^{24} \text{ kg})(m)}{(2.5 \times 6.37 \times 10^6 \text{ m})^2}$

$m = 50 \text{ kg}$ or $5.0 \times 10^1 \text{ kg}$

7. $\vec{F}_g = \dfrac{Gm_1 m_2}{r^2}$

$r^2 = \dfrac{Gm_1 m_2}{F_g}$

$= \dfrac{\left(6.67 \times 10^{-11} \dfrac{\text{N} \bullet \text{m}^2}{\text{kg}^2}\right)(75.0 \text{ kg})(7.90 \times 10^{25} \text{ kg})}{112 \text{ N}}$

$= 3.53 \times 10^{15} \text{ m}^2$

$r = 5.94 \times 10^7 \text{ m}$

9. $\vec{F}_{net} = 0$

$\vec{F}_f = -\vec{T} = -3.0$ N

$\vec{F}_f = \mu\vec{F}_N$ or $\vec{F}_f = \mu mg$

$\mu = \dfrac{\vec{F}_f}{mg}$

$= \dfrac{3.0 \text{ N}}{(2.5 \text{ kg})(9.80 \text{ m/s}^2)}$

$= 0.12$

11. $\vec{F}_g = mg$

$m = \dfrac{\vec{F}_g}{g}$

$= \dfrac{50.0 \text{ N}}{9.81 \text{ m/s}^2}$

$= 5.10$ kg

13. a) $\vec{F}_{net} = m\vec{a}$

$\vec{a} = \dfrac{\vec{F}_{net}}{m}$

$= \dfrac{85 \text{ N}}{(6.8 + 5.2) \text{ kg}}$

$= 7.1 \text{ m/s}^2$

b) Find the force acting to accelerate m_2.

$\vec{F} = m_2\vec{a}$

$= (5.2 \text{ kg})(7.1 \text{ m/s}^2)$

$= 37$ N

15. $\vec{F}_{net} = \mu mg + \vec{T}$

$T = \vec{F}_{net} - \mu mg$

$= 53 \text{ N} - (0.30)(4.0 \text{ kg})(9.81 \text{ m/s}^2)$

$= 41$ N

17. $(\vec{F}_g)_x = \vec{F}_g \sin\theta$

$= mg\sin\theta$

$= (25.0 \text{ kg})(9.81 \text{ m/s}^2)(\sin 30.0°)$

$= 122.6$ N

$\vec{F}_{net} = 0$

$0 = (\vec{F}_g)_x + F_f$

$\vec{F}_f = -(\vec{F}_g)_x$

$= -122.6$ N

$\vec{F}_f = \mu mg \cos\theta$

$\mu = \dfrac{\vec{F}_f}{mg\cos\theta}$

$= \dfrac{-122.6 \text{ N}}{(25.0 \text{ kg})(-9.81 \text{ m/s}^2)(\cos 30.0°)}$

$= 0.577$

19. $\vec{F}_f = \mu mg \cos\theta$

$= (0.20)(7.6 \text{ kg})(9.81 \text{ m/s}^2)(\cos 33°)$

$= 13$ N

21. $\vec{F}_g = \dfrac{Gm_1m_2}{r^2}$

$F_1 = \dfrac{\left(6.67\times10^{-11}\ \dfrac{\text{N}\bullet\text{m}^2}{\text{kg}^2}\right)(0.35 \text{ kg})(0.35 \text{ kg})}{(0.25 \text{ m})^2}$

$= 1.31\times10^{-10}$ N

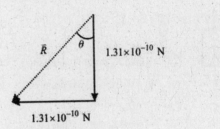

magnitude F_1 = magnitude F_2

$\vec{R} = \sqrt{a^2 + b^2}$

$= \sqrt{\left(1.31\times10^{-10}\text{ N}\right)^2 + \left(1.31\times10^{-10}\text{ N}\right)^2}$

$= 1.85\times10^{-10}$ N 45° N of E

23. $\vec{F}_g = \dfrac{Gm_1m_2}{r^2}$

$= \dfrac{\left(6.67\times10^{-11}\ \dfrac{\text{N}\bullet\text{m}^2}{\text{kg}^2}\right)(5.98\times10^{24} \text{ kg})(525 \text{ kg})}{\left(6.37\times10^6 \text{ m} + (3.0\times10^3 \text{ km}\times1\,000 \text{ m})\right)^2}$

$= 2.38\times10^3$ N

$\vec{F}_g = mg$

$g = \dfrac{\vec{F}_g}{m}$

$= \dfrac{2.38\times10^3 \text{ N}}{525 \text{ kg}}$

$= 4.53 \text{ m/s}^2$

25. $\vec{F}_g = mg$

$g = \dfrac{\vec{F}_g}{m}$

$= \dfrac{7.22 \times 10^2 \text{ N}}{1.10 \times 10^2 \text{ kg}}$

$= 6.56 \text{ N/kg}$

Practice Test

1. $\vec{F}_f = \mu \vec{F}_N$

$\therefore \mu = \dfrac{\vec{F}_f}{\vec{F}_N}$

D is the answer.

3. According to Newton's 2nd Law $\vec{a} \propto \vec{F}_{net}$

A is the answer.

5.

$\vec{F}_{net} = \vec{T} + \vec{F}_g$

$\vec{T} = \vec{F}_{net} - \vec{F}_g$

where $\vec{F}_{net}$ and $\vec{F}_g$ are both in a downward direction $(-)$

$\vec{T} = -x\vec{F}_{net} - (-625 \text{ N})$

$= (\text{some negative value}) + 625 \text{ N}$

which can be written as

$\vec{T} = 625 \text{ N} - \text{some value} \left(\vec{F}_{net} \right)$

$\therefore \vec{T}$ is less than 625 N

A is the answer.

7. $\vec{a} \propto \vec{F}$

A is the answer.

9. $\vec{F}_{net} = \vec{T} + \vec{F}_g$

$\vec{F}_{net} = 775 \text{ N} + (75 \text{ kg})(-9.81 \text{ m/s}^2)$

$= 39 \text{ N}$

Positive $\therefore$ upward

11. $\vec{F}_N = \vec{F}_g$ on a horizontal surface.

B is the answer.

13.

$\vec{F}_{net} = m\vec{a}$

$= (3.0 \text{ kg})(1.2 \text{ m/s}^2)$

$= 3.6 \text{ N}$

$\vec{F}_{net} = \vec{T} + \vec{F}_f$

$\vec{F}_f = \vec{F}_{net} - \vec{T}$

$= 3.6 \text{ N} - 5.2 \text{ N}$

$= -1.6 \text{ N}; \text{ magnitude only } = 1.6 \text{ N}$

A is the answer.

15. $\vec{F}_g \propto g$

Therefore, if g increases, so does $\vec{F}_g$.

B is the answer.

17. The velocity is constant; therefore there is no net force.

A is the answer.

19. The slope of the graph represents the acceleration; therefore we are looking for the section that has the greatest uniform slope.

$\vec{F}_{net} = m\vec{a}$

The greater the acceleration (slope), the greater the net force.

B is the answer.

21. $\vec{F}_N = \vec{F}_g$ on a horizontal surface. Because the three objects have the same masses, they have the same weights $\left(\vec{F}_g \right)$.

D is the answer.

23.

If the object is moving at a constant velocity, there is no net force.

$\Delta \vec{T} = \vec{F}_g = 5.0 \text{ N}$

B is the answer.

25.

$$\vec{F}_{net} = m\vec{a}$$
$$= (1.50 \text{ kg})(1.20 \text{ m/s}^2)$$
$$= 1.80 \text{ N}$$

$$\vec{F}_g = mg$$
$$= (1.50 \text{ kg})(-9.81 \text{ m/s}^2)$$
$$= -14.7 \text{ N}$$

$$\vec{F}_{net} = \vec{T} + \vec{F}_g$$
$$\vec{T} = \vec{F}_{net} - \vec{F}_g$$
$$= 1.80 \text{ N} - (-14.7 \text{ N})$$
$$= 16.5 \text{ N}$$

D is the answer.

27. $\vec{F}_{net} = m\vec{a}$

$$\frac{\vec{F}_{net}}{\vec{a}} = m$$

If we know the net force acting on an object and the acceleration of the object, it is possible for us to find the mass of the object.

D is the answer.

29. $\vec{F}_g = \dfrac{Gm_1m_2}{r^2}$

$$= \frac{\left(6.67\times10^{-11} \dfrac{\text{N}\bullet\text{m}^2}{\text{kg}^2}\right)(5.98\times10^{24} \text{ kg})(0.20 \text{ kg})}{\left(2(6.37\times10^6 \text{ m})\right)^2}$$

$$= 0.50 \text{ N}$$

A is the answer.

31. Object B has twice the mass of object A. Solving for weight $\left(\vec{F}_g = mg\right)$, we find that on Earth, object B will have twice the weight of object A. On the moon, object B will experience twice the gravitational force as object A $\left(\vec{F}_g = mg\right)$. Near the surface of the Earth, the acceleration due to gravity is a constant.

B is the answer.

33. $\vec{F}_{net} = \vec{F}_{g2}$

$$m_{net}\vec{a} = m_2g$$

$$\vec{a} = \frac{m_2g}{m_{net}}$$

$$= \frac{(7.5 \text{ kg})(9.81 \text{ m/s}^2)}{(7.5 \text{ kg} + 3.0 \text{ kg})}$$

$$= 7.0 \text{ m/s}^2$$

C is the answer.

35. $\vec{a} = \dfrac{\vec{v}_f - \vec{v}_i}{r}$

$$= \frac{0 - 22 \text{ m/s}}{9.0 \text{ s}}$$

$$= 2.44 \text{ m/s}^2$$

$$\vec{F}_{net} = m\vec{a}$$

$$= (1.2\times10^3 \text{ kg})(2.44 \text{ m/s}^2)$$

$$= 2.9\times10^3 \text{ N}$$

D is the answer.

CIRCULAR MOTION, WORK, AND ENERGY

Lesson 1—Uniform Circular Motion

1. $F_c = \dfrac{mv^2}{r}$

$\quad = \dfrac{(925 \text{ kg})(22 \text{ m/s})^2}{75 \text{ m}}$

$\quad = 6.0 \times 10^3 \text{ N}$

3. $\vec{F}_c = \dfrac{mv^2}{r}$

$\quad = \dfrac{(822 \text{ kg})(28.0 \text{ m/s})^2}{105 \text{ m}}$

$\quad = 6.14 \times 10^3 \text{ N}$

5. $F_c = \dfrac{mv^2}{r}$

$4.60 \times 10^{-14} \text{ N} = \dfrac{(9.11 \times 10^{-31} \text{ kg})(v^2)}{2.00 \times 10^{-2} \text{ m}}$

$v = \sqrt{\dfrac{(4.60 \times 10^{-14} \text{ N})(2.00 \times 10^{-2} \text{ m})}{9.11 \times 10^{-31} \text{ kg}}}$

$\quad = 3.18 \times 10^7 \text{ m/s}$

7. $F_c = \dfrac{mv^2}{r}$

$\quad = \dfrac{(2.7 \times 10^3 \text{ kg})(4.7 \times 10^3 \text{ m/s})^2}{1.8 \times 10^7 \text{ m}}$

$\quad = 3.3 \times 10^3 \text{ N}$

9. a) $2r = \text{diameter}$

$r = \dfrac{30.0 \times 10^{-2} \text{ m}}{2}$

$\quad = 1.50 \times 10^{-2} \text{ m}$

$T = \dfrac{1}{f}$

$\quad = \dfrac{60 \text{ s}}{33\frac{1}{3} \text{ Hz}}$

$\quad = 1.80 \text{ s}$

$v = \dfrac{2\pi r}{T}$

$\quad = \dfrac{2\pi(15.0 \times 10^{-2} \text{ m})}{1.80 \text{ s}}$

$\quad = 0.524 \text{ m/s}$

b) $a_c = \dfrac{v^2}{r}$

$\quad = \dfrac{(0.524 \text{ m/s})^2}{15.0 \times 10^{-2} \text{ m}}$

$\quad = 1.83 \text{ m/s}^2$

11. a) $\vec{F}_N = mg$

$\quad = (932 \text{ kg})(9.81 \text{ m/s}^2)$

$\quad = 9.14 \times 10^3 \text{ N}$

$\vec{F}_f = \mu \vec{F}_N$

$\quad = (0.95)(9.14 \times 10^3 \text{ N})$

$\quad = 8.69 \times 10^3 \text{ N}$

$F_c = \dfrac{mv^2}{r}$

$8.69 \times 10^3 \text{ N} = \dfrac{(932 \text{ kg})(v^2)}{82 \text{ m}}$

$v = \sqrt{\dfrac{(8.69 \times 10^3 \text{ N})(82 \text{ m})}{932 \text{ kg}}}$

$\quad = 28 \text{ m/s}$

b) $\vec{F}_f = \mu \vec{F}_N$

$\quad = (0.40)(9.14 \times 10^3 \text{ N})$

$\quad = 3.66 \times 10^3 \text{ N}$

$F_c = \dfrac{mv^2}{r}$

$3.66 \times 10^3 \text{ N} = \dfrac{(932 \text{ kg})(v^2)}{82 \text{ m}}$

$v = \sqrt{\dfrac{(3.66 \times 10^3 \text{ N})(82 \text{ m})}{932 \text{ kg}}}$

$\quad = 18 \text{ m/s}$

c) If the coefficient of friction is less on a wet road, the force of friction is also less; therefore the car will skid further when trying to stop quickly.

13. a) Speed:

$$F_c = \frac{mv^2}{r} \quad \text{or} \quad v = \sqrt{\frac{F_c r}{m}}$$

$$v = \sqrt{\frac{(0.0981 \text{ N})(0.350 \text{ m})}{0.0400 \text{ kg}}} = 0.926 \text{ m/s}$$

$$v = \sqrt{\frac{(0.196 \text{ N})(0.350 \text{ m})}{0.0400 \text{ kg}}} = 1.31 \text{ m/s}$$

$$v = \sqrt{\frac{(0.392 \text{ N})(0.350 \text{ m})}{0.0400 \text{ kg}}} = 1.85 \text{ m/s}$$

$$v = \sqrt{\frac{(0.589 \text{ N})(0.350 \text{ m})}{0.0400 \text{ kg}}} = 2.27 \text{ m/s}$$

$$v = \sqrt{\frac{(0.785 \text{ N})(0.350 \text{ m})}{0.0400 \text{ kg}}} = 2.62 \text{ m/s}$$

Period

$$v = \frac{2\pi r}{T} \quad \text{or} \quad T = \frac{2\pi r}{v}$$

$$T = \frac{2\pi(0.350 \text{ m})}{0.926 \text{ m/s}} = 2.37 \text{ s}$$

$$T = \frac{2\pi(0.350 \text{ m})}{1.31 \text{ m/s}} = 1.68 \text{ s}$$

$$T = \frac{2\pi(0.350 \text{ m})}{1.85 \text{ m/s}} = 1.19 \text{ s}$$

$$T = \frac{2\pi(0.350 \text{ m})}{2.27 \text{ m/s}} = 0.969 \text{ s}$$

$$T = \frac{2\pi(0.350 \text{ m})}{2.62 \text{ m/s}} = 0.839 \text{ s}$$

b) F_c vs v

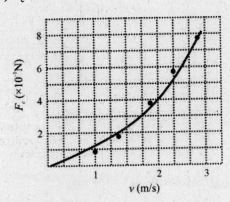

c) The slope of the graph is an increasing slope.

d) According to the formula $F_c = \frac{mv^2}{r}$, $F_c \propto v^2$.

This graph should be an exponential graph, which is an increasing slope.

e) F_c vs v^2

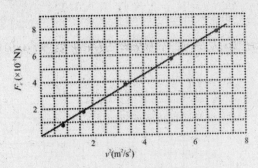

f) The slope of the graph is constant.

g) According to the equation $F_c = \frac{mv^2}{r}$, $F_c \propto v^2$.

This graph should be a straight line as drawn, which is a constant slope.

15. a) Speed:

$$v = \frac{2\pi r}{T} \quad \text{or} \quad v = \sqrt{\frac{F_c r}{m}}$$

$$v = \sqrt{\frac{2\pi(0.350 \text{ m})}{0.296 \text{ s}}} = 7.43 \text{ m/s}$$

$$v = \sqrt{\frac{2\pi(0.350 \text{ m})}{0.593 \text{ s}}} = 3.71 \text{ m/s}$$

$$v = \sqrt{\frac{2\pi(0.350 \text{ m})}{0.839 \text{ s}}} = 2.62 \text{ m/s}$$

$$v = \sqrt{\frac{2\pi(0.350 \text{ m})}{1.03 \text{ s}}} = 2.14 \text{ m/s}$$

$$v = \sqrt{\frac{2\pi(0.350 \text{ m})}{1.19 \text{ s}}} = 1.85 \text{ m/s}$$

$$v = \sqrt{\frac{2\pi(0.350 \text{ m})}{1.33 \text{ s}}} = 1.65 \text{ m/s}$$

b) v vs T

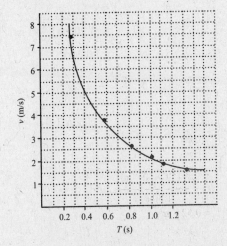

c) The slope of the graph is a decreasing slope.

d) According to the equation $v = \dfrac{2\pi r}{T}$, $v \propto \dfrac{1}{T}$.

This graph should be a decreasing slope.

e) v vs $\dfrac{1}{T}$

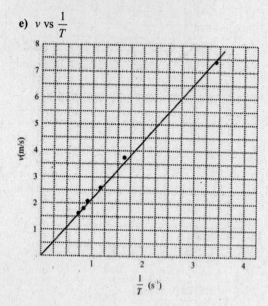

$\dfrac{1}{T}$ (s^{-1})

f) The slope of this graph is constant.

g) According to the formula $v = \dfrac{2\pi r}{T}$, $v \propto \dfrac{1}{T}$.

This graph should be a straight line as drawn, which is a constant slope.

Lesson 2—Vertical Circular Motion

1.

$T = 0$

$\therefore F_c = F_g$

$\dfrac{mv^2}{r} = mg$

$v = \sqrt{rg}$

$= \sqrt{(5.00 \text{ m})(9.81 \text{ m/s}^2)}$

$= 7.00 \text{ m/s}$

3.

$\vec{F}_c = \vec{F}_N - \vec{F}_g$

$= 1.96 \times 10^3 \text{ N} - 655 \text{ N}$

$= 1.31 \times 10^3 \text{ N}$

$\vec{F}_g = mg$

$m = \dfrac{\vec{F}_g}{g}$

$= \dfrac{655 \text{ N}}{9.81 \text{ m/s}^2}$

$= 66.8 \text{ kg}$

$\vec{F}_c = \dfrac{mv^2}{r}$

$v = \sqrt{\dfrac{\vec{F}_c r}{m}}$

$= \sqrt{\dfrac{(1.31 \times 10^3 \text{ N})(18.0 \text{ m})}{66.8 \text{ kg}}}$

$= 18.8 \text{ m/s}$

5.

$\vec{F}_g = mg$

$= (1.50 \text{ kg})(-9.81 \text{ m/s}^2)$

$= -14.7 \text{ N}$

$\vec{F}_c = \vec{T} + \vec{F}_g$

$= 186 \text{ N} + (-14.7 \text{ N})$

$= 171 \text{ N}$

$\vec{F}_c = \dfrac{mv^2}{r}$

$v = \sqrt{\dfrac{\vec{F}_c r}{m}}$

$= \sqrt{\dfrac{(171 \text{ N})(1.90 \text{ m})}{1.50 \text{ kg}}}$

$= 14.7 \text{ m/s}$

7.

$\vec{F}_g = mg$

$\vec{T} = 0$

$\therefore \vec{F}_c = \vec{F}_g$

$\dfrac{mv^2}{r} = mg$

$v = \sqrt{rg}$

$= \sqrt{(48 \text{ m})(9.81 \text{ m/s}^2)}$

$= 22 \text{ m/s}$

9. a)

High

$$\vec{F_c} = \vec{T} + \left(-\vec{F_g}\right)$$

$$\vec{T} = \vec{F_c} - \left(-\vec{F_g}\right)$$

or $\vec{T} = \vec{F_c} - \vec{F_g}$

Low

$$\vec{F_c} = \vec{T} + \vec{F_g}$$

$$\vec{T} = \vec{F_c} - \vec{F_g}$$

or $\vec{T} = \vec{F_c} + \vec{F_g}$

$$\vec{F_g} = mg$$

$$= (2.5\ \text{kg})\left(-9.91\ \text{m/s}^2\right)$$

$$= -24.5\ \text{N}$$

$$\vec{F_c} = \frac{mv^2}{r}$$

$$= \frac{(2.5\ \text{kg})(12\ \text{m/s})^2}{0.75\ \text{m}}$$

$$= 4.8 \times 10^2\ \text{N}$$

b) i) $\vec{T} = \vec{F_c} + \vec{F_g}$

$$= 480\ \text{N} + 24.5\ \text{N}$$

$$= 5.0 \times 10^2\ \text{N}$$

ii) $\vec{T} = \vec{F_c} - \vec{F_g}$

$$= 480\ \text{N} - 24.5\ \text{N}$$

$$= 4.6 \times 10^2\ \text{N}$$

Lesson 3—Banked Curves

1.

$$\tan\theta = \frac{v^2}{rg}$$

$$\tan 20.0° = \frac{v^2}{(125\ \text{m})\left(9.81\ \text{m/s}^2\right)}$$

$$v = \sqrt{(\tan 20.0°)(125\ \text{m})\left(9.81\ \text{m/s}^2\right)}$$

$$= 21.1\ \text{m/s}$$

3.

$$v = \frac{d}{t}$$

$$d = (115\ \text{m/s})\left(1.20 \times 10^2\ \text{s}\right)$$

$$= 1.38 \times 10^4\ \text{m}$$

$$C = 2\pi r$$

$$r = \frac{C}{2\pi}$$

$$= \frac{1.38 \times 10^4\ \text{m}}{2\pi}$$

$$= 2.20 \times 10^3\ \text{m}$$

$$\tan\theta = \frac{v^2}{rg}$$

$$= \frac{(115\ \text{m/s})^2}{\left(2.20 \times 10^3\ \text{m}\right)\left(9.81\ \text{m/s}^2\right)}$$

$$\theta = 31.5°$$

5.

$$\tan\theta = \frac{v^2}{rg}$$

$$r = \frac{v^2}{g(\tan\theta)}$$

$$= \frac{(205\ \text{m/s})^2}{\left(9.81\ \text{m/s}^2\right)(\tan 29.0°)}$$

$$= 7.73 \times 10^3\ \text{m}$$

Lesson 4—Motion in the Heavens

1.

$$\frac{T_e^2}{r_e^3} = \frac{T_m^2}{r_m^3}$$

$$\frac{(1.00\ \text{years})^2}{(1.49 \times 10^{11}\ \text{m})^3} = \frac{T_m^2}{(5.79 \times 10^{10}\ \text{m})^3}$$

$$T_m = 0.242\ \text{years}$$

3.

$$K = \frac{T^2}{r^3}$$

$$r^3 = \frac{T^2}{K}$$

$$= \frac{(24\ \text{h} \times 3\,600\ \text{s/h})^2}{9.84 \times 10^{-14}\ \text{s}^2/\text{m}^3}$$

$$r = 4.23 \times 10^7\ \text{m}$$

$$d = r - 6.38 \times 10^6\ \text{m}$$

$$= 4.23 \times 10^7\ \text{m} - 6.38 \times 10^6\ \text{m}$$

$$= 3.61 \times 10^7\ \text{m}$$

Lesson 5—Newton's Law of Universal Gravitation

1. $\vec{F}_c = \vec{F}_g$

$$\frac{mv^2}{r} = \frac{Gm_e m_m}{r^2}$$

or

$$v = \sqrt{\frac{Gm_e}{r}}$$

$$= \sqrt{\frac{\left(6.67\times10^{-11}\ \frac{N\bullet m^2}{kg^2}\right)\left(5.98\times10^{24}\ kg\right)}{3.85\times10^8\ m}}$$

$$= 1.02\times10^3\ m/s$$

3. $\vec{F}_c = \vec{F}_g$

$$\frac{mv^2}{r} = \frac{Gm_e m_m}{r^2}$$

or

$$v = \sqrt{\frac{Gm_e}{r}}$$

$$= \sqrt{\frac{\left(6.67\times10^{-11}\ \frac{N\bullet m^2}{kg^2}\right)\left(1.90\times10^{27}\ kg\right)}{\left(5.00\times10^6\ m + 7.18\times10^7\ m\right)}}$$

$$= 4.1\times10^4\ m/s$$

5. $\dfrac{T_e^{\ 2}}{r_e^{\ 3}} = \dfrac{T_m^{\ 2}}{r_m^{\ 3}}$

$$\frac{\left(1\ year\right)^2}{\left(1.49\times10^{11}\ m\right)^3} = \frac{\left(T_m\right)^2}{\left(2.3\times10^{11}\ m\right)^3}$$

$$T_m = 1.9\ years$$

7. $T = \dfrac{2\pi\sqrt{r^3}}{\sqrt{Gm_e}}$

$$\sqrt{r^3} = \frac{T\sqrt{Gm_e}}{2\pi}$$

$$r^3 = \frac{T^2 Gm_e}{4\pi^2}$$

$$r = \sqrt[3]{\frac{T^2 Gm_e}{4\pi^2}}$$

$$T = \left(1\ d\right)\left(24\ h/d\right)\left(3\ 600\ s/h\right)$$

$$= 8.64\times10^4\ s$$

$$= \sqrt[3]{\frac{\left(8.64\times10^4\ s\right)^2\left(6.67\times10^{-11}\ \frac{N\bullet m^2}{kg^2}\right)\left(5.98\times10^{24}\ kg\right)}{4\pi^2}}$$

$$= 4.23\times10^7\ m$$

Distance above the Earth's surface:

$$4.23\times10^7\ m - 6.37\times10^6\ m = 3.59\times10^7\ m$$

9. $v = \dfrac{2\pi r}{T}$

$$= \frac{2\pi\left(1.49\times10^{11}\ m\right)}{\left(1\ year\right)\left(365\ days/year\right)\left(24\ h/day\right)\left(3\ 600\ s/h\right)}$$

$$= 2.97\times10^4\ m/s\ \ or\ \ 29.7\ km/s$$

$$v = \sqrt{\frac{Gm_s}{r}}$$

$$v^2 = \frac{Gm_s}{r}$$

$$m_s = \frac{v^2 r}{G}$$

$$= \frac{\left(2.97\times10^4\ m/s\right)^2\left(1.49\times10^{11}\ m\right)}{6.67\times10^{-11}\ \frac{N\bullet m^2}{kg^2}}$$

$$= 1.97\times10^{30}\ kg$$

Lesson 6—Work

1. $W = \vec{F}\vec{d}$

$$= \left(20.0\ N\right)\left(1.50\ m\right)$$

$$= 30.0\ J$$

3. $W = \vec{F}\vec{d}$

$$= \left(2.20\ N\right)\left(0\right)$$

$$= 0$$

There is no work done because there is no displacement of the object.

5. Find horizontal component of the force

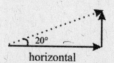

$$\vec{F}_x = \vec{F}\cos\theta$$

$$= \left(75.0\ N\right)\left(\cos 20.0°\right)$$

$$= 70.5\ N$$

$$W = \vec{F}\vec{d}$$

$$= \left(75.0\ N\right)\left(10.0\ m\right)$$

$$= 705\ J$$

7. $\vec{F}_{net} = m\vec{a}$

$= (20.0 \text{ kg})(0 \text{ m/s}^2)$

$= 0 \text{ N}$

9. Work done against friction

$W = \vec{F}\vec{d}$

$= (3.8 \text{ N})(6.0 \text{ m})$

$= 23 \text{ J}$

Work done to accelerate

$\vec{d} = \vec{v}_i t + \frac{1}{2}\vec{a}t^2$

$6.0 \text{ m} = \frac{1}{2}(\vec{a})(4.0 \text{ s})^2$

$\vec{a} = 0.75 \text{ m/s}^2$

$\vec{F}_{net} = m\vec{a}$

$= (25.0 \text{ kg})(0.75 \text{ m/s}^2)$

$= 19 \text{ N}$

$W = \vec{F}\vec{d}$

$= (19 \text{ N})(6.0 \text{ m})$

$= 1.13 \times 10^2 \text{ J}$

Total Work $= 1.1 \times 10^2 \text{ J} + 22.8 \text{ J} = 1.4 \times 10^2 \text{ J}$

11. $W =$ area under graph

$W = \vec{F}\vec{d}$

$= (3.5 \text{ N})(16.0 \text{ m})$

$= 56 \text{ J}$

Lesson 7—Power

1. $P = \frac{W}{t}$

$t = \frac{W}{P}$

$= \frac{(45.0 \text{ kg})(9.8 \text{ m/s}^2)(6.0 \text{ m})}{1.50 \times 10^3 \text{ W}}$

$= 1.8 \text{ s}$

3. $\vec{v}_{avg} = \frac{\vec{v}_f + \vec{v}_i}{2}$

$= \frac{(3.00 \text{ m/s}) + 0}{2}$

$= 1.50 \text{ m/s}$

$\vec{v}_f^2 = \vec{v}_i^2 + 2\vec{a}\vec{d}$

$(3.00 \text{ m/s}) = 2(\vec{a})(1.5 \text{ m})$

$\vec{a} = 3.0 \text{ m/s}^2$

$\vec{F}_{net} = m\vec{a}$

$= (2.00 \text{ kg})(3.0 \text{ m/s}^2)$

$= 6.0 \text{ N}$

$P = F\vec{v}$

$= (6.0 \text{ N})(1.50 \text{ m/s})$

$= 9.0 \text{ W}$

5. $\vec{v}_f^2 = \vec{v}_i^2 + 2\vec{a}\vec{d}$

$(6.0 \text{ m/s})^2 = 2(\vec{a})(2.0 \text{ m})$

$\vec{a} = 9.0 \text{ m/s}^2$

$\vec{F}_{net} = m\vec{a}$

$= (5.0 \text{ kg})(9.0 \text{ m/s}^2)$

$= 45 \text{ N}$

$\vec{F}_{net} = \vec{T} - \vec{F}_f$

$= 45 \text{ N} + 4.0 \text{ N}$

$= 49 \text{ N}$

$\vec{v}_{avg} = \frac{\vec{v}_f + \vec{v}_i}{2}$

$= \frac{(6.0 \text{ m/s}) + 0}{2}$

$= 3.0 \text{ m/s}$

$P = \vec{F}\vec{v}$

$= (49 \text{ N})(3.0 \text{ m/s})$

$= 1.5 \times 10^2 \text{ W}$

Lesson 8—Energy

1. $E_p = mgh$

$= (25.0 \text{ N})(2.10 \text{ m})$

$= 52.5 \text{ J}$

3. $E_p = \vec{F}\vec{d}$

$= (2.75 \text{ kg})(9.8 \text{ m/s}^2)(7.00 \text{ m})$

$= 1.9 \times 10^2 \text{ J}$

5. $E_p = mgh$

$$= (2.00 \times 10^2 \text{ kg})(9.8 \text{ m/s}^2)(6.0 \text{ m})$$

$$= 1.2 \times 10^4 \text{ J}$$

Lesson 9—Kinetic Energy

1. $E_k = \dfrac{1}{2}m\vec{v}^2$

$$= \dfrac{1}{2}(3.0 \text{ kg})(7.5 \text{ m/s})^2$$

$$= 84 \text{ J}$$

3. $\vec{v}_f^2 = \vec{v}_i^2 + 2\vec{a}\vec{d}$

$$= 2(2.5 \text{ m/s}^2)(15.0 \text{ m})$$

$\vec{v}_f = 8.7 \text{ m/s}$

$\vec{F}_g = mg$

$m = \dfrac{\vec{F}_g}{g}$

$$= \dfrac{10.0 \text{ N}}{9.8 \text{ m/s}^2}$$

$$= 1.0 \text{ kg}$$

$E_k = \dfrac{1}{2}m\vec{v}^2$

$$= \dfrac{1}{2}(1.02 \text{ kg})(8.66 \text{ m/s})^2$$

$$= 38 \text{ J}$$

5. $\vec{F}_g = mg$

$m = \dfrac{\vec{F}_g}{g}$

$$= \dfrac{10.0 \text{ N}}{9.8 \text{ m/s}^2}$$

$$= 1.0 \text{ kg}$$

$E_k = \dfrac{1}{2}m\vec{v}^2$

$\vec{v} = \sqrt{\dfrac{2E_k}{m}}$

$$= \sqrt{\dfrac{2(3.00 \times 10^2 \text{ J})}{1.0 \text{ kg}}}$$

$$= 24 \text{ m/s}$$

Lesson 10—Work-Energy Theorem for Net Force

1. $\vec{F}\vec{d} = \dfrac{1}{2}m\left(\vec{v}_f^2 - \vec{v}_i^2\right)$

$$\vec{v}_f^2 = \dfrac{2(23.0 \text{ N})(5.0 \times 10^{-2} \text{ m})}{0.12 \text{ kg}}$$

$$\vec{v}_f = \sqrt{\dfrac{2(23.0 \text{ N})(5.0 \times 10^{-2}\text{m})}{0.12 \text{ kg}}}$$

$$= 4.4 \text{ m/s}$$

3. Convert 5.00 km/h to m/s

$$\dfrac{(5.00 \text{ km/h})(1\,000 \text{ m/km})}{3\,600 \text{ s/h}} = 1.39 \text{ m/s}$$

$\vec{F}\vec{d} = \dfrac{1}{2}m\left(\vec{v}_f^2 - \vec{v}_i^2\right)$

$$= \dfrac{1}{2}(1.10 \times 10^3 \text{kg})\left((1.39 \text{ m/s})^2 - 0\right)$$

$$= 1.06 \times 10^3 \text{ J}$$

5. Convert weight to mass:

$\vec{F}_g = mg$

$m = \dfrac{\vec{F}_g}{g}$

$$= \dfrac{4.0 \text{ N}}{9.81 \text{ m/s}^2}$$

$$= 0.408 \text{ kg}$$

$\vec{F}\vec{d} = \dfrac{1}{2}m\left(\vec{v}_f^2 - \vec{v}_i^2\right)$

$$\vec{F} = \dfrac{\dfrac{1}{2}(0.408 \text{ kg})\left(0 - (2.1 \text{ m/s})^2\right)}{2.3 \times 10^{-2} \text{ m}}$$

$$= 39 \text{ N}$$

7.

$\vec{T} = 18 \text{ N}$

$\vec{F}_g$

$\vec{F}_g = mg$

$\quad = (1.0 \text{ kg})(-9.81 \text{ m/s}^2)$

$\quad = -9.81 \text{ N}$

$\vec{F}_{\text{net}} = \vec{T} + \vec{F}_g$

$\quad = 18 \text{ N} + (-9.81 \text{ N})$

$\quad = 8.19 \text{ N}$

$\vec{F}\vec{d} = \dfrac{1}{2}m\left(\vec{v}_f^{\,2} - \vec{v}_i^{\,2}\right)$

$v_f^{\,2} = \dfrac{2(8.19 \text{ N})(0.30 \text{ m})}{1.0 \text{ kg}}$

$\vec{v}_f = \sqrt{\dfrac{2(8.19 \text{ N})(0.30 \text{ m})}{1.0 \text{ kg}}}$

$\quad = 2.2 \text{ m/s}$

9. $\vec{F}\vec{d} = \dfrac{1}{2}m\left(\vec{v}_f^{\,2} - \vec{v}_i^{\,2}\right)$

$\vec{F} = \dfrac{\dfrac{1}{2}(0.65 \text{ kg})\left(0 - (2.0 \text{ m/s})^2\right)}{5.5 \text{ m}}$

$\quad = 0.24 \text{ N}$

11. Find net force first:

$\vec{T}$ $\vec{F}_g$

$(\vec{F}_N)$

$\vec{F}_g = mg$ $\vec{F}_g = mg$

$\quad = (6 \text{ kg})(9.81 \text{ m/s}^2)$ $\quad = (12 \text{ kg})(9.81 \text{ m/s}^2)$

$\quad = 58.9 \text{ N}$ $\quad = 117.7 \text{ N}$

$\vec{F}_{\text{net}} = 117.7 \text{ N} - 58.9 \text{ N}$

$\quad = 58.9 \text{ N}$

$\vec{F}\vec{d} = \dfrac{1}{2}m\left(\vec{v}_f^{\,2} - \vec{v}_i^{\,2}\right)$

$(58.9 \text{ N})(1.5 \text{ m}) = \dfrac{1}{2}(18 \text{ kg})\left(\vec{v}_f^{\,2} - 0\right)$

$\vec{v}_f = \sqrt{\dfrac{2(58.9 \text{ N})(1.5 \text{ m})}{18 \text{ kg}}}$

$\quad = 3.1 \text{ m/s}$

13. $P = \dfrac{W}{t}$

$W = Pt$

$\quad = (0.0290 \text{ J/s})(275 \text{ h})(3\,600 \text{ s/h})$

$\quad = 2.87 \times 10^4 \text{ J}$

$\vec{F}\vec{d} = \dfrac{1}{2}m\left(\vec{v}_f^{\,2} - \vec{v}_i^{\,2}\right)$

$2.87 \times 10^4 \text{ J} = \dfrac{1}{2}(0.145 \text{ kg})\left(\vec{v}_f^{\,2} - 0\right)$

$\vec{v}_f = \sqrt{\dfrac{2\left(2.87 \times 10^4 \text{ J}\right)}{0.145 \text{ kg}}}$

$\quad = 629 \text{ m/s}$

Lesson 11—Law of Conservation of Mechanical Energy

1. $\Delta E_k + \Delta E_p = 0$

$\Delta E_k = -\Delta E_p$

$\dfrac{1}{2}m\left(\vec{v}_f^{\,2} - \vec{v}_i^{\,2}\right) = -mg\Delta h$

$\dfrac{1}{2}\left(\vec{v}_f^{\,2} - \vec{v}_i^{\,2}\right) = -g\Delta h$

$\Delta h = \dfrac{\dfrac{1}{2}(3.2 \text{ m/s})^2}{9.81 \text{ m/s}^2}$

$\quad = 0.52 \text{ m}$

∴ object is dropped from a height of 0.52 m.

3. $\Delta E_k + \Delta E_p = 0$

$\Delta E_k = -\Delta E_p$

$\dfrac{1}{2}m\left(\vec{v}_f^{\,2} - \vec{v}_i^{\,2}\right) = -mg\Delta h$

$\dfrac{1}{2}\left(\vec{v}_f^{\,2} - \vec{v}_i^{\,2}\right) = -g\Delta h$

$\dfrac{1}{2}\left((37.0 \text{ m/s})^2 - 0\right) = -\left(-9.81 \text{ m/s}^2\right)(\Delta h)$

$\Delta h = \dfrac{\dfrac{1}{2}(37.0 \text{ m/s})^2}{\left(9.81 \text{ m/s}^2\right)}$

$\quad = 69.8 \text{ m}$

∴ building was 69.8 m tall

5. $\Delta E_k + \Delta E_p = 0$

$$\Delta E_k = -\Delta E_p$$

$$\frac{1}{2}m\left(\vec{v}_f^{\,2} - \vec{v}_i^{\,2}\right) = -mg\Delta h$$

$$\frac{1}{2}\left(\vec{v}_f^{\,2} - \vec{v}_i^{\,2}\right) = -g\Delta h$$

$$\frac{1}{2}\left(v_f^{\,2} - 0\right) = -\left(-9.81 \text{ m/s}^2\right)\left(4.0 \text{ m}\right)$$

$$\vec{v}_f = \sqrt{2\left(9.81 \text{ m/s}^2\right)\left(4.0 \text{ m}\right)}$$

$$= 8.9 \text{ m/s}$$

7. $\Delta E_k + \Delta E_p = 0$

$$0 = \frac{1}{2}m\vec{v}_f^{\,2} - \frac{1}{2}m\vec{v}_i^{\,2} + mg\Delta h$$

$$0 = \frac{1}{2}\vec{v}_f^{\,2} - \frac{1}{2}\vec{v}_i^{\,2} + g\Delta h$$

$$\vec{v}_f = \sqrt{-2g\Delta h}$$

$$= \sqrt{-2\left(-9.81 \text{ m/s}^2\right)\left(3.0 \text{ m}\right)}$$

$$= 7.7 \text{ m/s}$$

9. $\Delta E_k + \Delta E_p = 0$

$$\Delta E_k = -\Delta E_p$$

$$\frac{1}{2}m\left(\vec{v}_f^{\,2} - \vec{v}_i^{\,2}\right) = -mg\Delta h$$

$$\frac{1}{2}\left(\vec{v}_f^{\,2} - \vec{v}_i^{\,2}\right) = -g\Delta h$$

$$\frac{1}{2}\left(0 - \left(3.5 \text{ m/s}\right)^2\right) = -\left(-9.81 \text{ m/s}^2\right)\left(\Delta h\right)$$

$$\Delta h = \frac{\frac{1}{2}\left(0 - \left(3.5 \text{ m/s}\right)^2\right)}{9.81 \text{ m/s}^2}$$

$$= -0.62 \text{ m}$$

The student can swing 0.62 m high.

11. $\Delta E_k + \Delta E_p = 0$

$$\Delta E_k = -\Delta E_p$$

$$\frac{1}{2}m\left(\vec{v}_f^{\,2} - \vec{v}_i^{\,2}\right) = -mg\Delta h$$

$$\frac{1}{2}\left(\vec{v}_f^{\,2} - \vec{v}_i^{\,2}\right) = -g\Delta h$$

$$\frac{1}{2}\left(v_f^{\,2} - 0\right) = -\left(-9.81 \text{ m/s}^2\right)\left(0.25 \text{ m}\right)$$

$$\vec{v}_f = \sqrt{2\left(9.81 \text{ m/s}^2\right)\left(0.25 \text{ m}\right)}$$

$$= 2.2 \text{ m/s}$$

13. $\Delta E_k + \Delta E_p = 0$

$$\Delta E_k = -\Delta E_p$$

$$\frac{1}{2}m\left(\vec{v}_f^{\,2} - \vec{v}_i^{\,2}\right) = -\vec{F}\vec{d}$$

$$\frac{1}{2}\left(0.45 \text{ kg}\right)\vec{v}_f^{\,2} = -\left(12 \text{ N}\right)\left(0.30 \text{ m}\right)$$

$$\vec{v}_f = -4.0 \text{ m/s}$$

15. a) $E_p = mgh$

$$h = \frac{E_p}{mg}$$

$$= \frac{0.20 \text{ J}}{\left(0.40 \text{ kg}\right)\left(9.81 \text{ m/s}^2\right)}$$

$$= 5.1 \times 10^{-2} \text{ m}$$

b) Mechanical energy is conserved. At position B it has no gravitational potential energy. Therefore all the mechanical energy must be kinetic. Answer is 0.20 J.

c) Same answer is in **b)**.

d) $E_k = \frac{1}{2}mv^2$

$$0.20 \text{ J} = \frac{1}{2}\left(0.40 \text{ kg}\right)\vec{v}^2$$

$$\vec{v} = \sqrt{\frac{2\left(0.20 \text{ J}\right)}{0.40 \text{ kg}}}$$

$$= 1.0 \text{ m/s}$$

17. NOTE: There is friction!
TE = thermal energy
$$\Delta E_k + \Delta E_p + \Delta TE = 0$$

$$-\Delta TE = \frac{1}{2}mv_f^2 - \frac{1}{2}mv_i^2 + mg\Delta h$$

$$= \frac{1}{2}\left(15.0 \text{ kg}\right)\left(6.0 \text{ ms}\right)^2 +$$

$$\left(15.0 \text{ kg}\right)\left(-9.81 \text{ m/s}^2\right)\left(5.0 \text{ m}\right)$$

$$= 270 \text{ J} - 736 \text{ J}$$

$$= 4.7 \times 10^2 \text{ J}$$

Review Exercises—Circular Motion, Work, and Energy

1. $\bar{a}_c = \dfrac{v^2}{r}$

$= \dfrac{(26.0 \text{ m/s})^2}{225 \text{ m}}$

$= 3.00 \text{ m/s}^2$

3. $C = 2\pi r$

$= 2\pi r (0.750 \text{ m})$

$= 4.71 \text{ m}$

$v = \dfrac{d}{t}$

$= \dfrac{(2.50)(4.71 \text{ m})}{1 \text{ s}}$

$= 11.8 \text{ m/s}$

$\bar{T} = \bar{F}_c$

$\bar{F}_c = \dfrac{mv^2}{r}$

$= \dfrac{(0.150 \text{ kg})(11.8 \text{ m/s})^2}{0.750}$

$= 27.8 \text{ N}$

5.

$\bar{T}$
$(\bar{F}_N)$

$\bar{F}_g$

$\bar{F}_N = 0$

$\therefore \bar{F}_c = \bar{F}_g$

$\dfrac{mv^2}{r} = mg$

$v = \sqrt{rg}$

$= \sqrt{(10.0 \text{ m})(9.81 \text{ m/s}^2)}$

$= 9.90 \text{ m/s}$

7.

$\bar{T}$
$(\bar{F}_N)$

$\bar{F}_g$

$\bar{F}_g = mg$

$= (1.75 \text{ kg})(-9.81 \text{ m/s}^2)$

$= -17.2 \text{ N}$

$\bar{F}_c = \bar{T} + \bar{F}_g$

$= 262 \text{ N} + (-17.2 \text{ N})$

$= 245 \text{ N}$

$\bar{F}_c = \dfrac{mv^2}{r}$

$v = \sqrt{\dfrac{F_c r}{m}}$

$= \sqrt{\dfrac{(245 \text{ N})(1.10 \text{ m})}{(1.75 \text{ kg})}}$

$= 12.4 \text{ m/s}$

9. $K = \dfrac{T^2}{r^3}$

$r^3 = \dfrac{T^2}{K}$

$= \dfrac{(7.82 \times 10^9 \text{ s})^2}{(3.02 \times 10^{-19} \text{ s}^2/\text{m}^3)}$

$= 5.87 \times 10^{12} \text{ m}$

11. $v = \sqrt{\dfrac{Gm}{r}}$

$= \sqrt{\dfrac{\left(6.67 \times 10^{-11} \dfrac{\text{N} \cdot \text{m}^2}{\text{kg}^2}\right)(3.18 \times 10^{23} \text{ kg})}{(1.00 \times 10^6 \text{ m} + 2.43 \times 10^6 \text{ m})}}$

$= 2.49 \times 10^3 \text{ m/s}$

13. a) $v = \sqrt{\dfrac{Gm}{r}}$

$= \sqrt{\dfrac{\left(6.67 \times 10^{-11} \dfrac{\text{N} \cdot \text{m}^2}{\text{kg}^2}\right)(1.98 \times 10^{30} \text{ kg})}{(2.28 \times 10^{11} \text{ m})}}$

$= 2.41 \times 10^4 \text{ m/s}$

b) $v = \dfrac{2\pi r}{T}$

$T = \dfrac{2\pi r}{v}$

$= \dfrac{2\pi (2.28 \times 10^{11} \text{ m})}{2.41 \times 10^4 \text{ m/s}}$

$= 5.95 \times 10^7 \text{ s}$ or 689 days or 1.89 years

15.

$\bar{v}_i$	$\bar{v}_f$	$\bar{a}$	$\bar{d}$	t
15.0 m/s	20.0 m/s	?	?	4.30 s

$a = \dfrac{\bar{v}_f - \bar{v}_i}{t}$

$= \dfrac{20.0 \text{ m/s} - 15.0 \text{ m/s}}{4.30 \text{ s}}$

$= 1.16 \text{ m/s}^2$

$\bar{F}_{net} = m\bar{a}$

$= (11.0 \text{ kg})(1.16 \text{ m/s}^2)$

$= 12.8 \text{ N}$

$\bar{v}_i$	$\bar{v}_f$	$\bar{a}$	$\bar{d}$	t
15.0 m/s	20.0 m/s	1.16 m/s2	?	4.30 s

$$\vec{d} = \left(\frac{\vec{v}_f - \vec{v}_i}{2}\right)t$$

$$= \left(\frac{20.0 \text{ m/s} + 15.0 \text{ m/s}}{2}\right)(4.30 \text{ s})$$

$$= 75.3 \text{ m}$$

$$W = \vec{F}\vec{d}$$

$$= (12.8 \text{ N})(75.3 \text{ m})$$

$$= 963 \text{ J}$$

17. $E_p = mgh$

$$= (20.0 \text{ N})(2.0 \text{ m})$$

$$= 4.0 \times 10^1 \text{ J}$$

19.

$\vec{v}_i$	$\vec{v}_f$	$\vec{a}$	$\vec{d}$	t
0	1.5 m/s	?	?	4.0 s

$$\vec{a} = \frac{\vec{v}_f - \vec{v}_i}{t}$$

$$= \frac{1.50 \text{ m/s} - 0}{4.0 \text{ s}}$$

$$= 0.375 \text{ m/s}^2$$

$$\vec{d} = \left(\frac{\vec{v}_f - \vec{v}_i}{2}\right)t$$

$$= \left(\frac{1.50 \text{ m/s} - 0}{2}\right)(4.0 \text{ s})$$

$$= 3.00 \text{ m}$$

$$\vec{F}_{net} = m\vec{a}$$

$$= (50.0 \text{ kg})(0.375 \text{ m/s}^2)$$

$$= 18.8 \text{ N}$$

$$P = \frac{W}{t} = \frac{\vec{F}\vec{d}}{t}$$

$$= \frac{(18.8 \text{ N})(3.00 \text{ m})}{4.0 \text{ s}}$$

$$= 14 \text{ W}$$

21. $P = \dfrac{E}{t} = \dfrac{mgh}{t}$

$$= \frac{(1.50 \times 10^3 \text{ kg})(9.81 \text{ m/s}^2)(15.0 \text{ m})}{30.0 \text{ s}}$$

$$= 7.35 \times 10^3 \text{ W}$$

23. $\vec{F}\vec{d} = \dfrac{1}{2}m\left(\vec{v}_f^{\,2} - \vec{v}_i^{\,2}\right)$

$$(20.0 \text{ N})(6.00 \text{ m}) = \frac{1}{2}(10.0 \text{ kg})\left(v_f^2 - 0\right)$$

$$\vec{v}_f = \sqrt{\frac{2(20.0 \text{ N})(6.00 \text{ m})}{10.0 \text{ kg}}}$$

$$= 4.90 \text{ m/s}$$

25. $v = \dfrac{d}{t}$

$$d = vt$$

$$= (2.0 \text{ m/s})(4.0 \text{ s})$$

$$= 8.0 \text{ m}$$

$$E_p = mgh$$

$$= (3.0 \text{ kg})(9.81 \text{ m/s}^2)(8.0 \text{ m})$$

$$= 2.4 \times 10^2 \text{ J}$$

27. $v = \dfrac{d}{t}$

$$d = vt$$

$$= (1.2 \text{ m/s})(2.5 \text{ s})$$

$$= 3.0 \text{ m}$$

$$E_{k(bottom)} = E_{p(top)}$$

$$\frac{1}{2}mv^2 = mgh$$

$$v = \sqrt{2gh}$$

$$= \sqrt{2(9.81 \text{ m/s}^2)(3.0 \text{ m})}$$

$$= 7.7 \text{ m/s}$$

29. $\Delta E_k + \Delta E_p = 0$

$$\Delta E_k = -\Delta E_p$$

$$\frac{1}{2}m\left(\vec{v}_f^{\,2} - \vec{v}_i^{\,2}\right) = -mg\Delta h$$

$$\frac{1}{2}\left(\vec{v}_f^{\,2} - \vec{v}_i^{\,2}\right) = -g\Delta h$$

$$\frac{1}{2}\left((10 \text{ m/s})^2 - 0\right) = -\left(-9.81 \text{ m/s}^2\right)(\Delta h)$$

$$\Delta h = \frac{(10 \text{ m/s})^2}{2(9.81 \text{ m/s}^2)}$$

$$= 5.10 \text{ m}$$

31. **a)** If there is no air friction, mechanical energy is conserved. When the ball leaves the bat, all the mechanical energy is kinetic.

$$E_k = \frac{1}{2}mv^2$$

$$= \frac{1}{2}(0.145 \text{ kg})(15.0 \text{ m/s})^2$$

$$= 16.3 \text{ J}$$

b) When the ball reaches its maximum height, all the mechanical energy is gravitational potential energy.

$$\therefore E_p = 16.3 \text{ J}$$

c) maximum height

$$E_p = mgh$$

$$h = \frac{E_p}{mg}$$

$$= \frac{16.3 \text{ J}}{(0.145 \text{ kg})(9.81 \text{ m/s}^2)}$$

$$= 11.47 \text{ m}$$

∴ we want to find the spee when it is at

$$\frac{1}{2} \text{ of } 11.47 \text{ m}$$

$$= 5.73 \text{ m}$$

$$\Delta E_k + \Delta E_p = 0$$

$$\Delta E_k = -\Delta E_p$$

$$\frac{1}{2}m\left(\vec{v}_f^{\,2} - \vec{v}_i^{\,2}\right) = -mg\Delta h$$

$$\frac{1}{2}\left(\vec{v}_f^{\,2} - \vec{v}_i^{\,2}\right) = -g\Delta h$$

$$\frac{1}{2}\left(\vec{v}_f^{\,2} - (15.0 \text{ m/s})^2\right) = -\left(-9.81 \text{ m/s}^2\right)(5.73 \text{ m})$$

$$\vec{v}_f = \sqrt{2\left(9.81 \text{ m/s}^2\right)(5.73 \text{ m}) + (15.0 \text{ m/s})^2}$$

$$= 10.6 \text{ m/s}$$

33. **a)** $\Delta E_k + \Delta E_p = 0$

$$\Delta E_k = -\Delta E_p$$

$$\frac{1}{2}m\left(\vec{v}_f^{\,2} - \vec{v}_i^{\,2}\right) = -mg\Delta h$$

$$\frac{1}{2}\left(\vec{v}_f^{\,2} - \vec{v}_i^{\,2}\right) = -g\Delta h$$

$$\frac{1}{2}\left(\vec{v}_f^{\,2} - 0\right) = -\left(-9.81 \text{ m/s}^2\right)(1.0 \text{ m})$$

$$\vec{v}_f = \sqrt{2\left(9.81 \text{ m/s}^2\right)(1.0 \text{ m})}$$

$$= 4.4 \text{ m/s}$$

b) Because there is no friction, the mechanical energy is constant throughout the track. Therefore, find the mechanical energy at A.

mechanical energy at A = mechanical energy at C

All the mechanical energy at A is gravitational potential energy.

$$E_p = mgh$$

$$= (2.0 \text{ kg})\left(9.81 \text{ m/s}^2\right)(8.0 \text{ m})$$

$$= 1.6 \times 10^2 \text{ J}$$

35. $\Delta E_k + \Delta E_p = 0$

$$\frac{1}{2}m\left(\vec{v}_f^{\,2} - \vec{v}_i^{\,2}\right) + mg\Delta h = 0$$

$$\frac{1}{2}\left(\vec{v}_f^{\,2} - \vec{v}_i^{\,2}\right) = -g\Delta h$$

$$\frac{1}{2}\left(\vec{v}_f^{\,2} - 0\right) = -\left(-9.81 \text{ m/s}^2\right)(3.0 \text{ m})$$

$$\vec{v}_f^{\,2} = 58.9 \text{ m}^2/\text{s}^2$$

$$\vec{v}_f = 7.7 \text{ m/s}$$

37. $W = mgh$

$$= (12.0 \text{ N})(2.30 \text{ m})$$

$$= 27.6 \text{ J}$$

Practice Test—Circular Motion, Work, and Energy

1. $P = \dfrac{W}{t} = \dfrac{mgd}{t}$

Units therefore are: J/s or $\dfrac{\text{kg} \cdot \text{m}^2/\text{s}^2}{\text{s}}$

or $\text{kg} \cdot \text{m}^2/\text{s}^3$

D is the answer.

3. $E_k = \dfrac{1}{2}mv^2$

$$(2)(0.5)^2 = 0.5$$

We see that the right hand side changed by 0.5 times, therefore the left side also changed by 0.5 times.

C is the answer.

5. Zero. In order to be doing work on the object against gravity, we have to change the gravitational potential energy.

C is the answer.

7. $E_k = \dfrac{1}{2}mv^2$

If we triple the speed, the equation tells us that we increase the energy $3^2 = 9$ times.

D is the answer.

9. $W = \Delta E_k$

$\quad = \frac{1}{2}m\vec{v}_f^{\,2} - \frac{1}{2}m\vec{v}_i^{\,2}$

$\quad = \frac{1}{2}(2.50 \text{ kg})(10.0 \text{ m/s})^2 - 0$

$\quad = 125 \text{ J}$

C is the answer.

11. The energy does not depend on the speed that the student runs up the stairs. The change in her potential energy is still E_p.

A is the answer.

13. $\Delta E_k + \Delta E_p = 0$

$\quad \frac{1}{2}m\vec{v}_f^{\,2} - \frac{1}{2}m\vec{v}_i^{\,2} + mg\Delta h = 0$

$\quad \frac{1}{2}\vec{v}_f^{\,2} + \left(-9.81 \text{ m/s}^2\right)(0.40 \text{ m}) = 0$

$\quad\quad\quad\quad\quad\quad \vec{v}_f = 2.8 \text{ m/s}$

A is the answer.

15. Work is defined as the transfer of energy. There is energy transferred in all these cases.

D is the answer.

17. It is only in case iii) where there is a transfer of energy; therefore it is only in case iii) where there is work done.

A is the answer.

19. When an object is moved vertically at a constant speed, only the gravitational potential energy changes.

A is the answer.

21. There is no loss of potential energy here; but if there is friction, some mechanical energy will be changed to heat (thermal energy).

B is the answer.

23. $E_k = \frac{1}{2}mv^2 \quad\quad E_k \propto v^2$

This relationship is described by **D**.

D is the answer.

25. In circular motion, the direction of the velocity is tangent to the circular path.

C is the answer.

27. There are two forces acting on the object: the applied force (T) and the force of gravity. Both these forces are toward the centre or down.

B is the answer.

29. If the object if moving at a constant speed, the force acting on it is constant.

D is the answer.

31. $v = \sqrt{\dfrac{Gm_e}{r}}$, but the gravitational field depends on the mass of the object that the satellite is orbiting. Therefore the speed depends on both the gravitational field and the radius.

A is the answer.

33. The force of friction is the centripetal force.

$\quad \vec{F}_f = \mu mg \cos\theta$

$\quad\quad = 0.50 \text{ N}$

$\quad \vec{F}_c = \vec{F}_f$

$\quad \dfrac{mv^2}{r} = \mu mg \cos\theta$

$\quad \dfrac{v^2}{r} = \mu \cos\theta$

$\quad v = \sqrt{(\mu g \cos\theta)r}$

$\quad\quad = \sqrt{(0.50)(9.81 \text{ m/s}^2)(\cos\theta)(40.0 \text{ m})}$

$\quad\quad = 14 \text{ m/s}$

C is the answer

35. We can calculate the speed using $v = \dfrac{2\pi r}{T}$.

We can calculate the mass of the planet using $v = \sqrt{\dfrac{Gm_p}{r}}$.

C is the answer.

37. Centripetal means toward the centre.

C is the answer.

39. $E_k = \frac{1}{2}mv^2$

If you double the speed, the right hand side of this equation increases four times; therefore the left side must increase four times as well

D is the correct answer.

OSCILLATORY MOTION AND MECHANICAL WAVES

Lesson 1—Oscillatory Motion

1. $\vec{F}_s = -kx$

$= -(20.0 \text{ N/m})(0.100 \text{ m})$

$= -2.00 \text{ N}$

3. $\vec{F}_s = -kx$

$k = -\dfrac{F_s}{x}$

$= \dfrac{1.2 \text{ N}}{0.025 \text{ m}}$

$= 48 \text{ N/m}$

5. $\vec{F}_g = mg$

$= (5.0 \text{ kg})(-9.81 \text{ m/s}^2)$

$= 49.1 \text{ N}$

$\vec{F}_s = -kx$

$k = -\dfrac{\vec{F}_s}{x}$

$= -\dfrac{49.1 \text{ N}}{3.25 \times 10^{-2} \text{ m}}$

$= 1.5 \times 10^3 \text{ N/m}$

7. $\vec{F}_s = -kx$

$= (-4.2 \text{ N/m})(0.050 \text{ m})$

$= -0.21 \text{ N}$

$\vec{F}_{net} = m\vec{a}$

$\vec{a} = \dfrac{\vec{F}_{net}}{m}$

$= \dfrac{-0.21 \text{ N}}{0.25 \text{ kg}}$

$= -0.84 \text{ m/s}^2$

9. $\vec{F}_{max} = -kx_{max}$

$= -(0.37 \text{ N/m})(0.012 \text{ m})$

$= -4.4 \times 10^{-3} \text{ N}$

$\vec{F} = m\vec{a}$

$\vec{a}_{max} = \dfrac{\vec{F}_{max}}{m}$

$= \dfrac{-4.4 \times 10^{-3} \text{ N}}{0.042 \text{ kg}}$

$= -1.1 \times 10^{-1} \text{ m/s}^2$

Lesson 2—Energy of SHM

1. $T = 2\pi\sqrt{\dfrac{m}{k}}$

$= 2\pi\sqrt{\dfrac{0.50 \text{ kg}}{82 \text{ N/m}}}$

$= 0.49 \text{ s}$

3. $\vec{F}_g = mg$

$m = \dfrac{\vec{F}_g}{g}$

$= \dfrac{8.8 \text{ N}}{9.81 \text{ m/s}^2}$

$= 0.897 \text{ kg}$

$T = 2\pi\sqrt{\dfrac{m}{k}}$

$1.1 \text{ s} = 2\pi\sqrt{\dfrac{0.897 \text{ kg}}{k}}$

$k = \dfrac{(2\pi)^2}{(1.1 \text{ s})^2}(0.897 \text{ kg})$

$= 29 \text{ N/m}$

5. $f = \dfrac{1}{T}$

$T = \dfrac{1}{1.50 \text{ Hz}}$

$= 0.667 \text{ s}$

$T = 2\pi\sqrt{\dfrac{m}{k}}$

$0.667 \text{ s} = 2\pi\sqrt{\dfrac{m}{115 \text{ N/m}}}$

$m = \dfrac{(0.667 \text{ s})^2}{(2\pi)^2}(115 \text{ N/m})$

$= 1.29 \text{ kg}$

7. $f = \dfrac{1}{T}$

$T = \dfrac{1}{0.23 \text{ Hz}}$

$= 4.35 \text{ s}$

$T = 2\pi\sqrt{\dfrac{m}{k}}$

$4.35 \text{ s} = 2\pi\sqrt{\dfrac{75 \text{ kg}}{k}}$

$k = \dfrac{(2\pi^2)}{(4.35 \text{ s})^2}(75 \text{ kg})$

$= 1.6 \times 10^2 \text{ N/m}$

Lesson 3—The Simple Pendulum

1. $f = \dfrac{1}{T}$

$= \dfrac{1}{3.6 \text{ s}}$

$= 0.28 \text{ Hz}$

3. $T = 2\pi\sqrt{\dfrac{L}{g}}$

$2.0 \text{ s} = 2\pi\sqrt{\dfrac{L}{9.81 \text{ m/s}^2}}$

$L = \dfrac{(2.0 \text{ s})^2}{(2\pi)^2}\left(9.81 \text{ m/s}^2\right)$

$= 0.99 \text{ m}$

5. $f = \dfrac{1}{T}$

$T = \dfrac{1}{0.57 \text{ Hz}}$

$= 1.75 \text{ s}$

$T = 2\pi\sqrt{\dfrac{L}{g}}$

$1.75 \text{ s} = 2\pi\sqrt{\dfrac{0.75}{g}}$

$g = \dfrac{(2\pi)^2}{(1.75 \text{ s})^2}(0.75 \text{ m})$

$= 9.6 \text{ m/s}^2$

7. $T = 2\pi\sqrt{\dfrac{L}{g}}$

$= 2\pi\sqrt{\dfrac{1.0 \text{ m}}{9.81 \text{ m/s}^2}}$

$= 2.01 \text{ s}$

$f = \dfrac{1}{T}$

$= \dfrac{1}{2.01 \text{ s}}$

$= 0.50 \text{ Hz}$

9. $T = 2\pi\sqrt{\dfrac{L}{g}}$

$6.9 \text{ s} = 2\pi\sqrt{\dfrac{L}{9.81 \text{ m/s}^2}}$

$L = \dfrac{(6.9 \text{ s})^2}{(2\pi)^2}\left(9.81 \text{ m/s}^2\right)$

$= 12 \text{ m}$

Lesson 4—Energy of SHM (Mass-Spring System)

1. $E_T = \dfrac{1}{2}kA^2$

$= \dfrac{1}{2}(26 \text{ N/m})(0.15 \text{ m})^2$

$= 0.293 \text{ J}$

$E_T = \dfrac{1}{2}mv_i^2$

$v_i = \sqrt{\dfrac{2E_T}{m}}$

$= \sqrt{\dfrac{2(0.293 \text{ J})}{0.60 \text{ kg}}}$

$= 0.99 \text{ m/s}$

3. $E_T = \dfrac{1}{2}mv_i^2$

$= \dfrac{1}{2}(0.20 \text{ kg})(0.12 \text{ m/s})^2$

$= 1.44 \times 10^{-3} \text{ J}$

$E_T = \dfrac{1}{2}kA^2$

$A = \sqrt{\dfrac{2E_T}{k}}$

$= \sqrt{\dfrac{2\left(1.2 \times 10^{-2} \text{ J}\right)}{15 \text{ N/m}}}$

$= 1.4 \times 10^{-2} \text{ m}$

5. $E_p = \dfrac{1}{2}kx^2$

$x = \sqrt{\dfrac{2E_p}{k}}$

$= \sqrt{\dfrac{2(4.5 \text{ J})}{32 \text{ N/m}}}$

$= 0.53 \text{ m}$

7. $E_k = \dfrac{1}{2}mv^2$

$v = \sqrt{\dfrac{2E_k}{m}}$

$= \sqrt{\dfrac{2(7.32 \text{ J})}{0.46 \text{ kg}}}$

$= 5.6 \text{ m/s}$

9. $E_T = \frac{1}{2}kA^2$

$\quad = \frac{1}{2}(23 \text{ N/m})(0.20 \text{ m})^2$

$\quad = 0.46 \text{ J}$

$E_p = \frac{1}{2}kx^2$

$\quad = \frac{1}{2}(23 \text{ N/m})(0.15 \text{ m})^2$

$\quad = 0.26 \text{ J}$

$E_k = E_T - E_p$

$\quad = 0.46 \text{ J} - 0.26 \text{ J}$

$\quad = 0.20 \text{ J}$

$E_k = \frac{1}{2}mv^2$

$m = \dfrac{2(0.20 \text{ J})}{(0.12 \text{ m/s})^2}$

$\quad = 28 \text{ kg} + E_T = \frac{1}{2}mv_i^2$

$v_i = \sqrt{\dfrac{2E_T}{m}}$

$\quad = \sqrt{\dfrac{2(0.46 \text{ J})}{28 \text{ kg}}}$

$\quad = 0.18 \text{ m/s}$

11. $E_p = \frac{1}{2}kx^2$

$\quad = \frac{1}{2}(76.0 \text{ N/m})(0.0350 \text{ m})^2$

$\quad = 0.0466 \text{ J}$

Lesson 5—Energy: Transmission by Waves

1. $v = \lambda f$

$\lambda = \dfrac{v}{f}$

$\quad = \dfrac{3.3 \times 10^{-1} \text{ m/s}}{5.0 \times 10^{-1} \text{ Hz}}$

$\quad = 0.66 \text{ m}$

3. $v = \lambda f$

$f = \dfrac{2.5 \text{ m/s}}{5.0 \text{ m}}$

$\quad = 0.50 \text{ Hz}$

$T = \dfrac{1}{f}$

$\quad = \dfrac{1}{0.50 \text{ Hz}}$

$\quad = 2.0 \text{ s}$

5. $f = \dfrac{1}{T}$

$\quad = \dfrac{1}{1.00 \times 10^{-2} \text{ s}}$

$\quad = 1.00 \times 10^2 \text{ Hz}$

$v = \lambda f$

$\lambda = \dfrac{v}{f}$

$\quad = \dfrac{335 \text{ m/s}}{1.00 \times 10^2 \text{ Hz}}$

$\quad = 3.35 \text{ m}$

7. $\dfrac{4.0 \times 10^1 \text{ waves}}{300 \text{ s}} = \dfrac{f}{1 \text{ s}}$

$f = 0.133 \text{ Hz}$

$v = \lambda f$

$\quad = (4.0 \text{ m})(0.133 \text{ Hz})$

$\quad = 0.53 \text{ m/s}$

9. $v = \dfrac{d}{t}$

$d = vt$

$\quad = (1.46 \times 10^3 \text{ m/s})(0.31 \text{ s})$

$\quad = 4.5 \times 10^2 \text{ m}$

Lesson 6—Reflection of Waves

1. $\lambda = 2L$

$\quad = 2(1.2 \text{ m})$

$\quad = 2.4 \text{ m}$

$v = \lambda f$

$\quad = (2.4 \text{ m})(65 \text{ Hz})$

$\quad = 1.6 \times 10^2 \text{ m/s}$

3. 3rd harmonic = 3(Fundamental Frequency)

$\quad = 3(354 \text{ Hz})$

$\quad = 1.06 \times 10^3 \text{ Hz}$

5. 3rd harmonic = 3(Fundamental Frequency)

Fundamental Frequency $= \dfrac{3^{\text{rd}} \text{ harmonic}}{3}$

$\quad = \dfrac{1.2 \times 10^3 \text{ Hz}}{3}$

$\quad = 4.0 \times 10^2 \text{ Hz}$

2nd harmonic = 2(Fundamental Frequency)

$\quad = 2(4.0 \times 10^2 \text{ Hz})$

$\quad = 8.0 \times 10^2 \text{ Hz}$

7. $\lambda = 2L$

$\qquad = 2(27.0 \text{ cm})$

$\qquad = 54.0 \text{ cm}$

$v = \lambda f$

$\qquad = (54.0 \text{ cm})(637 \text{ Hz})$

$\qquad = 3.44 \times 10^4 \text{ cm/s}$

Frequency of 22.0 cm string

$\lambda = 2L$

$\qquad = 2(22.0 \text{ cm})$

$\qquad = 44.0 \text{ cm}$

$f = \dfrac{v}{\lambda}$

$\qquad = \dfrac{3.44 \times 10^4 \text{ cm/s}}{44.0 \text{ cm}}$

$\qquad = 782 \text{ Hz}$

9. $v = \sqrt{\dfrac{T}{m/L}}$

$\qquad = \sqrt{\dfrac{23 \text{ N}}{1.9 \times 10^{-3} \text{ kg}/0.80 \text{ m}}}$

$\qquad = 98 \text{ m/s}$

11. $v = \sqrt{\dfrac{T}{m/L}}$

$\qquad = \sqrt{\dfrac{80.0 \text{ N}}{(195 \times 10^{-3} \text{ kg})/5.0 \text{ m}}}$

$\qquad = 45.3 \text{ m/s}$

$\lambda = 2L$

$\qquad = 2(5.0 \text{ m})$

$\qquad = 10 \text{ m}$

$v = \lambda f$

$f = \dfrac{45.3 \text{ m/s}}{10 \text{ m}}$

$\qquad = 4.5 \text{ Hz}$

13. $v = \lambda f$

$v = \sqrt{\dfrac{T}{m/L}}$

$\therefore \lambda f = \sqrt{\dfrac{T}{m/L}}$

or $f \propto \sqrt{T}$

or $T \propto f^2$

Frequency

$\dfrac{\text{To}}{\text{From}} = \dfrac{231 \text{ Hz}}{224 \text{ Hz}}$

$\qquad = 1.03$

$f^2 = 1.06$

$T = (1.00 \times 10^2 \text{ N})(1.06)$

$\qquad = 1.06 \times 10^2 \text{ N}$

Lesson 7—Air Columns

1. $v = \lambda f$

$\lambda = \dfrac{v}{f}$

$\qquad = \dfrac{343 \text{ m/s}}{256 \text{ Hz}}$

$\qquad = 1.34 \text{ m}$

$L = \dfrac{\lambda}{4}$

$\qquad = \dfrac{1.34 \text{ m}}{4}$

$\qquad = 3.35 \times 10^{-1} \text{ m}$

3. 3rd harmonic $= 3$ (Fundamental Frequency)

$\qquad = 3(384 \text{ Hz})$

$\qquad = 1.15 \times 10^3 \text{ Hz}$

5. $v = \lambda f$

$\lambda = \dfrac{v}{f}$

$\qquad = \dfrac{341 \text{ m/s}}{4.40 \times 10^2 \text{ Hz}}$

$\qquad = 0.775 \text{ m}$

$L = \dfrac{\lambda}{4}$

$\qquad = \dfrac{0.775 \text{ m}}{4}$

$\qquad = 0.194 \text{ m}$

7. $\lambda = 2L$

$\qquad = 2(33.0 \times 10^{-2} \text{ m})$

$\qquad = 66.0 \times 10^{-2} \text{ m}$

$v = \lambda f$

$\qquad = (66.0 \times 10^{-2} \text{ m})(512 \text{ Hz})$

$\qquad = 338 \text{ m/s}$

9. 3rd Harmonic

3rd Harmonic $= 3$(Fundamental)

$\qquad = 3(384 \text{ Hz})$

$\qquad = 1.15 \times 10^3 \text{ Hz}$

Lesson 8—Doppler Effect

1. $f' = f_0 \left(\dfrac{v \pm v_o}{v \pm v_s} \right)$

$= \left(1.85 \times 10^3 \text{ Hz} \right) \left(\dfrac{341 \text{ m/s}}{341 \text{ m/s} - 32 \text{ m/s}} \right)$

$= 2.04 \times 10^3 \text{ Hz}$

3. $f' = f_0 \left(\dfrac{v \pm v_o}{v \pm v_s} \right)$

$= \left(2.15 \times 10^3 \text{ Hz} \right) \left(\dfrac{339 \text{ m/s} + 25 \text{ m/s}}{339 \text{ m/s}} \right)$

$= 2.31 \times 10^3 \text{ Hz}$

5. $f' = f_0 \left(\dfrac{v \pm v_o}{v \pm v_s} \right)$

$= \left(2.50 \times 10^3 \text{ Hz} \right) \left(\dfrac{341 \text{ m/s} + 15 \text{ m/s}}{341 \text{ m/s} - 27 \text{ m/s}} \right)$

$= 2.83 \times 10^3 \text{ Hz}$

7. $f' = f_0 \left(\dfrac{v \pm v_o}{v \pm v_s} \right)$

$3.13 \times 10^3 \text{ Hz} = \left(2.90 \times 10^3 \text{ Hz} \right) \left(\dfrac{343 \text{ m/s} + v_o}{343 \text{ m/s}} \right)$

$v_o = \dfrac{\left(3.13 \times 10^3 \text{ Hz} \right) \left(343 \text{ m/s} \right)}{2.90 \times 10^3 \text{ Hz}} - 343 \text{ m/s}$

$= 27.2 \text{ m/s}$

9. $f' = f_0 \left(\dfrac{v \pm v_o}{v \pm v_s} \right)$

$1.50 \times 10^3 \text{ Hz} = f_0 \left(\dfrac{3.40 \times 10^2 \text{ m/s} + 3.0 \times 10^1 \text{ m/s}}{3.40 \times 10^2 \text{ m/s}} \right)$

$f_0 = 1.38 \times 10^3 \text{ Hz}$

Review Exercises—Oscillatory Motion and Mechanical Waves

1. $F = ma$

$= \left(0.18 \text{ kg} \right) \left(0.13 \text{ m/s}^2 \right)$

$= 0.023 \text{ N}$

$F_s = -kx$

$x = \dfrac{F_s}{k}$

$= \dfrac{0.023 \text{ N}}{0.21 \text{ N/m}}$

$= -0.11 \text{ m}$

3. $F = ma$

$= \left(1.20 \text{ kg} \right) \left(8.20 \text{ m/s}^2 \right)$

$= 9.84 \text{ N}$

$F_s = -kx$

$k = \dfrac{F_s}{x}$

$= \dfrac{9.84 \text{ N}}{0.0500 \text{ m}}$

$= 197 \text{ N/m}$

5. $E_T = \dfrac{1}{2} m v_i^2$

$= \dfrac{1}{2} \left(0.300 \text{ kg} \right) \left(0.620 \text{ m/s} \right)^2$

$= 0.0577 \text{ J}$

$E_T = \dfrac{1}{2} k A^2$

$0.0577 \text{ J} = \dfrac{1}{2} \left(29.2 \text{ N/m} \right) A^2$

$A = \sqrt{\dfrac{2 \left(0.0577 \text{ J} \right)}{29.2 \text{ N/m}}}$

$= 0.0628 \text{ m}$

7. $E_T = \dfrac{1}{2} k A^2$

$= \dfrac{1}{2} \left(115 \text{ N/m} \right) \left(0.0450 \text{ m} \right)^2$

$= 0.116 \text{ J}$

$E_p = \dfrac{1}{2} k x^2$

$= \dfrac{1}{2} \left(115 \text{ N/m} \right) \left(0.0220 \text{ m} \right)^2$

$= 0.0278 \text{ J}$

$E_k = E_T - E_p$

$= 0.116 \text{ J} - 0.0278 \text{ J}$

$= 0.0886 \text{ J}$

$= 8.86 \times 10^{-2} \text{ J}$

9. $F_g = mg$

$m = \dfrac{F_g}{g}$

$= \dfrac{7.20 \text{ N}}{9.81 \text{ m/s}^2}$

$= 0.734 \text{ kg}$

$T = 2\pi\sqrt{\dfrac{m}{k}}$

$= 2\pi\sqrt{\dfrac{0.734 \text{ kg}}{21.3 \text{ N/m}}}$

$= 1.17 \text{ s}$

$f = \dfrac{1}{T}$

$= \dfrac{1}{1.17 \text{ s}}$

$= 0.857 \text{ Hz}$

11. $T = \dfrac{1}{f}$

$= \dfrac{1}{0.740 \text{ Hz}}$

$= 1.35 \text{ s}$

$T = 2\pi\sqrt{\dfrac{L}{g}}$

$1.35 \text{ s} = 2\pi\sqrt{\dfrac{0.450 \text{ m}}{\cdot g}}$

$g = 9.73 \text{ m/s}^2$

13. **a)** $E_k = \dfrac{1}{2}mv^2$

$v = \sqrt{\dfrac{2E_k}{m}}$

$= \sqrt{\dfrac{2(3.00\times10^{-3} \text{ J})}{0.20 \text{ kg}}}$

$= 0.173 \text{ m/s}$

b) $E_p = \dfrac{1}{2}kx^2$

$x = \sqrt{\dfrac{2E_p}{k}}$

$= \sqrt{\dfrac{2(3.00\times10^{-3} \text{ J})}{0.800 \text{ N/m}}}$

$= 8.66\times10^{-2} \text{ m}$

c) $\vec{F}_s = -kx$

This equation gives us the relationship between the restoring force (spring force) and the displacement. But when the displacement changes, the force changes. This means that when the spring is stretched from the equilibrium position to the end position, the average force will be:

$\dfrac{F_{max} + F_{min}}{2}$

$F_{min} = 0$

$\therefore F_{average} = \dfrac{F_{max}}{2}$

$\text{Work} = (F_{average})d$

$= \dfrac{1}{2}(kx)x$

$= \dfrac{1}{2}kx^2$

d) If there is no friction, mechanical energy is conserved. Therefore, the mechanical energy is always 3.00×10^{-3} J.

15. $v = \dfrac{d}{t}$

$d = vt$

$= (3.00\times10^8 \text{ m/s})(0.600 \text{ s})$

$= 1.80\times10^8 \text{ m}$

17. $f' = f_o\left(\dfrac{v \pm v_o}{v \pm v_s}\right)$

$= (2.00\times10^3 \text{ Hz})\left(\dfrac{341 \text{ m/s} - 25.0 \text{ m/s}}{341 \text{ m/s} - 30.0 \text{ m/s}}\right)$

$= 2.03\times10^3 \text{ Hz}$

19. $\lambda = 4L$

$= 4(0.330 \text{ m})$

$= 1.32 \text{ m}$

$v = \lambda f$

$= (1.32 \text{ m})(256 \text{ Hz})$

$= 338 \text{ m/s}$

21. $v = \dfrac{d}{t}$

$= \dfrac{25.5 \text{ m}}{60 \text{ s}}$

$= 0.425 \text{ m/s}$

$v = \lambda f$

$\lambda = \dfrac{v}{f}$

$= \dfrac{0.425 \text{ m/s}}{10.0 \text{ Hz}}$

$= 0.0425 \text{ m}$

Practice Test

1. All periodic motion is not simple harmonic motion, but all simple harmonic motion is periodic motion.

    B is the answer.

3. The direction of the acceleration will be in the direction of the restoring force. The restoring force is the component of the weight that is tangent to the direction that the pendulum bob is moving.

    B is the answer.

5. In simple harmonic motion, the speed is greatest at the equilibrium position.

    A is the answer.

7. In simple harmonic motion involving a frictionless system, mechanical energy is conserved.

    D is the answer.

9. Period is the time of one cycle.

    $\dfrac{100 \text{ cycles}}{60 \text{ s}} = \dfrac{1 \text{ cycle}}{T}$

    $T = 0.600 \text{ s}$

    A is the answer.

11. In simple harmonic motion involving a frictionless system, mechanical energy is conserved. Mechanical energy is the same at all times.

    C is the answer.

13. The frequency of a mass vibrating in simple harmonic motion at the end of a spring along a frictionless surface depends on both the mass and the spring constant. Remember the formula for period:

    $T = 2\pi \sqrt{\dfrac{m}{k}}$.

    C is the answer.

15. Amplitude is related to the energy.

    B is the answer.

17. $v = \lambda f$, but $f = \dfrac{1}{T}$, $\therefore v = \dfrac{\lambda}{T}$

    B is the answer.

19. $v = \lambda f$

    $f = \dfrac{v}{\lambda}$

    $= \dfrac{10.0 \text{ cm/s}}{2.0 \text{ cm}}$

    $= 5.0 \text{ Hz}$

    B is the answer.

21. When waves meet crest to crest or trough to trough, they are meeting in phase. When waves meet in phase, constructive interference results.

    B is the answer.

23. A point on a wave moves in simple harmonic motion.

    D is the answer.

25. Constructive interference is explained using the superposition principle.

    C is the answer.

27. Destructive interference results when waves meet out of phase.

    B is the answer.

29. The speed of a wave (sound) does not depend on the frequency. All frequencies of sound travel at the same speed. The wavelength does depend on the frequency. The higher the frequency, the shorter the wavelength.

    $v = \lambda f$

    $\lambda = \dfrac{v}{f}$

    A is the answer.

NOTES

ORDERING INFORMATION

SCHOOL ORDERS

Please contact the Learning Resource Centre (LRC) for school discount and order information.

THE KEY **Study Guides** are specifically designed to assist students in preparing for unit tests, final exams, and provincial examinations.

THE KEY **Study Guides** – $29.95 each plus G.S.T.

SENIOR HIGH		JUNIOR HIGH	ELEMENTARY
Biology 30	Biology 20	Language Arts 9	Language Arts 6
Chemistry 30	Chemistry 20	Math 9	Math 6
English 30-1	English 20-1	Science 9	Science 6
English 30-2	Pure Math 20	Social Studies 9	Social Studies 6
Applied Math 30	Physics 20	Math 8	Math 4
Pure Math 30	Social Studies 20-1	Math 7	Language Arts 3
Physics 30	English 10-1		Math 3
Social Studies 30-1	Pure Math 10		
Social Studies 30-2	Science 10		
	Social Studies 10-1		

Student Notes and Problems (SNAP) Workbooks contain complete explanations of curriculum concepts, examples, and exercise questions.

SNAP Workbooks – $29.95 each plus G.S.T.

SENIOR HIGH		JUNIOR HIGH	ELEMENTARY
Biology 30	Biology 20	Math 9	Math 6
Chemistry 30	Chemistry 20	Science 9	Math 5
Applied Math 30	Pure Math 20	Math 8	Math 4
Pure Math 30	Physics 20	Science 8	Math 3
Math 31	Pure Math 10	Math 7	
Physics 30	Applied Math 10	Science 7	
	Science 10		

Visit our website for a tour of resource content and features or order resources online at
www.castlerockresearch.com

#2340, 10180 – 101 Street
Edmonton, AB Canada T5J 3S4
e-mail: learn@castlerockresearch.com

Phone: 780.448.9619
Toll-free: 1.800.840.6224
Fax: 780.426.3917

CASTLE ROCK
RESEARCH CORP

ORDER FORM

PAYMENT AND SHIPPING INFORMATION

Name: _____
School Telephone: _____
SHIP TO
School: _____
Address: _____
City: _____ Postal Code: _____

PAYMENT
☐ by credit card
VISA/MC Number: _____
Expiry Date: _____
Name on card: _____
☐ enclosed cheque
☐ invoice school   P.O. number: _____

THE KEY	QUANTITY
Biology 30	
Chemistry 30	
English 30-1	
English 30-2	
Applied Math 30	
Pure Math 30	
Physics 30	
Social Studies 30-1	
Social Studies 30-2	
Biology 20	
Chemistry 20	
English 20-1	
Pure Math 20	
Physics 20	
Social Studies 20-1	
English 10-1	
Pure Math 10	
Science 10	
Social Studies 10-1	
Language Arts 9	
Math 9	
Science 9	
Social Studies 9	
Math 8	
Math 7	
Language Arts 6	
Math 6	
Science 6	
Social Studies 6	
Math 4	
Language Arts 3	
Math 3	

STUDENT NOTES AND PROBLEMS WORKBOOKS	QUANTITY	
	SNAP Workbooks	Solution Manuals
Math 31		
Biology 30		
Chemistry 30		
Applied Math 30		
Pure Math 30		
Physics 30		
Biology 20		
Chemistry 20		
Pure Math 20		
Physics 20		
Applied Math 10		
Pure Math 10		
Science 10		
Math 9		
Science 9		
Math 8		
Science 8		
Math 7		
Science 7		
Math 6		
Math 5		
Math 4		
Math 3		

TOTALS
KEYS
SNAP WORKBOOKS
SOLUTION MANUALS

CASTLE ROCK
RESEARCH CORP

#2340, 10180 – 101 Street, Edmonton, AB T5J 3S4   **Phone:** 780.448.9619 **Fax:** 780.426.3917
Email: learn@castlerockresearch.com **Toll-free:** 1.800.840.6224
www.castlerockresearch.com